Fast Track 5

Preparing for the AP*
U.S. Government and Politics Examination

To Accompany
American Government & Politics Today 2011–2012 and 2013–2014 Editions
by Steffen W. Schmidt, Mack C. Shelley, Barbara A. Bardes, and Lynne E. Ford

Karen K. Waples
Cherry Creek High School, Greenwood Village, Colorado

Benwari Singh
Cherry Creek High School, Greenwood Village, Colorado

David G. Benson
Cherry Creek High School, Greenwood Village, Colorado

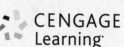

CENGAGE Learning·

Australia • Brazil • Mexico • Singapore • United Kingdom • United States

*AP and Advanced Placement Program are registered trademarks of the College Entrance Examination Board, which was not involved in the production of, and does not endorse, this product.

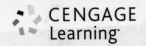

Holt McDougal is pleased to distribute Cengage Learning college-level materials to high schools for Advanced Placement*, honors, and college-prep courses. Our Advanced & Elective Programs department is dedicated to serving teachers and students in these courses.

To contact your Advanced & Elective Programs representative, please call us toll-free at **1-800-479-9799** or visit us at **www.HoltMcDougal.com**.

ISBN-13: 978-1-133-99780-1
ISBN-10: 1-133-99780-5

Cengage Learning
20 Channel Center Street
Boston, MA 02210
USA

Cengage Learning is a leading provider of customized learning solutions with office locations around the globe, including Singapore, the United Kingdom, Australia, Mexico, Brazil, and Japan. Locate your local office at: **www.cengage.com/global**.

Cengage Learning products are represented in Canada by Nelson Education, Ltd.

To learn more about Cengage Learning Solutions, visit **www.cengage.com**.

*AP and the Advanced Placement Program are registered trademarks of the College Entrance Examination Board, which was not involved in the production of, and does not endorse, this product.

Printed in the United States of America
2 3 4 5 6 7 17 16 15 14 13

CONTENTS

PREFACE

We hope this book helps you review all of the material covered in an AP U.S. Government and Politics course and prepares you well for the AP exam. AP Government is an exciting and engaging course, and there is no substitute for what you learn in the classroom. However, some of the most important learning happens during review, when you can tie together all of the facts and concepts to see the big picture. The content in this book is condensed, but we are confident that it covers most of what you will see on the AP exam.

We are indebted to Kenneth Wedding, who as our reviewer brought enormous brainpower to the project. Although he has retired from teaching, Ken remains one of the nation's preeminent authorities on AP U.S. Government and Politics. He has graded AP exams and has written his own review book for AP Comparative Government and Politics. Ken's editorial suggestions were invaluable for our writing and often extended our own knowledge of American government. Margot Mabie is perhaps the most supportive project manager anywhere, and she has an extraordinary eye for detail. Her gift of language in writing and editing shows up even in mundane e-mails.

We are lucky to work at Cherry Creek High School. It is one of the finest public high schools in the nation, and we are surrounded by supportive and professional colleagues and a top-notch support staff and administration. Finally, we thank our students, whose intelligence, energy, humor, and enthusiasm inspire us. We learn from them every day.

Benwari Singh
Karen K. Waples
David G. Benson
Cherry Creek High School
Greenwood Village, Colorado
March 2013

ABOUT THE AUTHORS

KAREN K. WAPLES has taught since 1989. Coordinator of the Social Studies Department at Cherry Creek High School, she has taught three Advanced Placement courses—U.S. History, U.S. Government and Politics, and Comparative Government and Politics. In 1997 she received the Colorado Governor's Award for Excellence in Education. A presenter at conferences nationwide, she is an author of two other review books in the *Fast Track to a 5* series and several Teacher's Resource Guides. Prior to teaching, Ms. Waples practiced law.

BENWARI SINGH, a teacher since 1992, is a member of the Cherry Creek High School Social Studies Department. Beginning with AP U.S. History, he now teaches both AP Comparative Government and Politics and AP U.S. Government and Politics. A reader and now a table leader for AP examination scoring, he has written two lessons in AP Comparative Government and Politics for the College Board. Mr. Singh is an author of another *Fast Track to a 5* and a Teacher's Resource Guide to accompany *The Challenge of Democracy*.

DAVID G.BENSON has been teaching since 1979. A member of the Cherry Creek High School Social Studies Department, he comes to AP U.S. Government and Politics by way of U.S. History, Humanities, Law, World History, International Relations, World Geography, and AP Comparative Government and Politics. He has been an AP examination reader for the College Board and is an author of another *Fast Track to a 5*.

Part I

Strategies for the AP Examination

PREPARING FOR THE AP*EXAM

Advanced Placement can be exhilarating. Whether you are taking an AP course at your school or you are working on AP independently, the stage is set for a great intellectual experience. As the school year progresses and you burrow deeper and deeper into the course work, you will begin to make connections between the ideas and concepts that form the basis of government and politics in the United States. Fleshing out those concepts with a growing collection of nuances is exciting. More exciting still is recognizing examples of these concepts in the media.

But sometime after New Year's Day, when the examination begins to loom on a very real horizon, Advanced Placement can seem downright intimidating—in fact, offered the opportunity to take the examination for a lark, even adults long out of high school refuse. If you dread taking the test, you are in good company.

The best way to deal with an AP examination is to master it, not let it master you. If you can think of these examinations as a way to show off how your mind works, you have a leg up: attitude does help. If you are not one of those students, there is still a lot you can do to sideline your anxiety. This book is designed to put you on a fast track. Focused review and practice time will help you master the examination so that you can walk in with confidence and get a 5.

WHAT'S IN THIS BOOK

This book is keyed to *American Government & Politics Today*, by Steffen W. Schmidt, Mack C. Shelley, Barbara A. Bardes, and Lynne E. Ford; but because it follows the College Board Topic Outline, it is compatible with all textbooks. It is divided into three sections. Part I offers suggestions for getting yourself ready, from signing up to take the test and sharpening your pencils to organizing a free-response question. At the end of Part I you will find a Diagnostic Test. This test has all of the elements of the U.S. Government and Politics examination, but the multiple-choice questions are organized according to the College Board Topic Outline. When you go through the answers at the end of the Diagnostic Test, you will see how the examination is weighted for each content area; a cluster of wrong answers in one area will show you where you are weak. Page references at the end of each answer indicate where you will find the discussion on that particular point in both the 2011–2012 and the 2013–2014 edition of *American Government & Politics Today*. Scoring is explained, so you will have some idea of how well you can do.

Part II, made up of sixteen chapters—again following the College Board Topic Outline—is especially valuable for those who took the course in the fall semester and are taking the examination months later, in the spring. These chapters are not a substitute for your textbook and class discussion; they simply review the U.S. Government and Politics course. At the end of each chapter you will find multiple-choice and free-response questions based on the material in that chapter. Again,

*AP and the Advanced Placement Program are registered trademarks of the College Entrance Examination Board, which was not involved in the production of, and does not endorse, this product.

you will find page references at the end of each question directing you to the discussion on that particular point in *American Government & Politics Today*.

Part III has two AP U.S. Government and Politics examinations. At the end of each test you will find the answers, explanations, and references to *American Government & Politics Today* for the multiple-choice and free-response questions. Following the answers and explanations is a worksheet that you can fill in to calculate your score and give you an approximation of how you might score on the AP exam

At the end of the book you will find a glossary of the terms commonly used in U.S. government and politics.

SETTING UP A REVIEW SCHEDULE

If you have been steadily doing your homework and keeping up with the course work, you are in good shape. But even if you've done all that—or if it's too late to do all that—there are some more ways to get it all together.

Read Part I of this book, which explains the format of the AP exam and provides advice about how to prepare for it. You will be much more comfortable going into the test if you understand how the test questions are designed and how best to approach them. Then take the Diagnostic Test and see where you are right now.

Take out a calendar and set up a schedule for yourself. If you begin studying early, you can chip away at the review chapters in Part II. You'll be surprised—and pleased—by how much material you can cover with half an hour a day for a month or so before the test. Look carefully at the sections of the Diagnostic Test; if you missed a number of questions in one particular area, allow more time for the chapters that cover that area of the course. The practice tests in Part III will give you more experience with different kinds of multiple-choice questions and the wide range of free-response questions. If time is short, skip reading the review chapters. Look at the Key Terms and Key Concepts at the beginning of each chapter to be sure that you are familiar with the vocabulary and broad ideas you will find in the examination, and work on the multiple-choice and free response questions at the end of each review. This will give you a good idea of your understanding of that particular topic. Then take the tests in Part III.

If time is *really* short, go straight from Part I to Part III. Taking practice tests over and over again is the fastest, most practical way to prepare.

BEFORE THE EXAMINATION

By February, long before the exam, you need to make sure that you are registered to take the test. Many schools take care of the paperwork and handle the fees for their AP students, but check with your teacher or the AP coordinator to make sure that you are on the list. This is especially important if you have a documented disability and need test accommodations. If you are studying AP independently, call AP Services at the College Board for the name of the local AP coordinator, who will help you through the registration process.

The evening before the exam is not a great time for partying. Nor is it a great time for cramming. If you like, look over class notes or drift through your textbook, concentrating on the broad outlines, not the small details, of the course. You might also want to skim through this book and read the AP tips.

The evening before the exam is a great time to get your things together for the next day. Sharpen a fistful of no. 2 pencils with good erasers for the multiple-choice section; set out several black or dark-blue ballpoint pens for the free-response questions; set out a wristwatch (you may want to borrow one from a parent) and turn off the alarm; get a piece of fruit or a power bar and a bottle of water for the break; make sure you have whatever identification is required. Check that you have removed your cell phone from your backpack or purse. Cell phones are not allowed during the exam. Then relax. And get a good night's sleep.

On the day of the examination it is wise not to skip breakfast—studies show that students who eat a hot breakfast before testing get higher grades. Be careful not to drink a lot of liquids, necessitating a trip to the bathroom during the test. Breakfast will give you the energy you need to power you through the test—and more. You will spend some time waiting while everyone is seated in the right room for the right test. That's before the test has even begun. With a short break between Section I and Section II, the U.S. Government and Politics exam lasts for over two and a half hours. So be prepared for a long morning. You do not want to be distracted by a growling stomach or hunger pangs.

Be sure to wear comfortable clothes, taking along a sweater in case the heating or air-conditioning is erratic. Be sure, too, to wear clothes you like—everyone performs better when they think they look better—and by all means wear your lucky socks.

You have been on the fast track. Now go get a 5.

TAKING THE AP U.S. GOVERNMENT AND POLITICS EXAM

The AP U.S. Government and Politics examination consists of two sections: Section I has sixty multiple-choice questions; Section II has four free-response questions. You will have 45 minutes for the multiple-choice portion. The questions and answer sheets are collected, and you will be given a short break. You will then have 100 minutes for the free-response portion. You must write a response for each of the four questions—some AP examinations allow you to choose among the free-response questions, but this is not one of them. Keep an eye on the time and devote 25 minutes to each free-response question. Remember: alarms and cell phones are not allowed.

STRATEGIES FOR THE MULTIPLE-CHOICE SECTION

Here are some general guidelines to help you work your way through the multiple-choice questions:

- **Read the question carefully** Pressured for time, many students make the mistake of reading the questions too quickly or merely skimming them. By reading a question carefully, you may already have some idea about the correct answer. You can then look for it in the responses. Careful reading is especially important in EXCEPT questions.

- **Eliminate any answer you know is wrong** You may write on the multiple-choice questions in the test book. As you read through the responses, draw a line through any answer you know is wrong.

- **Answer all questions** There is no longer a penalty for wrong answers, so it is in your interest to answer all questions, even if you have to guess. Some students like to go through the questions quickly, answering the ones they know, and then go back to the more difficult questions.

- **Read all of the possible answers, then choose the most accurate response** AP examinations are written to test your precise knowledge of a subject. Sometimes there are a few probable answers but one of them is more specific. For example, the Fifteenth Amendment gave the vote to African Americans, but only men could vote at that time. An answer that referred to black men would be more correct than an answer that referred simply to African Americans.

- **Avoid absolute responses** These answers often include the words "always" or "never." For example, the statement "Voter turnout in presidential elections is always slightly above 50 percent" is incorrect because in the 1996 presidential election, turnout was a little below 50 percent.

■ **Mark tough questions** If you are hung up on a difficult question or are getting bogged down in a complicated chart, mark the question in the margin of the test booklet. Fill in a random space on the answer sheet for that question so that you get the answer to the next question in the correct place. Go back to the marked questions when you have gotten to the end of the multiple-choice test. You want to answer all the questions; there is no longer a penalty for wrong answers, and you might just guess right.

Types of Multiple-Choice Questions

There are various kinds of multiple-choice questions. Here are some suggestions for how to approach each kind:

Classic/Best Answer Questions

This is the most common type of multiple-choice question. It simply requires you to read the question and select the most correct answer. For example:

1. How is the president of the United States usually selected?
   (A) by direct vote of the populace
   (B) by the House of Representatives
   (C) by the Senate
   (D) in a runoff election between the top two vote getters
   (E) by the electoral college
2. (E) The electoral college usually selects the president, although the House of Representatives decides on the rare occasion when no candidate receives a majority of electoral college votes. The word "usually" is very important in this question. This is a standard question that has one correct answer.

Except Questions

In the EXCEPT question, all of the answers are correct but one. The best way to approach these questions is as true/false. Mark a T or F in the margin next to each possible answer. There should be only one false answer, and that is the one you should select. For example:

1. Congress has the expressed power to do all of the following EXCEPT
   (A) lay and collect taxes.
   (B) regulate interstate commerce.
   (C) establish uniform standards for weights and measures.
   (D) declare war.
   (E) regulate intrastate commerce.
2. (E) Congress does not have the power to regulate intrastate commerce (commerce within a state), so that is a false statement. You should have put an "F" next to it. All of the other statements are true.

LIST AND GROUP QUESTIONS

In this type of question, there is a list of possible answers, and you must select the answer that contains the correct group of responses. These questions look hard, but you can simplify them by crossing out items from the list and then eliminating them in the answers below. For example:

1. According to the Constitution, as amended, which of the following is elected directly?
   I.   the president and vice president
   II. members of the House of Representatives
   III. justices of the Supreme Court
   IV. senators
   (A) I and II
   (B) II and III
   (C) I, II, and III
   (D) I and IV
   (E) II and IV

To approach the question, draw a line through choice I because the president and vice president are not elected directly but are chosen by the electoral college. Then cross out any response that contains choice I. At this point, you have eliminated responses (A), (C), and (D). Continue to cross out items that are wrong and the responses that contain them. Justices of the Supreme Court are appointed, not elected. Draw a line through III and answer (B), which contains choice III. Now you have narrowed down the possible responses.

The correct answer is (E) because under the Constitution, including the Seventeenth Amendment, which provides for the direct election of senators, members of the House of Representatives and the Senate are elected directly.

CHART/GRAPH/TABLE QUESTIONS

These questions require you to examine the data on a chart, graph, or table. While these questions are not difficult, spending too much time interpreting a chart or graph may slow you down. To avoid this, first read the question and all of the possible answers so that you know what the question is asking. You may be able to eliminate some obviously incorrect responses even before you look at the chart.

FREE-RESPONSE QUESTIONS

There are four mandatory free-response questions on the U.S. Government and Politics examination. Usually at least one of the questions requires interpretation of a chart or graph. The question is printed at the top of the page. Free-response questions can be written in any order. Questions are broken into parts, such as (a) and (b). Label each part of your response.

These are not traditional essay questions. Free-response questions do not require an introduction, thesis, or conclusion. Many of these questions may be written in a short-answer format. Although this may sound easier than writing a traditional essay, it is important that you know the material very well because these are targeted questions. Examination readers want specifics. They are looking for accurate information presented in clear, concise prose. You cannot mask vague information with elegant prose.

You will have a 100-minute block of time for this section, so watch your time. Allow 25 minutes for each question. Spend 5 minutes reading the question and jotting down a few words on each point you want to cover in your answer. Then spend 15 minutes writing your response. Save the last 5 minutes to read over your response to make sure you have covered each point with enough detail. If 25 minutes have passed and you are not finished with a question, leave some space, and start a new question. You can come back later if you have time.

Students often have time left over after writing the free-response portion of the exam. This is a good time to reread each of the free-response questions and make sure that you have answered all of the sections. For example, if a question asked you to identify and explain a term, make sure you completed both tasks. If you still have time remaining, sit quietly. You may not read outside material during the testing period.

Vocabulary

In answering the free-response questions, carefully read the question, and do exactly what it asks. It is important to note the word choices used in the questions:

- **Define** to state the meaning of a word or phrase or to give a specific example. For instance, if a question asks you to define "political party," the response is "A political party is an organization that sponsors candidates for political office under the organization's name." Definitions are usually just one sentence.

- **Identify** to select a factor, person, or idea and give it a name. For instance, if a question asks you to identify one advantage of incumbency, one possible response is "One advantage of incumbency is the opportunity to do *casework* for constituents."

- **Explain why/explain how** to give a cause or reason. Explanations usually include the word *because*. For instance, if a question asks you why the ability to do casework gives incumbents an advantage, one possible response is "By doing casework, such as helping a constituent get her Social Security check, members of Congress are able to leave a favorable impression on members of their district. This increases their chances of reelection *because* they are able to get positive results for their constituents, who will vote for them in the next election."

Scoring for Free-Response Questions

These questions are scored using a rubric that assigns points for each part of the answer. For example, if Part (a) requires you to identify and explain two factors, that part of the response will usually be worth 4 points (1 point for each identification and 1 point for each explanation). If Part (b) requires you to identify and explain one factor, that part of the response will usually be worth 2 points (1 point for the identification and 1 point for the explanation), for a total of 6 points possible on the question.

For the following free-response question you will find three sample responses—one excellent, one mediocre, and one poor—and an explanation of how the responses were scored.

QUESTION Congress has several ways of checking the power of the executive branch.

a. Identify and explain two formal powers that Congress may use to limit executive authority.
b. Identify and explain one informal power that Congress may use to limit executive authority.

SAMPLE ESSAY 1

Part (a): The Constitution provides several formal, expressed powers that Congress can use to limit executive authority. One is by overriding a veto. When the president vetoes a bill passed by Congress, that bill does not usually become law. However, Congress can override a presidential veto by a two-thirds vote in each house. This limits presidential power, because the president does not have the final say over legislation. If two-thirds of the members of both houses of Congress feel strongly enough about the legislation, it can still become law. Sometimes presidents are aware that their vetoes will be overridden and will sign bills they do not support in order to avoid the negative press that may come later with a defeat in Congress.

Another formal power that Congress has to limit executive authority is that Congress has the power to declare war. The president is commander in chief and has substantial authority in foreign affairs. He may commit troops for sixty days without congressional approval under the War Powers Act. However, for prolonged conflict, the president must turn to Congress to get an official declaration of war.

Part (b): An informal power that Congress has to limit executive authority is legislative oversight. Congress can conduct investigations and hold hearings to supervise the activities of the executive branch. This may pressure the executive to make changes in those agencies. For example, after Hurricane Katrina, Congress held hearings to investigate the effectiveness of the nation's disaster relief agencies.

SCORING 6/6. In Part (a) the response identifies overriding a veto as a formal power of Congress (1 point for identification). The response explains that by overriding a veto, presidential power is limited because the president does not have the final say over legislation (1 point for explanation).

The student also identifies the power to declare war as a check on the presidency (1 point for identification). The response explains that presidential power is limited because the president must turn to Congress in prolonged conflicts (1 point for explanation). Part (a) earns all 4 points.

In Part (b) the response identifies legislative oversight as an informal limit on the power of the executive (1 point for identification).The response explains that this limits the power of executive agencies because their activities are investigated and their effectiveness may be challenged (1 point for explanation). Part (b) earns 2 points.

Sample Essay 2

Part (a): Under the Constitution, all appropriations bills must originate in the House. This means that the House has the power of the purse over executive proposals. This limits executive authority because Congress can reduce or eliminate funding altogether for presidential initiatives. Likewise, Congress must approve the budget. This limits executive authority because the president may not get everything he wants in his budget.

In addition, Congress can limit executive authority, because the Senate must ratify treaties. Although the executive branch negotiates treaties, often through the State Department, the Senate must ratify them in order for them to become law.

Part (b): One informal power that Congress has over the executive branch is the ability to go to the press. If Congress does not like a presidential proposal, a press conference can be held to get the public to oppose the president's policies.

SCORING 3/6. In Part (a) the student is awarded 3 points. The response identifies the power of the purse as a limitation on the executive (1 point for identification). The response explains that Congress can limit executive power by refusing to fund presidential initiatives by cutting the budget proposed by the president (1 point for explanation).

The student also identifies Senate ratification of treaties as a limit on executive power (1 point for identification), but there is no meaningful explanation of how this limits presidential power.

In Part (b) the student does not receive any points. While congressional leaders may call press conferences as a way to put public pressure on the president, Congress is made up of 535 members. Congress as a whole cannot appeal to the press.

Sample Essay 3

Part (a): One formal power of Congress that limits the executive branch is the power to declare war. However, the president is the commander in chief. As a result, he is able to commit troops to foreign conflicts without a formal declaration of war. This is what Lyndon Johnson did during the Vietnam conflict.

Another formal power of Congress is the power to regulate interstate commerce. This gives Congress the power to enact laws affecting the economy. Such laws have been used to provide civil rights to African Americans, as well as to provide consumer protection nationwide.

Part (b): One informal power of Congress is the ability to support a president's reelection campaign. If the president does not do what Congress wants, it can oppose his reelection.

SCORING 1/6. The student identifies the power to declare war as a limit on the executive (1 point for identification). However, the response does not explain how this power limits the president. Instead, it discusses how the president has not been limited by this power.

While the power to regulate interstate commerce is a power of Congress, it does not generally limit the power of the presidency. The student does not earn any points for the rest of Part (a).

In Part (b) the response indicates that Congress may not support a president's reelection. While this may be true of individual members of Congress, it is not true of Congress as a whole. The student earns no points for Part (b).

A DIAGNOSTIC TEST

This diagnostic test will give you some indication of how you might score on the multiple-choice portion of the AP U.S. Government and Politics exam. Of course, the exam changes every year, so it is never possible to predict a student's score with certainty. This test will also pinpoint strengths and weaknesses on the key content areas covered by the exam.

UNITED STATES GOVERNMENT AND POLITICS EXAMINATION
Section I: Multiple-Choice Questions
Time: 45 minutes

Directions The questions or incomplete statements below are each followed by five suggested answers. Select the best answer.

1. The framers of the Constitution addressed the issue of slavery. Which of the following statements best describes the compromise they made?
   (A) Slavery would be prohibited after 1808.
   (B) Slavery would continue where it existed, but it would not be allowed to expand into new territory.
   (C) Three-fifths of all slaves would be given citizenship.
   (D) Three-fifths of all slaves would be counted for purposes of representation in the House of Representatives.
   (E) Three-fifths of all slaves would be counted for purposes of representation in the Senate.

2. James Madison believed that various groups, or factions, would compete within our democratic system. The result would be effective policy making. Which of the following best describes Madison's theory?
   (A) pluralism
   (B) Marxism
   (C) group dominance theory
   (D) two-party competition
   (E) elitism

3. Which of the following statements best describes most of the framers?
   (A) They were more interested in lofty ideals than in pragmatic politics.
   (B) They were wealthy, well educated, and experienced politicians.
   (C) They were representative of the population as a whole.
   (D) They were radicals who favored states' rights and the protection of individual liberties.
   (E) They were young and inexperienced.

4. What is the result of the Great Compromise?
   (A) Both the House of Representatives and the Senate directly represent the population as a whole.
   (B) The House of Representatives represents the interests of the states, while the Senate represents individuals within a district.
   (C) The Senate represents state interests, while the House of Representatives mirrors the population proportionally.
   (D) The electoral college vote does not always mirror the popular vote.
   (E) Large states have more power in the Senate than small states.

5. The president nominates Supreme Court justices, who must be confirmed by the Senate. Once appointed, those justices usually serve for life terms. This is an example of
   I. separation of powers
   II. Federalism
   III. checks and balances
   IV. judicial review
   (A) I and II
   (B) I and III
   (F) II and III
   (G) III and IV
   (H) I, II, and IV

6. The United States is characterized by cooperative federalism, whereby the national government shares money with the states through grants. Which of the following is most favored by the states?
   (A) categorical grants, because the states can spend the money on broad categories of projects
   (B) formula grants, because the states can use a precise equation to determine how to spend the money
   (C) categorical grants, because they rarely have any strings attached
   (D) block grants, because they give states considerable freedom in deciding how to spend the money
   (E) project grants, because the states can compete to build specific projects, such as libraries and airports

7. Which of the following best exemplifies political equality in the United States?
   (A) All citizens who are charged with a crime have a right to counsel.
   (B) All citizens have the right to compete in the economic marketplace.
   (C) All citizens have the right to peacefully protest against the government's policies without fear of retaliation.
   (D) Government policies like food stamps seek to equalize wealth.
   (E) Each citizen has one vote.

8. Which of the following best describes a nation's set of values and beliefs about the government?
   (A) political framework
   (B) political socialization
   (C) party identification
   (D) political culture
   (E) ideological theory

9. Which of the following statements best describes conservative ideology?
   (A) the belief that the private sector can outperform government in economic activity
   (B) the belief that government should promote civil rights
   (C) the belief that government should promote economic equality
   (D) the belief that the government should be actively involved in regulating private economic activity
   (E) the belief that the government should support gay rights

10. Which of the following statements about political socialization is the most accurate?
    (A) Political parties play a role in family life.
    (B) The family has a significant effect on political socialization.
    (C) Republicans socialize their children more than Democrats.
    (D) Children tend to follow their parents' political ideology, but they tend to reject their parents' beliefs when they become young adults.
    (E) Teenagers are more likely to identify themselves as Republicans than as Democrats.

11. Which of the following statements best describes the difference between the way men and women vote?
    (A) There is no significant difference between men and women about most issues.
    (B) More men than women identify themselves as independents.
    (C) Women are more likely than men to vote for Republicans.
    (D) Men are more likely than women to switch political parties as they age.
    (E) There is a gender gap in political views between men and women on issues such as affirmative action and government spending for social programs.

12. All of the following might suppress voter turnout EXCEPT
    (A) the electorate is large.
    (B) many states allow voting by mail.
    (C) many elections are not close.
    (D) voters must meet residency requirements.
    (E) voters must register prior to the Election.

13. Which of the following persons is most likely to vote?
    (A) an 18-year-old high school graduate
    (B) a 50-year-old union member
    (C) a 40-year-old soccer mom with an associate's degree
    (D) a 65-year-old attorney who works for the federal government
    (E) a 21-year-old married father of two

14. Which of the following statements best describes split-ticket voting?
    (A) voting for a Democratic presidential candidate and a Republican candidate for the Senate
    (B) voting for Democratic candidates in one election and Republican candidates in the next election
    (C) voting for Republican candidates on the first half of the ballot and Democratic candidates on the second half of the ballot
    (D) changing party registration from Republican to Democrat in order to vote in the primary election
    (E) voting for a presidential candidate from one major party and a vice-presidential candidate from the other major party

15. What is the impact of third parties on the American political system?
    (A) Minor parties develop ideas that the major parties later come to adopt.
    (B) Minor parties join together, weakening the two major parties.
    (C) Minor parties tend to develop around charismatic personalities, who are recruited as candidates by the major parties.
    (D) Minor parties usually get enough votes to prevent a majority vote in the electoral college.
    (E) Minor parties have had no significant impact on the American political system.

16. All of the following are examples of interest groups EXCEPT
    (A) Greenpeace
    (B) The National Right to Life Committee
    (C) The Christian Coalition
    (D) The Libertarian Party
    (E) The National Organization of Women

17. How do interest groups differ from PACs?
    (A) Interest groups donate money to candidates, while PACs hire lobbyists to influence policymaking.
    (B) Interest groups can hire PACs to help them conduct polls, create direct mail solicitations, and produce TV ads.
    (C) PACs are committees, often set up by interest groups, to raise and spend money on campaigns and causes.
    (D) Interest groups are required to register with the Federal Election Commission, but there are no registration requirements for PACs.
    (E) PACs run candidates for election, while interest groups do not.

18. African Americans and women led campaigns to gain more rights as a group. This is an example of
    (A) an interest group.
    (B) a social movement.
    (C) a political action committee.
    (D) a third party.
    (E) lobbying.

19. How do the rules governing conduct of the House of Representatives compare with the rules governing conduct of the Senate?
    (A) There are fewer rules governing the conduct of the House of Representatives because it is the lower house and has less power.
    (B) There are fewer rules governing the conduct of the House of Representatives because the House is so big that its individual members lack power.
    (C) There are fewer rules governing the conduct of the Senate because it relies on unanimous consent agreements.
    (D) There are fewer rules governing the Senate because senators tend to vote along party lines.
    (E) The same rules of conduct govern both the House and the Senate.

20. Which of the following statements best describes the incumbency effect?
    (A) Incumbency is an important advantage for reelection, and it is a greater advantage in the House than in the Senate.
    (B) When the economy is poor, most incumbents are not reelected.
    (C) Incumbents are less likely to get reelected in times of divided government.
    (D) Incumbency is less of an advantage in mid-term congressional elections than it is in presidential election years.
    (E) Incumbency is an important advantage in elections, and it is a greater advantage in the Senate than in the House.

21. In the 2010 midterm elections, Republicans won control of the House of Representatives. What was the impact on committees in the House?
    I.   Each committee will have a majority of members who are Republicans.
    II. The committee chairs will be Republicans.
    III. Republicans will decide which bills to assign to a particular committee.
    IV. Most committees will have no members from the Democratic Party.
    (A) I and II
    (B) II and III
    (C) I, II, and III
    (D) II, III, and IV
    (E) I, II, III, and IV

22. The filibuster has been criticized for which of the following reasons?
    (A) It allows members of the Senate to block legislation being considered by the House.
    (B) It is a means for limiting meaningful debate on a bill.
    (C) It was placed in the Constitution because the framers did not trust majority rule.
    (D) There is no formal procedure for ending a filibuster.
    (E) It allows a small group of committed senators to thwart the will of the majority.

23. The Foreign Investors Act, a bill designed to solve the balance-of payments problem, had riders added to it giving assistance to hearse owners, the mineral ore business, importers of scotch whiskey, and presidential candidates. These spending provisions are called
    (A) earmarks.
    (B) revenue.
    (C) authorizations.
    (D) mandates.
    (E) federal grants.

24. Which of the following statements best describes party leadership in Congress?
    (A) The most important leadership position in both the House and the Senate is the majority leader.
    (B) The vice president takes an active role in leading the Senate.
    (C) The minority party leader often works closely with the majority party leader in the House.
    (D) Leadership in the House is fluid, depending upon the particular issue being debated.
    (E) The Senate is led by a majority leader, and the House is led by the Speaker of the House.

25. All of the following statements about the president are true EXCEPT
    (A) the president often faces a Congress led by the opposing party
    (B) most U.S. presidents have not served in Congress
    (C) presidents often choose Cabinet members from outside Congress
    (D) the president is both the head of state and the head of government
    (E) the president relies on the vice president to push legislation through the Senate

26. Which of the following statements best describes the impact of divided government on the legislative process?
    (A) It is harder to pass legislation because the Constitution ensures that the president and Congress will be rivals for power.
    (B) Most presidents have so much political clout that they can force members of the opposing party to support their key legislative proposals.
    (C) Legislation is passed during periods of divided government because members of the opposing party are willing to compromise with the president on important policy issues.
    (D) Legislation is passed in times of divided government because Congress frequently overrides presidential vetoes.
    (E) Divided government occurs most frequently in wartime. Congress is forced to pass legislation in order to meet the needs of the nation.

27. All of the following are formal constitutional powers of the president EXCEPT .
    (A) signing executive agreements.
    (B) signing bills into law.
    (C) vetoing legislation.
    (D) appointing judges to the federal bench.
    (E) receiving ambassadors.

28. Under the Constitution, the president can
    I.   grant reprieves and pardons in federal offenses
    II. call a special session of Congress
    III. declare war
    IV. serve as commander in chief of the armed forces
    (A) I and II
    (B) I, II, and III
    (C) I, II, and IV
    (D) III and IV
    (E) II, III, and IV

29. All of the following statements about the president's Cabinet are true EXCEPT
    (A) in theory, the Cabinet is supposed to serve as an advisory body.
    (B) the number of Cabinet members has grown significantly over time.
    (C) most appointees have served in Congress.
    (D) most appointees share the president's ideology.
    (E) most appointees have limited expertise outside their department's policy area.

30. Which of the following statements best describes the president's role in policy making?
    (A) The president does not usually make policy; he reacts to policy proposals from Congress and interest groups.
    (B) Congress rarely lets the president take credit for policy making.
    (C) Congress generally agrees to pass the president's entire program of policies.
    (D) The policy-making process involves bargaining and struggle between the president and Congress.
    (E) Presidents veto most pieces of legislation, and policy making is difficult.

31. What was the intent of Congress in passing the War Powers Resolution of 1973?
    (A) to cut military appropriations when presidents commit troops without a formal declaration of war
    (B) to clarify that Congress must approve troop commitments once war has been declared
    (C) to require presidents to declare war before troops can be committed overseas
    (D) to require presidents to brief the Senate Intelligence Committee before sending troops overseas
    (E) to end the president's ability to pursue armed conflict without explicit congressional approval

32. When candidates run for office, they often promise to present certain legislative programs once elected. Why is it difficult for presidents to get these promised programs passed?
    I.   Presidents do not have the power to influence a majority of votes in Congress.
    II. The president must choose his battles carefully because he will not win all of them.
    III. Low approval ratings can make it difficult for the president to be persuasive.
    IV. The public rarely expects politicians to deliver on their promises, so their promises are frequently abandoned.
    (A) I and II
    (B) II and III
    (C) II, III, and IV
    (D) I, II, and IV
    (E) I, II, and III

33. When is it most likely that a presidential veto will be overridden by Congress?
    (A) when the president does not write a veto message
    (B) when the president attempts to veto a few select portions of a bill
    (C) when the majority in the House of Representatives is from the opposing party
    (D) when the majority in the Senate is from the opposing party
    (E) when a large majority in both the House and Senate is from the opposing party

34. All of the following are part of the Executive Office of the President EXCEPT
    (A) the Cabinet.
    (B) the White House staff.
    (C) the Office of Management and Budget.
    (D) the Office of the Vice President.
    (E) the National Security Council.

35. What is the process for impeachment and removal of the president?
    (A) The House must vote to impeach a president by a two-thirds vote, and the president is tried in the Senate, which must vote to convict by a three-fourths vote.
    (B) The House must vote to impeach a president by a majority vote, and the president is tried in the Senate, which must vote to convict by a two-thirds vote.
    (C) Both houses of Congress must vote on impeachment charges, and the Supreme Court has original jurisdiction to hear the case.
    (D) The House votes on articles of impeachment, a trial is held in the Senate, and then the case is sent back to the House for a final vote on conviction.
    (E) The House and Senate appoint members to a joint committee on impeachment, which then holds hearings and makes a final recommendation to the Congress as a whole.

36. The president can exercise authority over the bureaucracy in all of the following ways EXCEPT
    (A) the president appoints a majority of federal employees.
    (B) presidential appointees fill the top policy-making positions.
    (C) presidential aides review agency policy making.
    (D) the president sets up a review process requiring agencies to submit draft regulations to a White House office.
    (E) presidential appointees are politically compatible with the president's ideology.

37. How has the role of the bureaucracy changed since the start of the twentieth century?
    (A) The bureaucracy used to regulate the economy, but now its primary role is to provide services to the public.
    (B) The bureaucracy has less power to regulate the economy than it had prior to the New Deal.
    (C) The bureaucracy now provides a wide variety of programs and plays an active role in regulating economic activity.
    (D) The bureaucracy has fewer employees today because of the devolution of powers to state and local governments.
    (E) The role of the bureaucracy has become less controversial.

38. How are most members of the federal bureaucracy selected?
    (A) The president, often on the basis of party loyalty, appoints them.
    (B) They are selected by the Congressional Committee on Hiring and usually reflect the political affiliations of Congress.
    (C) They are appointed after they have passed a written exam or have met certain selection criteria.
    (D) Federal positions are filled using strict affirmative action guidelines that require the bureaucracy to mirror the population as a whole.
    (E) They are interviewed by the OPM, and the top three candidates are sent to the agency head, who makes the final selection.

39. How can Congress supervise the bureaucracy?
    I.   No agency may exist without congressional approval.
    II. No money can be spent unless it has been authorized by Congress.
    III. Congressional committees may fire agency heads.
    IV. Congressional committees may hold oversight hearings.
    (A) I and II
    (B) I, II, and III
    (C) II and III
    (D) II, III, and IV
    (E) I, II, and IV

40. What is judicial review?
    (A) the right of the Supreme Court to rewrite a federal law to make it constitutional
    (B) the right of the Supreme Court to review the evidence in a trial and hear new testimony
    (C) the right of the Supreme Court to hear appeals in cases involving constitutional issues
    (D) the right of the Supreme Court to declare an act of the president or Congress void if it violates the Constitution
    (E) the right of the Supreme Court to reduce a defendant's criminal sentence upon review if that sentence is excessive

41. The Supreme Court has ruled that the Fourth Amendment contains a right of privacy, even though the amendment does not contain the word "privacy." This is an example of which judicial approach?
    (A) strict construction
    (B) restraint
    (C) activism
    (D) statutory construction
    (E) discretionary construction

42. Partisanship affects judicial selection in all of the following ways EXCEPT
    (A) the president usually nominates candidates who are members of his political party.
    (B) senatorial courtesy allows the senior senator from the state where the judicial district is located to object to a nominee.
    (C) the opposing party in the Senate often delays judicial confirmations.
    (D) during confirmation hearings, prospective judges can be asked how they would rule in specific cases.
    (E) during confirmation hearings, prospective judges can be asked about their judicial philosophy.

43. All of the following are permissible restraints on free speech EXCEPT
    (A) libel.
    (B) clear and present danger.
    (C) prior restraint.
    (D) obscenity.
    (E) slander.

44. A state decides to provide funding for math textbooks. This law will provide tax dollars for both public and private schools. What would be the most likely result if this law were challenged in court on grounds that it violates the establishment clause?
    (A) It will be overturned because it fosters an excessive government entanglement with religion.
    (B) It will be overturned because it violates the principle of separation of church and state by using tax dollars to benefit private schools.
    (C) It will be overturned because it advances religious beliefs.
    (D) It will be upheld because tax dollars can be spent for primary or secondary educational purpose.
    (E) It will be upheld because it has a secular purpose, does not advance religion, and will not cause excessive government entanglement with religion.

45. Which of the following are true regarding searches?
    I.   A warrant is usually required prior to a search.
    II. Evidence taken without a valid warrant may be excluded in court.
    III. There is a good faith exception to the exclusionary rule.
    IV. If a search is conducted illegally, the defendant must be freed.
    (A) I and II
    (B) I, II, and III
    (C) I, II, and IV
    (D) II, III, and IV
    (E) I, II, III, and IV

46. What was the Court's decision in *Bakke v. University of California*?
    (A) Affirmative action programs are reverse discrimination and violate the Fourteenth Amendment.
    (B) Affirmative action programs are designed to provide racial equality and are required by the Fourteenth Amendment.
    (C) Schools can take race into account in making admissions decisions, but the use of quotas will be viewed with strict scrutiny.
    (D) Schools can take race into account in making admissions decisions, and using quotas is the best way to accomplish this.
    (E) Affirmative action programs are permissible but not required; states may abolish them if they wish.

47. What is the result of *Roe v. Wade* and subsequent Supreme Court decisions about abortion?
    (A) There is an unlimited right to abortion throughout pregnancy.
    (B) Abortion is legal during the first six months of pregnancy, and may be regulated, but not unduly restricted.
    (C) There is an unrestricted right to abortion.
    (D) States may regulate, and even prohibit, abortion, but the national government may not restrict access to abortion.
    (E) Although abortion is legal during the first two trimesters of pregnancy, protests can occur at entrances to abortion clinics.

48. All of the following were involved in the *Brown v. Board* of Education decisions EXCEPT
    (A) de facto segregation.
    (B) de jure segregation.
    (C) a ruling that states must act "with all deliberate speed".
    (D) separate-but-equal segregation.
    (E) desegregation.

49. Which of the following are required by the No Child Left Behind Act?
    I.   state testing of students
    II. a yearly measure of adequate progress
    III. retraining for poorly qualified teachers
    IV. allowing students in underperforming schools to transfer
    (A) I, II, and IV
    (B) II, III, and IV
    (C) I, II, and III
    (D) I and II
    (E) III and IV

50. How does a regulation differ from legislation?
    (A) Congress passes legislation, and regulations are rules set forth by administrative agencies.
    (B) Legislation is usually much more specific and detailed than regulations.
    (C) Legislation has the force of law, and regulations do not.
    (D) The Supreme Court may overturn legislation, but it may not overturn regulations.
    (D) Congress can pass legislation over a presidential veto, but presidents may kill regulations.

51. What is the difference between monetary policy and fiscal policy?
    (A) Monetary policy involves taxing, and fiscal policy involves spending.
    (B) Fiscal policy occurs when there is a deficit, and monetary policy is used when there is a surplus.
    (C) Fiscal policy uses tax cuts to stimulate the economy, while monetary policy uses government spending to stimulate the economy.
    (D) Fiscal policy involves the budget, and monetary policy involves interest rates and the money supply.
    (E) There is no difference; these terms are synonymous.

52. The economic theory that emphasizes government spending to stimulate the economy is
    (A) supply-side economics.
    (B) Keynesianism.
    (C) monetarism.
    (D) fiscal federalism.
    (E) New Deal activism.

53. What is the difference between an income-based social welfare program and an entitlement?
    (A) Income-based programs, like Medicaid, are available to everyone, regardless of income.
    (B) Entitlement programs, like Social Security, are available regardless of income.
    (C) Entitlement programs, like Social Security, are available only to people who fall below certain income levels.
    (D) Income-based programs, like food stamps, are available only to people who do not work fulltime.
    (E) Income-based programs were eliminated in the Welfare Reform Act.

54. Which of the following is a provision of the Welfare Reform Act?
    (A) Welfare recipients may only receive one year of welfare assistance at a time.
    (B) Welfare recipients must be employed at least 20 hours per week.
    (C) There is a lifetime limit on welfare assistance of five years.
    (D) Welfare recipients must be working toward a GED or high school diploma.
    (E) Welfare recipients who marry receive a housing bonus.

IF YOU FINISH BEFORE TIME IS CALLED, YOU MAY CHECK YOUR WORK ON THIS SECTION. DO NOT GO ON TO SECTION II UNTIL YOU ARE TOLD TO DO SO.

UNITED STATES GOVERNMENT AND POLITICS EXAMINATION
Section II: 4 Free-Response Questions
Time: 100 minutes

Directions You have 100 minutes to answer all four of the following questions. Unless the directions indicate otherwise, respond to all parts of each question. It is recommended that you take a few minutes to plan and outline each answer. Spend approximately 25 minutes on each question. In your response, use specific examples where appropriate. Be sure to number each of your answers.

1. The due-process clause of the Fourteenth Amendment has been used by the Supreme Court to protect individuals from state actions that violate fundamental rights. For TWO of the following cases, complete the following tasks:
    a. Identify the issue the Court was asked to resolve.
    b. Describe the Court's ruling.
    c. Explain how the ruling expanded individual rights.
    Mapp v. Ohio
    Miranda v. Arizona
    Gideon v. Wainright
2. The United States has evolved from a system of dual federalism (in which the powers of the national and state governments are clearly delineated) to a system of cooperative federalism (in which federal and state powers overlap). In the past two decades, some powers have shifted from the federal government back to the states (devolution).
    a. Identify and explain one factor that led to the national government having significantly more power than the states.
    b. Identify and explain one factor that led to cooperative federalism.
    c. Identify and explain one factor that has led to devolution.
3. Several factors impact whether a president will be successful in getting Congress to pass the policies he favors.
    a. Explain why presidents tend to be more successful in getting their policies passed at the beginning of their terms..
    b. Identify and explain two other relevant factors that have affect the ability of a president to get Congress to pass the policies he favors.
4. Congress is made up of the House of Representatives and Senate, both of which must approve the same legislation before it is sent to the president. Despite this similarity of purpose, each house functions differently.
    a. Identify and explain two differences in the way the House of Representatives and the Senate pass legislation.
    b. Identify and explain one similarity in the way the House and the Senate pass legislation.

END OF EXAMINATION

ANSWER KEY FOR THE MULTIPLE-CHOICE QUESTIONS

Using the table below, determine how many questions you answered correctly and how many you answered incorrectly.

1. D	8. D	15. A	22. E	29. C	36. A	43. C	50. A
2. A	9. A	16. D	23. A	30. D	37. C	44. E	51. D
3. B	10. B	17. C	24. E	31. E	38. C	45. B	52. B
4. C	11. E	18. B	25. E	32. E	39. E	46. C	53. B
5. B	12. B	19. C	26. A	33. E	40. D	47. B	54. C
6. D	13. D	20. A	27. A	34. A	41. C	48. A	
7. E	14. A	21. C	28. C	35. B	42. D	49. A	

Your score for the multiple-choice section will give you some idea of how well you might do on the AP exam. (Keep in mind that your answers for the free-response questions count for 50 percent and also determine your score.) The practice multiple-choice test consisted of 54 questions. To calculate your percentage, divide the number of questions you answered correctly by 54. The following is a rough estimate of how you might do on the AP exam:

Potential Score	
88–100%	5
73–87%	4
60–72%	3
45–59%	2
Below 59%	1

ANSWERS TO THE MULTIPLE-CHOICE QUESTIONS

The AP exam covers key content areas in certain percentages. This answer key will give you an indication of how much weight each area is given and your knowledge of each of the important content areas. Page numbers at the end of each answer refer to the pages in the 2011–2012 and 2013–2014 editions of *American Government & Politics Today* where that issue is discussed.

Questions 1–6 are about the Constitution and Federalism (covered in both editions of American Government & Politics Today, Chapters 2 and 3). These topics will be 5–15 percent of the multiple-choice portion of the AP exam.

1. **(D)** Slaves would be counted as three-fifths of a person in the census. This would increase the South's representation in the House of Representatives, which is based on population (*American Government, 2011–2012, pp. 48–49/ 2013–2014, pp. 43–44*).

2. **(A)** Pluralism is the belief that groups compete within a democratic system. Because no single group can dominate the policy-making process, the result is that all relevant interests can affect policy-making outcomes (*American Government, 2011–2012, pp. 12–14/ 2013–2014, pp. 16–17*).

3. **(B)** The framers were politically experienced. They were wealthier and more educated than the general population (*American Government, 2011–2012, p. 44/ 2013–2014, pp. 39–40*).

4. **(C)** There are two senators per state. Thus states are represented equally in the Senate. Seats in the House are awarded based on a state's population, as determined by the census. The number of members in the House of Representatives reflects a state's population (*American Government, 2011–2012, pp. 47–48/ 2013–2014, pp. 42–43*).

5. **(B)** The appointment process for the Supreme Court is an example of both separation of powers and checks and balances. The executive and legislative branches have distinct roles. By confirming presidential nominees, Congress has a check on the presidency. Lifetime tenure is a check on both the executive and the legislature, because justices cannot be removed for political reasons (*American Government, 2011–2012, pp. 51–52/ 2013–2014, pp. 45–46*).

6. **(D)** States prefer block grants because, in theory, they allow states more freedom in deciding how to spend the money, as long as the money is spent on the specific purpose determined by the federal government (*American Government, 2011–2012, pp. 108–109/ 2013–2014, pp. 83, 86*).

Questions 7–13 are about Political Beliefs and Behavior (covered in American Government & Politics Today, Chapters 1, 6, and 9). These topics will be 10–20 percent of the multiple-choice portion of the AP exam.

7. **(E)** The United States provides political equality. Each adult citizen has one vote, which means there is equal opportunity to participate at the polls. While political equality is an American ideal, economic equality is not a goal of the American political system (*American Government, 2011–2012, p. 16/ 2013–2014, pp. 9–10*).

8. **(D)** Political culture consists of the community's beliefs and attitudes toward government (*American Government, 2011–2012, p. 14/ 2013–2014, p. 6*).

9. **(A)** Conservatives believe that private businesses can outperform the government in most economic activities (*American Government, 2011–2012, pp. 18–19/ 2013–2014, p. 19*).

10. **(B)** The majority of young people identify with their parents' political party. This is a result of political socialization (*American Government, 2011–2012, p. 215/ 2013–2014, pp. 183–185*).

11. **(E)** There is a gender gap, with more women than men voting for the Democratic Party. This may be caused by economic disparities between men and women (*American Government, 2011–2012, pp. 222–224/ 2013–2014, pp. 192–194*).

12. **(B)** Mail-in ballots make voting easier than going to the polls. However, many Americans don't vote because they don't think their vote will make a difference in the election, or they haven't met residency or registration requirements (*American Government, 2011–2012, p. 321/ 2013–2014, pp. 285–286*).

13. **(D)** This person has the most demographic factors that favor voting. He is older, well educated, and works for the government (*American Government*, 2011–2012, pp. 317–319/ 2013–2014, pp. 284–285).

Questions 14–18 are about Political Parties, Interest Groups, and Elections (covered in American Government & Politics Today, Chapters 7, 8, 9, and 10). These topics will be 10–20 percent of the multiple-choice portion of the AP exam.

14. **(A)** Split-ticket voting is selecting a candidate from one major party for president and a candidate from the other major party for Congress. Split-ticket voting may result in divided government and policy gridlock (*American Government*, 2011–2012, p. 283, 285/ 2013–2014, 263).

15. **(A)** Sometimes minor parties develop ideas that the major parties later adopt. (*American Government*, 2011–2012, p. 304/ 2013–2014, pp. 267–269).

16. **(D)** An interest group is an organization that seeks to influence public policy. In America, these groups do not usually run candidates for office. The Libertarian Party is a political party, rather than an interest group, because it holds positions on a variety of issues and frequently runs candidates for office (*American Government*, 2011–2012, p. 245/ 2013–2014, pp. 212, 244).

17. **(C)** Political action committees are set up by and represent a corporation, labor union, or interest group. They raise and spend campaign contributions on behalf of candidates or causes (*American Government*, 2011–2012, pp. 349–351/ 2013–2014, pp. 320–321).

18. **(B)** A social movement represents the demands of a large segment of the public for political, economic, or social change (*American Government*, 2011–2012, pp. 246–247/ 2013–2014, pp. 213–214).

Questions 19-42 are about Institutions of Government, including Congress, the Presidency, the Courts, and the Bureaucracy (covered in American Government & Politics Today, 2012–2013 edition, Chapters 12–15, and 2013–2014 edition, Chapters 11–14). These topics will be 35–45 percent of the multiple-choice portion of the AP exam.

19. **(C)** There are fewer rules governing the conduct of the Senate because it has only 100 members, and it relies on unanimous consent agreements. As a result, it is easier to manage than the House of Representatives, which has 435 members (*American Government*, 2011–2012, pp. 428–432/ 2013–2014, p. 348).

20. **(A)** A greater percentage of incumbents in the House is reelected than in the **Senate** (*American Government*, 2011–2012, pp. 415–416/ 2013–2014, p. 353).

21. **(C)** Committees usually reflect party membership in the chamber as a whole. Chairs are appointed by the majority party, which also decides which bills will be sent to particular committees. After the 2010 midterm elections, committees in the House were chaired by Republicans, who made up the majority on each committee (*American Government*, 2011–2012, p. 427/ 2013–2014, pp. 363–364).

22. **(E)** A **filibuster** allows one senator, or a small group, to talk a bill to death. Filibusters are difficult to end because sixty senators must vote for cloture. As a result, it allows a small group to block the will of the majority (*American Government, 2011–2012, p. 411–412/ 2013–2014, pp. 348–349*).

23. **(A)** Federal funds appropriated by Congress to benefit a particular **constituency** or district are called "earmarks" or "pork barrel" spending (*American Government, 2011–2012, p. 434/ 2013–2014, p. 368*).

24. **(E)** The most important leadership position in the House is the Speaker. The **majority** leader guides the Senate (*American Government, 2011–2012, pp. 428–429 and 431–432/ 2013–2014, pp. 364–367*).

25. **(E) While** the vice president supports the president, the vice president does not preside over the Senate unless there is a tie vote (*American Government, 2011–2012, p. 472/ 2013–2014, p. 366*).

26. **(A)** Divided government is a result of separation of powers. Opposing parties must compromise to pass legislation (*American Government, 2011–2012, p. 456/ 2013–2014, p. 263*).

27. **(A)** The Constitution does not expressly grant the president the power to sign an executive order; however, these directives carry the force of law (*American Government, 2011–2012, p. 465/ 2013–2014, p. 398*).

28. **(C) The** president is the commander in chief, may grant reprieves and pardons for federal offenses, and can call Congress into special session. Congress has the power to declare war (*American Government, 2011–2012, pp. 452–456/ 2013–2014, pp. 381–386*).

29. **(C)** The president's Cabinet appointees usually have not served in the **legislature** (*American Government, 2011–2012, p. 469/ 2013–2014, p. 402*).

30. **(D)** Legislative-executive relations involve hard bargaining and struggle **between** these two branches of government (*American Government, 2011–2012, pp. 456–457/ 2013–2014, pp. 388–389*).

31. **(E)** The War Powers Resolution was passed in response to the Vietnam War. It requires presidents to consult Congress prior to committing troops for more than sixty days. Most presidents have ignored it (*American Government, 2011–2012, p. 453/ 2013–2014, pp. 386, 547–548*).

32. **(E)** People expect presidents to deliver on their promises. However, presidents must be careful in choosing which programs to advocate. The president has the power to persuade, but he cannot force Congress to act (*American Government, 2011–2012, pp. 456–457 and 461–462/ 2013–2014, pp. 388–390*).

33. **(E)** It takes a two-thirds vote by both houses of Congress to override a **presidential** veto. This is most likely to occur during divided government, when a large majority of both houses of Congress are from the opposing party (*American Government, 2011–2012, pp. 296 and 460/ 2013–2014, p. 368–369, 393*).

34. **(A)** The Executive Office of the Presidency provides staff assistance to the **president** and helps coordinate the executive bureaucracy. The Cabinet is separate, and consists of 15 large departments (*American Government, 2011–2012, pp. 470–472 and 487/ 2013–2014, pp. 401–402*).

35. **(B)** The House votes, by a simple majority, on impeachment charges. The Senate holds an impeachment trial. A conviction requires a two-thirds vote in the Senate (*American Government, 2011–2012, p. 468/ 2013–2014, pp. 400–401*).

36. **(A)** **Political** appointees make up a small percentage of federal employees (*American Government, 2011–2012, pp. 494–495/ 2013–2014, pp. 425–427*).

37. **(C)** Since the start of the twentieth century, the government has been **expected** to play a more active role in dealing with economic and social problems. The bureaucracy manages a wide variety of government programs and plays an active role in regulating the economy (*American Government, 2011–2012, pp. 485–486/ 2013–2014, pp. 414–415, 420*).

38. **(C)** Most bureaucrats are hired under the requirements of the civil service, in **which** positions are filled through written examinations or are based upon certain selection criteria (*American Government, 2011–2012, p. 497/ 2013–2014, pp. 427–428*).

39. **(E)** Congress must approve the creation of agencies, and no money may be spent **until** Congress authorizes it. In addition, congressional committees hold hearings to investigate the efficiency and effectiveness of agencies (*American Government, 2011–2012, pp. 494–495/ 2013–2014, pp. 438–440*).

40. **(D)** In *Marbury v. Madison*, the Supreme Court asserted its authority to **invalidate** congressional laws that violate the Constitution. Subsequent cases extended the power to cover presidential acts as well (*American Government, 2011–2012, pp. 520–522/ 2013–2014, pp. 446, 449, 450, 463*).

41. **(C)** Judicial activism is the philosophy whereby judges take an active role in creating new policy or in checking other branches of government when they have exceeded their authority. When the Supreme Court held that the Bill of Rights contains a right to privacy, this was an example of judicial activism, because the Supreme Court interpreted several amendments as creating a zone of privacy (*American Government, 2011–2012, pp. 535–536/ 2013–2014, pp.117, 464*).

42. **(D)** During confirmation hearings, prospective judges can be asked about their judicial philosophy but cannot be asked how they would rule on specific cases (*American Government, 2011–2012, pp. 533–534/ 2013–2014, pp. 462–463*).

Questions 43–48 are about Civil Rights and Civil Liberties (covered in American Government & Politics Today, Chapters 4 and 5). These topics will be 5–15 percent of the multiple-choice portion of the AP exam.

43. **(C)** Although the First Amendment protects freedom of speech, there are prohibitions against defamation (libel and slander), speech that presents a clear and present danger to the public, and obscenity. However, as a general rule, the government may not restrain speech prior to its publication (*American Government, 2011–2012, pp. 136–139/ 2013–2014, pp. 105–111*).

44. **(E)** This funding for math books will probably be upheld. It has a secular purpose (improve math skills), does not advance religion, and will not cause excessive government entanglement in religion. This is the standard established in *Lemon v. Kurtzman* (*American Government, 2011–2012, pp. 127–128/ 2013–2014, pp. 99–100*).

45. **(B)** The exclusionary rule bars illegally obtained evidence from being used in court. However, there is an exception when police act in good faith. Defendants may still be tried, however, if there is additional evidence against them (*American Government, 2011–2012, p. 155/ 2013–2014, p. 126*).

46. **(C)** In the Bakke case, the University of California's racial quota system was found to violate the prohibition against race discrimination in the Fourteenth Amendment. The Court did not abolish affirmative action, stating that race can be a factor in admissions decisions (*American Government, 2011–2012, p. 198/ 2013–2014, p. 167*).

47. **(B)** Abortion is legal during the first two trimesters of pregnancy. States may pass regulations, such as a mandatory waiting period, as long as they do not unduly restrict abortion (*American Government, 2011–2012, pp. 148–149/ 2013–2014, pp. 95, 118–120*).

48. **(A)** *Brown v. Board of Education* involved the invidious segregation of public school by law (de jure). This followed the "separate but equal" doctrine. In the second Brown decision the Court ordered desegregation "with all deliberate speed." This is not a case of de facto segregation because the separation was required by law (*American Government, 2011–2012, pp. 172–173/ 2013–2014, pp. 141–142*).

Questions 49–54 are about Public Policy (covered in American Government & Politics Today, 2011–2012 edition, Chapters 16–18, and 2013-2014 edition, Chapters 15–17). These topics will be 10–20 percent of the multiple-choice portion of the AP exam.

49. **(A)** NCLB requires testing to determine whether students are making adequately yearly progress. Children in under-performing schools may transfer (*American Government, 2011–2012, p. 552/ 2013–2014, pp. 82–83*).

50. **(A)** Legislation consists of the bills passed by Congress. Regulations are rules that intervene in the workings of a business market to promote some socially desirable goal. Agencies create regulations, which have the force of law (*American Government, 2011–2012, pp. 488–491/ 2013–2014, p. 420–422*).

51. **(D)** Monetary policy involves government decisions that control interest rates and the money supply. Fiscal policy concerns the budget (American Government, 2011–2012, pp. 600–603/ *2013–2014, pp. 512–513*).

52. **(B)** Keynesianism is the theory that the government should actively stimulate economic growth. On the other hand, supply-side economists favor less government planning, more deregulation, and tax cuts to stimulate economic growth (American Government, 2011–2012, pp. 595– 596/ *2013–2014, pp. 513–514*).

53. **(B)** Entitlement programs are available to everyone who meets certain requirements, such as the age requirement for receiving Social Security retirement benefits, regardless of income (*American Government*, 2011–2012, pp. 555 and 572/ *2013–2014, p. 522–523*).

54. **(C)** The Welfare Reform Act of 1994 limits welfare assistance to two years at a time, with maximum limit of five years (*American Government*, 2011–2012, pp. 572–573/ *2013–2014, p. 498*).

ANSWERS TO THE FREE-RESPONSE QUESTIONS

QUESTION 1

This question required you to write about TWO of three cases (*American Government, 2011–2012, pp. 152–155/ 2013–2014, pp. 123–126*).

In *Mapp v. Ohio*, the Supreme Court was asked to consider whether evidence obtained in an illegal search could be used against a defendant at trial. Police entered Mapp's home in search of drugs. They did not find any drugs, but they found pornography. The police had plenty of time to obtain a search warrant, but they did not get one. The Supreme Court held that the evidence could not be used in Mapp's trial. The *Mapp v. Ohio* case established the exclusionary rule. This rule protects defendants from having illegally obtained evidence used against them in court. The right being protected is provided in the Fourth Amendment, which prohibits unreasonable searches and seizures. This right is protected to make sure police will be diligent in getting proper warrants.

In *Miranda v. Arizona*, the Supreme Court considered whether a confession could be used in court if the suspect was not informed of his rights. Miranda was arrested for kidnapping and rape. Police did not inform him that he had the right to remain silent, that his statements could be used against him, or that he had a right to have an attorney present during questioning. Miranda confessed. In *Miranda v. Arizona*, the Supreme Court threw out Miranda's confession because defendants have a right to be protected against self-incrimination. This right is meaningful only when suspects are fully aware of their rights. As a result of this ruling, it is now standard police procedure to read from a "Miranda card" when taking suspects into custody.

In *Gideon v. Wainwright*, the Supreme Court considered whether the Sixth Amendment requires that poor defendants be provided with attorneys at trial, and whether Gideon's conviction should be overturned because he was not provided with legal counsel. Gideon was a penniless vagrant accused of breaking into and robbing a pool hall. Although he asked for an attorney to represent him at trial, his request was denied. He tried to defend himself as best he could, but he was convicted anyway. From his jail cell, he appealed to the Supreme Court. In *Gideon v. Wainright*, the Court extended the Sixth Amendment's right to counsel to indigent defendants in state criminal proceeding. The Court reasoned that a defendant could not receive a fair trial unless he or she had the opportunity to receive the assistance of an attorney. As a result, defendants who cannot afford legal counsel are entitled to have an attorney, paid for by the state.

SCORING This essay is worth 8 points. The discussion of each of the two cases you choose is worth 4 points.

Part (a) is worth 1 point for identifying the issue. The issue in *Mapp v. Ohio* was whether illegally obtained evidence could be used in court. In *Miranda v. Arizona*, the issue was whether the use in court of a confession made when the suspect has not been read his rights violates the prohibition against self-incrimination. The issue in *Gideon v. Wainright* was whether the Sixth Amendment requires states to provide counsel in state criminal court proceedings.

Part (b) is worth 1 point for explaining the Court's decision. In *Mapp*, the Court established the exclusionary rule. In *Miranda*, the Court held that confessions cannot be used in court if the suspect has not been read his rights. In *Gideon*, the Court held that states must provide legal counsel for indigent defendants.

Part (c) is worth 2 points for explaining how the decision expands rights. An incomplete but correct explanation would receive 1 point. In *Mapp*, the exclusionary rule protects people from illegal searches (1 point) because police will be more diligent (1 point). In *Miranda*, suspects will be protected from self-incrimination (1 point) because police now read Miranda cards when taking suspects into custody (1 point). In *Gideon*, defendants have a right to legal counsel provided by the state (1 point), because they cannot receive a fair trial unless they have the assistance of an attorney (1 point).

QUESTION 2

Part (a): One way the federal government became significantly more powerful than the states is through rulings of the Supreme Court. For example, in *McCulloch v. Maryland*, the Court held that the national government could establish a bank even though this power is not expressly granted in the Constitution. The Court interpreted the elastic clause (also known as the "necessary and proper" clause) broadly. Because the national government has the expressed power to regulate commerce and currency, establishing a bank was necessary to carry out those powers. In addition, the Court held that Maryland could not tax the bank because "the power to tax involves the power to destroy." This gave the federal government significant economic powers not specifically in the Constitution and paved the way for broad federal powers in comparison with the states (*American Government, 2011–2012*, pp. 100–101/ *2013–2014*, pp. 69, 72, 75–76). There are other possible responses. Another way the federal government has become significantly more powerful than the states is due to globalization. Because of increased trade and interaction with foreign countries and international organizations, situations arise—like tainted products from China—that only the national government can address. Similarly, economic crises and natural disasters may call for the resources of the national government. Hurricane Katrina is an example. These situations led to an increase in the power of the national government in order to meet the demands caused by these events.

Part (b): Grants-in-aid have encouraged cooperative federalism. These grants of money allow states to build projects, like airports and universities. Although states enjoy receiving federal money, the money comes with strings attached, known as conditions-of-aid. This means that in order to receive funding, the states must comply with certain requirements, such as raising the drinking age to 21 in order to receive full highway construction funds. The state and federal governments often jointly manage federally funded projects, and this shared administration requires state and federal government to work together (*American Government, 2011–2012*, pp. 107–109/ *2013–2014*, pp. 82–84). There are other possible responses. For example, during times of natural disasters and terrorist attacks, the state and national governments must work together to provide relief and assistance to those in need.

Part (c): One factor that has shifted power back to the states has been Supreme Court rulings. For example, in *United States v. Lopez*, the Court ruled that the Congress exceeded its authority under the commerce clause in banning the possession of guns in schools. As a result of this ruling, it is up to states to establish the criminal penalties for bringing a gun to school, rather than the federal government (American Government, 2011–2012, p. 113/ 2013–2014, pp. 87–88). There are other possible responses. For example, the Reagan administration actively pursued devolution—the policy of granting more power to the states (*American Government, 2011–2012*, p. 112/ *2013–2014, p. 86*).

SCORING This essay is worth 6 points.

Part (a) is worth 2 points—1 point is awarded for identifying a reason for more federal power (court cases), and 1 point is awarded for an explanation (the elastic clause was interpreted in a manner that gives the national government power beyond its expressed powers).Other factors could be discussed, including the use of the commerce clause by the federal government to regulate private businesses.

Part (b) is worth 2 points—1 point is awarded for identifying a factor that results in cooperative federalism (grants-in-aid), and 1 point is awarded for explaining the influence of that factor (shared administration requires levels of government to work together). Other factors could be discussed, such as land grants to the states and the federal income tax, which provided funds that could be given by the federal government to the states.

Part (c) is worth 2 points—1 point is awarded for identifying a reason for devolution (court cases), and 1 point is awarded for explaining how this returns power to the states (states, rather than the federal government, set the penalties for bringing a gun to school).Block grants could also be mentioned as a factor that returns some decision making to the states.

QUESTION 3

Part (a): One factor that impacts presidential victories in Congress is the honeymoon period immediately following an election. Presidents are often most popular right after an election, and they can persuade Congress to enact legislation they favor by claiming to have a mandate from the public supporting their terms.(*American Government, 2011–2012, p. 456/ 2013–2014, p. 389*).

Part (b): Another factor affecting presidential victories in Congress is divided government. When one or both houses of Congress are controlled by the political party opposite of the president's, the president is less likely to get his proposed legislation enacted. (*American Government, 2011–2012, pp. 456–460/ 2013–2014, pp. 388–389*). Also, lame duck presidents will be leaving office soon and are unable to promise rewards in the future and Congress is less likely to cooperate with them.

SCORING This essay is worth 5 points.

Part (a) is worth 1 point for describing why it is easier for the president to get his policies passed at the beginning of his term.

Part (b) is worth 4 points, with 1 point awarded for identifying each factor affecting presidential victories in Congress (divided government lame duck period), and 1 point awarded for each explanation (divided government makes it difficult for the president to get his program enacted, during the lame duck period the president cannot promise rewards in exchange for votes). Points would be awarded for other factors, such as a crisis or high approval ratings, that would cause Congress to support the president's program.

QUESTION 4

Part (a): The House of Representatives, with 435 members, is much larger than the Senate, with 100 members. Because of its size, the House has more rules to keep it organized. One difference between the House of Representatives and the Senate is that the Senate is run more informally. In the House, the Rules Committee sets the limits for debate on a bill. This can include time limits, as well as limits on the kinds of amendments that may be proposed. In the Senate, there is no rule limiting debate, and senators can speak for as long as they want. Another difference is the requirement that amendments in the House have to pertain to the topic of the bill being considered. No such requirement exists in the Senate (*American Government, 2011–2012, pp. 428–432/ 2013–2014, pp. 348–349*).

Another difference between the House and Senate is that senators can filibuster legislation, and filibusters are not allowed in the House of Representatives. A filibuster allows senators to talk a bill to death. This allows senators who are in the minority to block actions favored by the majority. During the fifties and sixties, southern senators used it to block civil rights legislation. More recently, it has been used to block appointments to the federal bench. Filibusters give senators more power than representatives, because one determined senator can block legislation (*American Government, 2011– 2012, pp. 411–412/ 2013–2014, pp. 348–349*).

Part (b): One similarity in the way the House of Representatives and the Senate are run is committees. Both houses have standing and select committees. These committees review legislation, make changes, and give recommendations to the House and Senate as a whole. In addition, a conference committee irons out legislation when it has been passed in different versions. Joint committees have members from both houses. Committees allow members of Congress to develop expertise in certain policy areas. Committees also create a division of labor that makes the legislative process more efficient (*American Government, 2011–2012, pp. 424–427/ 2013–2014, pp. 360–363*).

SCORING This essay is worth 6 points.

Part (a) is worth 4 points; 1 point is awarded for identifying each difference between the House and the Senate (the House has a Rules Committee; senators can filibuster) and 1 point is awarded for explaining each difference (the Rules Committee can limit the time for debate; the filibuster allows senators to block legislation favored by the majority). Points would be awarded for other differences, such as different leaders (the Speaker of the House and the Majority Leader as head of the Senate).

Part (b) is worth 2 points, with 1 point awarded for identifying a similarity between the House and the Senate (both have committees) and 1 point awarded for the explanation (committees allow members to develop expertise and make the legislative process more efficient). Points would be awarded for other similarities, such as majority and minority leaders and whips.

CALCULATING YOUR SCORE

SECTION I: MULTIPLE-CHOICE QUESTIONS

(Because the practice test contains 54 questions and the AP exam contains 60 questions, you will need to multiply the number you answered correctly by 1.11. This is the number of questions you might have answered correctly on a 60-question test).

Number answered correctly (multiplied by 1.11) equals ___

SECTION II: FREE-RESPONSE QUESTIONS

Question 1 _____ × 1.875 equals _____
out of 8   do not round
Question 2 _____ × 2.5 equals _____
out of 6   do not round
Question 3 _____ × 3.0 equals _____
out of 5   do not round
Question 4 _____ × 2.5 equals _____
out of 6   do not round
Total for Section II _____

COMPOSITE SCORE

_____ + _____ = _____
Section I   Section II   Composite Score

Student scores are weighted differently each year to determine the final
AP grade. The chart below is an estimate.

COMPOSITE SCORE RANGE	AP GRADE
93–120	5
82–92	4
66–81	3
48–65	2
0–47	1

Part II

A Review of AP U.S. Government and Politics

Part II

A Review of AP U.S. Government and Politics

1

THE CONSTITUTION

The Constitutional Convention that met in Philadelphia in the summer of 1787 created a constitution that has remained largely unchanged for more than 200 years. The U.S. Constitution addressed the weaknesses of the failed Articles of Confederation and was the result of several philosophical and moral compromises.

KEY TERMS

Anti-Federalists
bicameral legislature
Bill of Rights
checks and balances
confederation
Declaration of
Independence
federal system
Federalist Papers
Federalists
Great Compromise
Madisonian model
natural rights
New Jersey Plan
ratification
representative assembly
separation of powers
social contract
state
three-fifths compromise
unicameral legislature
Virginia Plan

39

KEY CONCEPTS

- Prior to 1763, the colonies exercised a large degree of self-government. The colonists did not want to give up self-government as Britain tried to assert more control after 1763.

- The Articles of Confederation, which formed the nation's first constitution, created a number of problems for the new nation.

- Called to revise the Articles of Confederation, the Constitutional Convention instead scrapped them and drafted the Constitution, under which we live today.

- Proponents of the Constitution (Federalists) argued that it provided for a much needed and stronger national government; opponents (Anti-Federalists) preferred that state governments remain stronger.

- To ensure ratification of the Constitution, a Bill of Rights was added.

- The Constitution has two amendment processes—formal and informal—that account in large measure for its endurance

For a full discussion of the Constitution, see the 2011–2012 and 2013–2014 editions of *American Government & Politics Today*, Chapter 2.

COLONIAL BACKGROUND

Life for most colonial Americans was good by the standards of the day. Colonists, except for slaves, enjoyed more liberty, wealth, and even equality than most of the rest of the world. The British monarchy and Parliament generally ventured only into matters of trade and foreign relations. This benign relationship changed abruptly when Britain gained extensive new North American territory by winning the French and Indian War (also known as the Seven Years' War) in 1763. The expense of defending the newly won territory was overwhelming. Britain reasoned that the colonists should share in the burden of paying for the administration and defense of the new land through taxes on items such as newspapers, glass, paint, official documents, paper, and tea.

Colonial leaders, including Benjamin Franklin, John Adams, Thomas Jefferson, James Madison, Robert Morris, and Alexander Hamilton, were heavily influenced by European political philosophies of the Enlightenment. Perhaps the most influential of these European philosophers was John Locke, an Englishman. In *The Second Treatise of Civil Government* (1689), Locke posited several basic ideas about government and how it should operate, including the following:

- All human beings have natural rights. They are inherent rights; they are not bestowed by government and cannot be taken away or given up. Among them are life, liberty, and property.

- Government exists for the purpose of securing these rights and must therefore be built upon the consent of the governed.

- Citizens create government by giving their consent and creating a social contract. Government must be limited. Laws should be written, and government should not take any part of a man's property without his consent.

Colonial resentment toward the new taxes, levied without their representation, crystallized political and philosophical values in the colonies that had been evolving for some time. As colonial unhappiness with various British taxes escalated, war broke out. Colonial leaders met almost continuously during 1775 and 1776 as the Continental Congress. By May 1776, resolutions concerning independence were being openly debated, resulting in the Declaration of Independence, which was formally adopted on July 4, 1776. Written primarily by Thomas Jefferson, the document is both political and philosophical, emphasizing many of Locke's ideas. It announced and rationalized the revolution, listing 27 specific ways that King George III had abused the Americans. Its philosophical statements, however, set forth many of the underlying assumptions of American government, then and now.

THE ARTICLES OF CONFEDERATION

The newly independent Americans sought to avoid what they saw as the tyranny of a strong central government, so they set out to create a government that had few restraints on local communities. To do this, the Continental Congress appointed a committee to devise a framework for government. The result of the committee's work was the Articles of Confederation, the nation's first constitution. The Articles created a national legislature that was unicameral. Several delegates could be sent to the new Congress by a particular state, but each state had only one vote. Passing a new law required nine of the thirteen states to vote in favor. The executive was powerless, no judicial branch was included in the national government, and legislative powers were severely limited. Most power was reserved for the state legislatures. The Continental Congress adopted the Articles in 1777, but they didn't go into effect until 1781 because unanimous consent was required for them to become operative.

From the beginning, the Articles appeared to create more problems than they solved. Among the notable weaknesses were the following:

- Congress had no power to tax. To obtain money, Congress had to request funds from the states, which often refused.

- Congress had no power to regulate commerce. This severely hindered efforts to create a national economy.

- The national government had no court system to deal with disputes between states.

- Congress *did* have the power to maintain an army and navy, yet it lacked the resources to adequately do even that.

The ineffectiveness of the Articles was further revealed in 1786, when a band of farmers in western Massachusetts staged a rebellion to protest the loss of their land to creditors. Led by a Revolutionary War captain, Shays' Rebellion was a series of attacks on courthouses to keep judges from foreclosing on farms. Neither the national government nor the Commonwealth of Massachusetts was able to raise a militia to put down the rebellion. A force privately funded by Boston merchants was organized to do the job. National leaders cringed at the seeming chaos. Shays's Rebellion and the perceived weaknesses of the Articles of Confederation convinced many that bold solutions were needed to mend the country's post–Revolutionary War problems. A handful of leaders met in Annapolis, Maryland, in September 1786 to offer suggestions for putting the country on better footing. Because only five states were represented, the meeting had little effect. The Annapolis delegates petitioned Congress for a meeting of all the states the following year. Congress agreed, and in May 1787, delegates convened in Philadelphia for the Constitutional Convention.

THE CONSTITUTIONAL CONVENTION

Although the 55 delegates to the convention were commissioned only to revise the Articles of Confederation, they dismissed this as impossible because it would have required the unanimous consent of the states. Instead, they set about writing a new constitution.

Of the 55 delegates, only about 40 participated consistently, and Rhode Island refused to send any delegates. Most delegates were relatively young, though Benjamin Franklin was already past 80. They were mostly wealthy plantation owners, lawyers, and merchants.

Some of the most contentious and difficult issues were the following:

■ **Representation** The composition of the new Congress was hotly contested. The Virginia Plan called for representation based on each state's population (also called proportional representation). The New Jersey Plan insisted on equal representation for each state. The solution is known as the Connecticut Compromise, or the Great Compromise: the Senate would have two members from each state, and the House of Representatives would be based on population.

■ **Slavery** The contradictions between the Declaration of Independence and slavery were evident. States were allowed to count three-fifths of slaves for representation and taxation purposes. This was a compromise between Southern delegates, who wanted to count all slaves, and Northern delegates, who did not want slaves counted at all. Congress was given the power to end the importation of slaves—though not slavery itself—after 1808.

■ **Economic issues** Because their economy was based on exports, many Southern delegates worried that a tax would be levied on exports, thus hurting their economic interests. These delegates worked to ensure that exports would not be taxable under the new constitution.

AP Tip

The solution to the problem of representation at the Constitutional Convention still resonates within our government today. The Great Compromise led to the creation of the U.S. House of Representatives and the U.S. Senate, each with its own responsibilities and powers. Representation and the powers of each house of Congress are likely to appear on the AP exam in some form.

There were several other small compromises made at the Convention, such as the structure of the judiciary and whether the executive or the legislative branch would have the power to appoint justices and other officials.

THE MADISONIAN MODEL

More than any other delegate, James Madison was the principal visionary of the government's structure. Madison feared factions of self-interested individuals banding together to create tyranny. To prevent the possible evils of powerful factions, Madison drew on examples from state constitutions and proposed (and eventually saw instituted within the Constitution) the following:

- **Separation of powers** Each of the three branches of government—executive, legislative, and judicial—would be given independent powers so that no one branch could control the others, yet no branch could operate with total independence. Power would be shared among the three, rather than divided absolutely.

- **Checks and balances** Because the three branches would share power, each could, to a certain extent, check the powers of the other two. For instance, the president could veto legislation passed by Congress, Congress could confirm or deny certain presidential appointments, and the Supreme Court could interpret laws.

- **Federalism** Political authority was divided between the national government and the various state governments. Madison assumed that this would check any tyranny by the national government.

RATIFICATION OF THE CONSTITUTION

The proposed Constitution called for nine of the thirteen states to approve the document at special state ratifying conventions. This was technically illegal, because the Articles of Confederation, which were still in effect, called for approval by all 13 state legislatures for any changes to the Articles to take effect. The framers of the Constitution wanted to evade this requirement; they feared that the legislatures would resist the new document, thus retaining their extensive powers.

Advocates of the Constitution called themselves Federalists. Their opponents, those wanting to thwart the ratification of the Constitution, became known as Anti-Federalists. Of the two groups, the Federalists were better financed and organized.

To help persuade the public of the merits of the Constitution, Alexander Hamilton published a series of articles in New York newspapers. He recruited John Jay and James Madison to help him, and the trio wrote 85 articles from late 1787 through 1788. Known as the *Federalist Papers*, these articles provide rare glimpses into the Philadelphia meetings and important elaborations regarding the Constitution itself. Although Hamilton wrote most of the articles, Madison penned the most famous: *Federalist* No. 10 offers Madison's warning about factions and strategies to deal with the problems that they might cause. The Anti-Federalists countered with articles of their own that made scathing and insightful attacks on the proposed Constitution. The Anti-Federalists' core argument was that the new Constitution would create an overbearing central government that would be prone to limiting personal liberty. The Anti-Federalists, and later historians including Charles Beard, also argued that wealthy individuals created the Constitution in an attempt to protect and expand their wealth.

Anti-Federalists argued that if a strong national government were to be created, it should be restrained by more explicit guarantees of individual liberties than those found in this Constitution. Despite the protections written into the Constitution, such as the prohibition of *ex post facto* laws and the protection of the writ of habeas corpus, leading Federalists were persuaded by this argument and promised to add amendments to the document with explicit protections of individual liberties. Later, at the First Congress, in 1789, James Madison proposed 12 constitutional amendments designed to restrain the national government from limiting civil liberties. By 1791, 10 of those amendments had been ratified by the states. Collectively, they are known as the Bill of Rights. Another of Madison's original amendments, one regarding congressional salaries, was ratified 201 years later as the Twenty-seventh Amendment.

On December 7, 1787, Delaware became the first state to ratify the Constitution. Although bitter opposition in Virginia and New York seemed to threaten ratification, within six months, New Hampshire became the ninth state to ratify the Constitution. Virginia and New York joined shortly thereafter, seeing that further resistance was futile. North Carolina and Rhode Island waited for the Bill of Rights to be ratified before they joined in 1791.

ALTERING THE CONSTITUTION

The framers of the Constitution wisely allowed for changes to be made in accord with the needs of later times. Constitutional changes can be made either through a formal amendment process or through informal processes. Article V of the Constitution sets forth procedures for formal amendments. For an amendment to pass, it must survive two stages of the process—proposal and ratification. In turn, each of these stages has two possible courses of action. An amendment may be proposed by either a two-thirds vote of both houses of Congress or a national convention called by Congress at the request of two-thirds of the state legislatures. An amendment may be ratified by either the legislatures of three-fourths of the states or by special state conventions in three-fourths of the states. The formal amendment process is arduous. Since its ratification, Congress has considered some 11,000 amendments; only 33 have been submitted to the states. Of these 33, only 27 have been ratified. The framers made the process difficult to protect minority rights from majority rule.

There are several ways the Constitution can change informally:

- **Congressional action** The Constitution granted broad powers to Congress. The commerce clause (Art. I, Sec. 8) has been used by Congress to regulate a wide variety of activities. Congress has also delegated a great deal of authority to the bureaucracy to implement programs.

- **Presidential actions** Presidential power has grown tremendously since the ratification of the Constitution. Presidents today propose legislation, use executive orders and agreements (which have the force of law), and have sent troops into combat without a declaration of war.

- **Judicial interpretation** Although the Constitution only implies the power of the Supreme Court to consider the constitutionality of a case, the Court has exercised such power since the 1803 case of *Marbury v. Madison*. The power of judicial review enables the Court to settle disputes regarding interpretations of the Constitution.

- **Changing political practices** As the size of the national government has grown, so has the bureaucracy. Today's issues are too complex to be dealt with by the small government envisioned by the Founders. This has led to a greater role for the executive branch than they anticipated. Also, many Americans would be surprised to know that the Constitution mentions nothing of political parties, much less a two-party system. The electoral college system as outlined in the Constitution does not include any provisions that require an elector to vote for the winner of the popular vote in a particular state, yet this is now a firm tradition, and even the law in most states.

The flexibility of the Constitution has served the nation well for over 200 years. Despite the enormous changes and the diversity and size of the nation, the American Constitution continues to operate effectively and legitimately.

MULTIPLE-CHOICE QUESTIONS

1. What was the most serious weakness in the Articles of Confederation?
   (A) Congress did not have the power to conduct foreign policy.
   (B) Congress did not have the power to raise revenue.
   (C) Congress did not have the right to declare war.
   (D) The national government had too much power over the states.
   (E) The actions of Congress required the consent of nine states.

2. What was the result of the Great Compromise?
   (A) States were represented in the upper house, and citizens were represented in the lower house.
   (B) Citizens were represented in the upper house, and states were represented in the lower house.
   (C) Citizens were given proportional representation in both the House of Representatives and the Senate.
   (D) All members of Congress were selected by direct election.
   (E) Slaves were not counted in the census.

3. Under the original Constitution, which branch or branches of government were selected directly by the citizens?
   I.   the president and vice president
   II. the Supreme Court
   III. the Senate
   IV. the House of Representatives
   (A) I and II
   (B) I, III, and IV
   (C) III and IV
   (D) III only
   (E) IV only

4. Some historians, including Charles Beard, have argued that the Constitution was written by the elite to protect their interests. All of the following might form the basis for Beard's argument EXCEPT
   (A) property rights are expressly protected in the Constitution
   (B) there was never a popular vote on whether to hold the convention
   (C) the House of Representatives is not directly elected
   (D) states restricted voting rights to white males
   (E) proceedings of the Constitutional Convention were not open to the press or the public

5. All of the following are ways to formally amend the Constitution EXCEPT
   (A) a proposal accepted by a two-thirds vote of both houses of Congress
   (B) a proposal accepted at a national convention called by Congress as requested by two-thirds of the states
   (C) a national referendum (by popular vote) with two-thirds voter approval
   (D) ratification by three-fourths of the state legislatures
   (E) ratification by three-fourths of the states in special conventions

6. How does the Constitution provide an executive check on the judicial branch?
   (A) It allows the president to remove Supreme Court justices from office for cause.
   (B) It allows the executive to change the number of judges sitting on the Supreme Court.
   (C) It gives the president the power to veto a decision made by the Supreme Court.
   (D) It gives the president the power to nominate federal judges, subject to Senate confirmation.
   (E) It gives the president the power to appoint and remove federal judges at will.

7. What was the main argument of the Anti-Federalists?
   (A) They believed that the national government was too weak under the Constitution.
   (B) They criticized the Federalists for protecting state sovereignty.
   (C) The Anti-Federalists believed the Constitution did not take strong enough steps to eliminate factions.
   (D) The Anti-Federalists believed that a strong central government would destroy liberty.
   (E) The Anti-Federalists were opposed to representative democracy.

8. Which of the following guarantees of individual liberties is found in the original Constitution?
   (A) freedom of speech, press, and assembly
   (B) no official state religion
   (C) a prohibition against double jeopardy
   (D) no unreasonable searches and seizures
   (E) a prohibition against *ex post facto* laws

9. All of the following statements about the electoral college are true EXCEPT
   (A) a group of electors is chosen for the sole purpose of selecting the president
   (B) if there is no majority winner in the electoral college, the election is determined by the House of Representatives, with one vote per state
   (C) the electoral college allows citizens to vote directly for the president
   (D) each state has the same number of electoral college votes as the number of members of Congress
   (E) the winner of the electoral college vote may not be the winner of the majority of the popular votes

10. In theory, each branch of government has independent and distinct functions. This is a result of
    (A) checks and balances
    (B) the separation of powers
    (C) the Great Compromise
    (D) (D) federalism
    (E) the full faith and credit clause

11. A government that divides power among institutions that have the authority to check one another's power is known as
    (A) a constitutional government
    (B) a Republican government
    (C) Federalist
    (D) a government under the Madisonian model
    (E) a government under the Jeffersonian model

12. Which of the following was accomplished under the Articles of Confederation?
    (A) A pattern of government was established for new territories.
    (B) States developed effective and powerful militias.
    (C) Freedom of religion was guaranteed throughout the United States.
    (D) The United States paid its Revolutionary War debt to France.
    (E) The United States created a uniform and stable currency.

13. What was the impact of the three-fifths compromise?
    (A) It gave Southern states more representation in the Senate.
    (B) It gave Northern states more representation in the Senate.
    (C) It gave Southern states more representation in the House of Representatives.
    (D) It gave Northern states more representation in the House of Representatives.
    (E) It gave Southern states fewer votes in the electoral college.
14. Which of the following best describes judicial review?
    (A) The Supreme Court may amend the Constitution.
    (B) The Supreme Court may nullify state laws if they provide more rights than are included in the federal Bill of Rights.
    (C) The Supreme Court may remove state government officials who violate the Constitution.
    (D) The Supreme Court may recommend impeachment proceedings against the president.
    (E) The Supreme Court may nullify government acts that conflict with the Constitution.
15. Congress has broad powers to carry out its duties as the nation's legislative body. Which of the following has been interpreted broadly to expand Congressional power?
    (A) the power to regulate commerce
    (B) the power to establish a uniform currency
    (C) the power to declare war
    (D) the power of impeachment
    (E) the power to establish bankruptcy laws

FREE-RESPONSE QUESTIONS

1. It has been said that "even the word *democracy* was distasteful to the founders."
   a. Identify and explain one feature of the Constitution that reflects a distrust of popular government.
   b. Identify and explain a second feature of the Constitution that reflects a distrust of popular government.
   c. Explain one way in which the Constitution has become more democratic over time.
2. The Constitution is based on the Madisonian model of government.
   a. Define separation of powers.
   b. Define checks and balances.
   c. Identify and explain one way in which the executive can check the power of the legislature.
   d. Identify and explain one way in which the executive can check the power of the judiciary.

Answers

MULTIPLE-CHOICE QUESTIONS

1. **(B)** Although Congress had the power to declare war and conduct foreign affairs, it lacked the power to tax. This was the most fundamental weakness in the Articles of Confederation (*American Government, 2011–2012*, p. 42/ *2013–2014*, p. 38).

2. **(A)** Under the Great Compromise, the House of Representatives is proportional and elected directly, and there are two senators per state (*American Government, 2011–2012*, pp. 47–48 / *2013–2014*, pp. 42–43).

3. **(E)** Under the original Constitution, only members of the House of Representatives were elected directly. Senators were not elected directly until ratification of the Seventeenth Amendment in 1913. The president is chosen by the electoral college, and the Supreme Court is appointed (*American Government, 2011–2012*, pp. 48, 50/ *2013–2014*, pp. 42, 50).

4. **(C)** Charles Beard argued that the Constitution was written to protect elite interests and was not truly democratic. The direct election of the House of Representatives goes against his argument because it is an example of direct election (*American Government, 2011–2012*, pp. 54–55/ *2013–2014*, p. 49).

5. **(C)** A proposed amendment must receive a two-thirds vote in Congress or in a national convention called by Congress. It must then be approved by a three-fourths vote in state legislatures or by conventions in three-fourths of the states. (*American Government, 2011–2012*, pp. 58–59/ *2013–2014*, p. 53).

6. **(D)** The president nominates federal judges, and the Senate confirms them (*American Government, 2011–2012*, pp. 51–52/ *2013–2014*, p. 46).

7. **(D)** The Anti-Federalists argued that a strong national government would take away powers that belong to the states and destroy liberty (*American Government, 2011–2012*, pp. 52–53/ *2013–2014*, pp. 48–49).

8. **(E)** The Constitution protects citizens against *ex post facto* lawmaking. In other words, states may not criminalize past behavior (*American Government, 2011–2012*, p. 55/ *2013–2014*, p. 50).

9. **(C)** The electoral college is an indirect method of choosing the president. Voters are actually choosing electors, who then cast their votes for a presidential candidate (*American Government, 2011–2012*, pp. 50, 329–332/ *2013–2014*, pp. 46, 298–300).

10. **(B)** In theory, separation of powers means that each branch of government has distinct powers. This prevents one branch from dominating the others (*American Government, 2011–2012*, pp. 49–50/ *2013–2014*, pp. 45–46).

11. **(D)** James Madison proposed a model of government that divided power among the executive, legislative, and judicial branches and provided for checks and balances among the branches (*American Government, 2011–2012*, pp. 49–50/ *2013–2014*, pp. 45-46).

12. **(A)** The Northwest Ordinance of 1787 established a basic pattern of government for new territories north of the Ohio River (*American Government, 2011–2012*, pp. 41–42/ *2013–2014*, p. 37).

13. **(C)** Under this compromise, slaves counted as three-fifths of a person when the census was taken. This determined the number of representatives each state had in the House of Representatives, increasing representation for Southern states (*American Government, 2011–2012*, pp. 48–49/ *2013–2014*, pp. 43–44).

14. **(E)** Judicial review is the Supreme Court's power to interpret the Constitution and nullify state and federal laws that conflict with it (*American Government, 2011–2012, pp. 62–63/ 2013–2014, p. 57*).

15. **(A)** Congress has used the Commerce Clause as the broad basis for passing thousands of laws (*American Government, 2011–2012, pp. 61–62/ 2013–2014, p. 56*).

FREE-RESPONSE QUESTIONS

1. (a) The electoral college is a feature of the Constitution that reflects a distrust of direct popular government, because the majority does not directly elect the president. Instead, votes are cast by members of the electoral college. This was a check on the passions of the majority.

   (b) Voting requirements were left to the states, which imposed property requirements. These requirements reflect a distrust of popular government, because citizens could vote directly only for members of the House of Representatives—the lower house, whose members have two-year terms of office. In addition, property requirements prevented many citizens from voting at all.

   (c) Through amendments, the Constitution has become more democratic over time. For example, the Seventeenth Amendment provided for the direct election of senators and the Nineteenth Amendment gave women the right to vote (*American Government, 2011–2012, pp. 50, 58–60/ 2013–2014, pp. 53–54, 56-58,*).

2. (a) Separation of powers is giving the executive, legislative, and judicial branches differing authority.

   (b) Checks and balances is a system that ensures each branch of government some authority over the actions of the other branches.

   (c) One check that the executive has over the legislative branch is veto power. This means that the president may stop a bill from becoming law even though it was passed by both houses of Congress. However, Congress may override a veto with a two-thirds vote by both houses.

   (d) One check the executive has over the judiciary is that the president can refuse to enforce the Supreme Court's decisions. The Court has no enforcement powers, and it must rely on the executive branch to support its decisions (*American Government, 2011-2012, pp. 49–50/ 2013–2014, 45–46*).

2

FEDERALISM

Federalism is a philosophy of government based on the division of power between state and national governments. In the United States, federalism has been a persistent source of political conflict.

KEY TERMS

categorical grants
commerce clause
concurrent powers
confederal system
cooperative federalism ·
devolution
dual federalism
elastic or necessaryand proper clause
extradite
federal mandate
full faith and credit
clause
interstate compact
picket-fence federalism
police powers
privileges and
immunities
supremacy clause
unitary system

KEY CONCEPTS

- Federalism is the sharing of power between local and national governments.

- Defining the relationship between the national government and state governments has been—and continues to be—a major issue in the nation's history.

51

- The cornerstone of national and state government relations today is the system of grants and funds distributed by Congress to state and local governments.

- The national government influences state government activities and policies through mandates and conditions of aid.

- For a full discussion of federalism, see the 2011–2012 and 2013–2014 editions of *American Government & Politics Today*, Chapter 3.

SYSTEMS OF GOVERNMENT

Federalism is a political system in which power is shared between local units of government—states—and a national government. Only a handful of the world's governments are federal. Most countries have unitary systems, in which the national government has final authority over all government activities. A third, uncommon way to organize a government is the confederal system, where most power resides with subnational governments. The United States under the Articles of Confederation was a confederal system.

The Founders originally settled on a federal system as a practical compromise. The Constitution would not have been ratified if the states lost all of their power, and it was obvious that a confederal system was not working.

Among Americans, federalism has both advocates and opponents. Advocates argue that because the states have their own authority, federalism has provided a training ground for political leaders and an arena to experiment with new public policies before trying these policies on a national level. Federalism also allows for the existence of many political subcultures that vary based on region, race, and wealth, among other factors. Federalism allows these multiple subcultures a greater chance to influence government and policy. Finally, federalism in American government helps create a system of vertical checks and balances. The national and state governments often check each other, ensuring that neither becomes abusive of citizens' rights.

Critics of federalism argue that it allows minority interests to thwart the will of the majority and results in inequities across the states. For example, there is a large range of education funding among the states.

THE CONSTITUTIONAL BASIS OF FEDERALISM

The Constitution creates the outlines of the federal system by delineating how power is shared while also regulating relationships among the states.

The Constitution divides governmental power into three basic categories:

- **Powers of the national government** These are either expressed or implied. Expressed, or enumerated, powers are those that are specifically listed in the Constitution. Some of these include the power to declare war and the power to regulate interstate commerce. Implied powers are those possessed by the national government that are suggested or inferred by its expressed powers. Implied powers came about because of the necessary and proper, or elastic, clause. This clause has allowed the national government to take on additional powers in the course of carrying out its expressed powers. For example, the first Bank of the United States was created using the concept of implied powers. Alexander Hamilton argued that the Constitution's power to levy and collect taxes implied the government's power to create a bank.

■ **Powers of the state governments** The Tenth Amendment of the Constitution protects the states' powers to act in areas not allotted to the federal government or prohibited to the states. This vague definition has come to mean that states are usually free to regulate commerce within their borders. States also retain the majority of police power, or the ability to create laws for the well-being of citizens, in the federal system. Certain powers, such as the power to tax, are shared by the national and state governments. These powers are called concurrent powers.

■ **Prohibited powers** The Constitution denies the national government, state governments, or both the ability to do certain things. For example, the national government is not allowed to tax exports and the state governments are not allowed to enter into treaties.

If there is a conflict between national and state policy or power, the supremacy clause of the Constitution states that the actions and laws of the national government will overrule the actions and laws of a state government.

Not only does the Constitution divide power between the national and state governments, it also regulates relations among the states themselves. The Constitution provides that "full faith and credit" shall be given by each state to the laws, records, and court decisions of other states. It also provides that the citizens of each state shall have the "privileges and immunities" of the citizens of every other state. Extradition (the return of an accused criminal to the state where the crime was committed) is also ensured under the Constitution.

THE EVOLUTION OF FEDERALISM

The Constitution does not—and could not—account for every possibility or situation the government might face. Because of this vagueness, disputes between the states and the national government develop often. Over the years, the Supreme Court has become the final arbiter in these federalism disputes. The evolution of federalism can be observed in several distinct cases and periods:

■ The first important case to define federalism arose in 1819, when James McCulloch, the cashier of the Baltimore branch of the Bank of the United States, refused to pay a tax levied on the bank by the state of Maryland. The Court's ruling on the case answered two questions that expanded the powers of Congress and confirmed the supremacy of the federal government. The first question was whether Congress even had the right to charter a bank, since such power was not explicitly stated in the Constitution. Chief Justice John Marshall held that while the federal government possessed only those powers mentioned in the Constitution, the meaning of those powers required interpretation. Because the power to manage money is in the Constitution, Congress may reasonably charter a national bank as "necessary and proper" (referring to the elastic clause). The second question was whether a federal bank could be taxed by a state. Here Marshall advanced the idea that the government of the United States was not established by the states but by the people. The federal government was therefore supreme in those powers conferred upon it. The states could not challenge those powers and destroy them, as a tax might do. *McCulloch v. Maryland* was clearly a victory for those favoring the supremacy of the national government.

■ On the heels of *McCulloch* came another case that furthered the supremacy of the national government. The Constitution gives Congress the power to regulate interstate and international commerce. An 1824 case, *Gibbons v. Ogden,* forced clarification of the difference between intrastate and interstate commerce. In that case the Supreme Court broadly defined commerce to include virtually any form of commercial activity, again strengthening federal power.

■ After the early Marshall Court decisions, Supreme Court decisions began to favor states' rights over the power of the national government. During the early to mid-1800s, the issues of the tariff and slavery dominated national politics. The slavery issue finally led to the secession of the Southern states and the Civil War, which, in turn, greatly expanded the power of the national government. National power increased not only because of the demands of the war, but also because of the passage of the Civil War Amendments (Thirteenth, Fourteenth, and Fifteenth Amendments), which began to redefine the place of African Americans in U.S. society.

■ After the Civil War, the concept of dual federalism became dominant. In dual federalism, both the national government and the state governments were considered distinct and sovereign within their respective spheres. In practice, this meant that the Supreme Court significantly limited the power of the national government.

■ The doctrine of dual federalism dominated until the Great Depression in the 1930s. To deal with the economic problems caused by the depression, the national government created dozens of programs to create jobs and ease the suffering of the unemployed. In doing this, the New Deal helped to establish the concept of cooperative federalism, meaning the national and state governments work together to create policies. Cooperative federalism has also been referred to as picket-fence federalism. The primary tool of cooperative federalism is the use of federal grants to the states.

Federal grants to the states can be broken into two broad categories:

■ **Categorical grants** are given to states to fund specific programs and projects. Categorical grants come in two types:

- **Formula grants** are given states based on a pre-determined criteria or formula. For example, funding for school lunch programs is based on the number of students who qualify for free or reduced lunches.

- **Program grants** are competitive. States have to apply for money to fund specific programs. Each application is evaluated by the national government, and the money is awarded based on the merits of the application.

- **Block grants** give money to states for a broad program. These grants offer states more flexibility in designing programs. An example of a block grant is federal aid to state welfare programs.

Regardless of the type of grant, money from the national government comes with strings attached. When states accept grant money from the central government, they are forced to accept conditions for the use of that money. These conditions are used by the U.S. government to influence policies related to education and the drinking age. The central government also creates mandates, or requirements, that states must meet regardless of whether there is a grant involved. Most mandates concern civil rights and environmental protection. States may not discriminate in their programs and must comply with national environmental standards.

FEDERALISM TODAY

The relationship between the national and state governments is an ongoing source of political disagreement in modern American politics. In recent years, it has also become a partisan issue. Starting in 1968, Republicans began to favor devolution, or granting more power to the states. Nixon coined the term "New Federalism" to describe his program of revenue sharing and increasing emphasis on block grants. Also in recent years, the Supreme Court has limited the power of the national government, in cases such as *Lopez v. United States* and *Printz v. United States*.

Federalism was built into the Constitution to prevent a concentration of power and threats to liberty. It no doubt expands democracy in many ways. However, the multitude of state and local governments has also created problems, such as inequalities among states in several vital areas, including education. The inevitability of some policies being controlled by the national government because of global, technological, economic, and social changes has given the states a reduced role in American government.

The states nevertheless continue to play a central role in American political life.

AP Tip

Because conditions of aid and mandates are the primary pressures the national government puts on state governments to make them do what it wants, they are a significant aspect of federalism and are likely to appear on the AP exam.

Multiple-Choice Questions

1. Which of the following is the best example of devolution?
   - (A) the No Child Left Behind Act, which provides states with monetary incentives for meeting national educational guidelines
   - (B) the *McCullough v. Maryland* case, which allowed the federal government to maintain a national bank
   - (C) civil rights legislation mandating that states not discriminate
   - (D) block grants, which allow the provision of federal funds to states for discretionary use in a general area
   - (E) the federal tax code, which provides deductions for local charities

2. The Founding Fathers devised a federal system for all of the following reasons EXCEPT
   - (A) federalism is one method for checking government's power and protecting personal liberties
   - (B) geography created travel and communications difficulties, which made it hard to create unified policy when the Constitution was written
   - (C) under the Articles of Confederation, the national government was too dependent on the states for survival
   - (D) a federal system provides a balance of power between state and national governments
   - (E) federal systems were common throughout the world and were proven to be effective

3. Which of the following statements best describes the impact of the Tenth Amendment?
   - (A) It has been effective in protecting and expanding the powers of the states.
   - (B) It had little impact at first but has been expanded over time to protect state powers.
   - (C) The ambiguity of the Tenth Amendment has allowed it to be interpreted differently at different times.
   - (D) The Supreme Court has interpreted it more narrowly over time, restricting states' rights.
   - (E) It has protected the powers of the states, but not those of individual citizens.

4. Which of the following constitutional provisions has been interpreted as weakening the Tenth Amendment and strengthening the scope of federal authority?
   - (A) the full faith and credit clause
   - (B) the supremacy clause
   - (C) the Ninth Amendment
   - (D) the necessary and proper clause
   - (E) the extradition clause

5. What did the Supreme Court determine in *McCulloch v. Maryland*?
   - I. To carry out its economic powers, Congress may reasonably decide to create a national bank.
   - II. The necessary and proper clause enables Congress to take actions not specifically listed in the Constitution.
   - III. States have the right to tax all economic activity within their borders.
   - IV. States may not tax any federal institution.

(A) I and II
(B) I, II, and III
(C) I and IV
(D) I, II, and IV
(E) II and IV

6. The idea that the national government is supreme in its own sphere whereas the states are co-equal in their sovereign powers is known as
   (A) cooperative federalism
   (B) balanced federalism
   (C) home rule
   (D) emerging federalism
   (E) dual federalism

7. Why do states prefer block grants to categorical grants?
   (A) Categorical grants require the states to spend matching funds.
   (B) Block grants have fewer restrictions and can be used for broad purposes.
   (C) Categorical grants are often rescinded.
   (D) The amounts given in block grants are stable from year to year.
   (E) Block grants allow local officials to satisfy the needs of interest groups.

8. The Americans with Disabilities Act (ADA) requires states and local governments to provide equal access for the disabled. This is an example of a(n)
   (A) categorical grant
   (B) block grant
   (C) revenue sharing
   (D) mandate
   (E) administrative regulation

9. In *Kelo v. City of New London* (2005), the Supreme Court upheld a local government's power of eminent domain to take private property to be developed by private companies. How does this case relate to federalism?
   (A) Many state and local governments passed laws to protect property owners from having their land taken and given to a private developer.
   (B) The Court gave the power of eminent domain to the national government, rather than the states.
   (C) The Court overturned a law passed by a local government.
   (D) The Court substituted its own judgment for the judgment of state and local officials.
   (E) The Court strengthened private property rights at the expense of state and local governments.

10. What was the impact of the Supreme Court's decision in *United States v. Lopez* (1995)?
    (A) It revitalized state powers under the Tenth Amendment.
    (B) It prohibited Congress from regulating guns.
    (C) It allowed students to bring handguns to school.
    (D) It broadened the meaning of the commerce clause.
    (E) It created an unfunded mandate that states conduct background checks on gun purchasers.

11. The states play a key role in all of the following
    (A) public education
    (B) law enforcement and criminal justice
    (C) managing the economy
    (D) health and hospitals
    (E) social welfare
12. A husband and wife were married in Virginia and moved to Florida. Must Florida accept the couple's marriage as valid?
    (A) No, because each state may set its own requirements for marriage.
    (B) Yes, but Florida may charge an additional fee for authenticating the marriage certificate.
    (C) Yes, because of the privileges and immunities clause.
    (D) Yes, because of the full faith and credit clause.
    (E) It depends whether Virginia and Florida have reached a reciprocity agreement.

FREE-RESPONSE QUESTIONS

1. The United States Constitution created a federal system of government, and the powers of the state and national governments have shifted over time.
   a. Define federalism.
   b. Identify and explain the constitutional provision that protects state powers.
   c. Pick ONE topic from the list below and explain how it expanded federal power relative to the states.
   McCulloch v. Maryland   Gibbons v. Ogden
   Fourteenth Amendment
2. One way for the national government to influence the states is through the grant process.
   a. Define TWO of the terms from the list below.
   b. Explain how they affect policy making, giving an example for each.
   block grants
   categorical grants
   mandates

Answers

MULTIPLE-CHOICE QUESTIONS

1. **(D)** Devolution is an effort by the national government to return some powers to the states. Block grants, which allow states to spend federal money using some discretion, are an example of devolution (*American Government, 2011–2012*, pp. 112–113/ 2013-2014, 83, 86).
2. **(E)** Federal systems were uncommon when the Constitution was written, and they are relatively rare today (*American Government, 2011–2012*, pp. 87–88/ 2013-2014, pp. 64-65).

3. **(C)** The Supreme Court has tried to interpret the Tenth Amendment as giving the states certain powers beyond the reach of the federal government, but there is a pattern of contradictory decisions by the Supreme Court over time (*American Government, 2011–2012,* pp. 113–115/ 2013-2014, p. 89).

4. **(D)** The necessary and proper clause, also known as the elastic clause, gives the national government any power that is important in carrying out its expressed powers. As a result, the power of the national government was expanded relative to state power (*American Government, 2011–2012,* p. 94/ 2013-2014, pp. 75-76).

5. **(D)** In *McCulloch v. Maryland* the Supreme Court ruled that the necessary and proper clause enables Congress to take actions not specifically mentioned in the Constitution, including the creation of a national bank. Maryland could not tax the national bank, because "the power to tax is the power to destroy" (*American Government, 2011–2012,* pp. 94, 100–101/ 2013-2014, pp. 75-76).

6. **(E)** Dual federalism is the idea that national and state governments are supreme in their respective spheres. This has been replaced by cooperative federalism, with each level of government sharing overlapping powers (*American Government, 2011–2012,* pp. 104–105/ 2013-2014, pp. 79-81).

7. **(B)** Block grants allow states to spend federal money for general functional areas, such as criminal justice or mental health programs. They have fewer conditions attached than do categorical grants (*American Government, 2011–2012,* pp. 108–109/ 2013-2014, p. 83).

8. **(D)** A mandate forces state and local governments to comply with certain rules. For example, the federal government has enacted legislation requiring states to improve environmental conditions and civil rights. When federal funding does not accompany the requirement, this is known as an unfunded mandate (*American Government, 2011–2012,* pp. 109, 201/ 2013-2014, pp. 82-83).

9. **(A)** Many state and local governments passed laws to protect private property owners from having their property taken under eminent domain and given to private developers, even though the Supreme Court approved this use of eminent domain. These state and local governments disagreed with the Court's decision (*American Government, 2011–2012,* p. 115/ 2013-2014, p. 10).

10. **(A)** The Court ruled that Congress exceeded its authority under the commerce clause in passing the Gun-Free School Zones Act. This was the first decision in 60 years that limited the federal government's authority in relation to the states (*American Government, 2011–2012,* pp. 113– 114/ 2013-2014, p. 87).

11. **(C)** States provide a wide array of public services. While the states have some responsibility to manage the local economy, the national government sets monetary and fiscal policy (*American Government, 2011–2012,* pp. 93–94/ 2013-2014, p. 71).

12. **(D)** The full faith and credit clause requires states to respect one another's laws, records, and court decisions (*American Government, 2011–2012,* p. 98/ 2013-2014, p. 73).

Free-Response Questions

1. (a) Federalism is a system of government in which power is divided between the national and state governments.

   (b) The Tenth Amendment is the constitutional basis of state power. It provides that all power not expressly delegated to the national government nor prohibited to the states is reserved to the states and the people.

   (c) In *McCulloch v. Maryland*, the establishment of a national bank was allowed under the necessary and proper clause, which gives Congress the authority to make all laws necessary for carrying out its express powers—in this case, the powers to control interstate commerce and the currency. This decision expanded the power of the national government to take actions not specifically mentioned in the Constitution and limited the states' authority over these actions.

   In *Gibbons v. Ogden*, the Supreme Court ruled that the term "commerce" should be defined broadly, that the national government's power to regulate commerce extended to commerce within a state, and that the power to regulate interstate commerce was an exclusive national power. This expanded the national government's power. Thousands of laws have been passed by Congress under the commerce clause.

   The Fourteenth Amendment defined citizenship. States must accept this definition. It also provided that states may not deprive citizens of due process or equal protection under the law. This limits states' powers. (*American Government, 2011–2012*, pp. 99–102, 104/ 2012–2013, pp. 64, 71, 75–77, 78–79).

2. (a) Block grants are given for use in broad policy areas with few restrictions on their use.   Categorical grants are given to the states to be used for specific purposes or projects defined by federal law.

   Mandates are laws enacted by the national government that the states must follow. Sometimes mandates require the states to spend money, and when the national government doesn't accompany the requirement with funding, this is called an "unfunded mandate."

   (b) This enables states to create policies to address issues identified by the national government in ways that will most benefit their unique circumstances. Welfare money, for example, is given to states in a block grant.

   This affects policy making within the states because it restricts each state's ability to make new policy. States must spend the money in relatively narrowly defined ways, as prescribed by the national government, such as highway construction.

   Mandates make states act in a certain way. They often cost money that could be spent on other programs, and this limits policy making by the states (*American Government, 2011–2012*, pp. 108–109/ 2012–2013, pp. 82–84).

3

THE DEMOCRATIC REPUBLIC

All governments have the same basic goals, such as providing security and order. What distinguishes different types of governments from one another is the emphasis they place on specific goals and how they accomplish these goals. The fundamental values that American democracy emphasizes and attempts to balance are freedom, equality, order, and security.

KEY TERMS

anarchy
aristocracy
authoritarianism
authority
capitalism
conservatism
democracy
democratic republic
direct democracy
elite theory
eminent domain
equality
political socialization
politics
property
recall
government
ideology
initiative
institution
legislature
liberalism
libertarianism
liberty
limited government
majoritarianism

61

majority rule
oligarchy
order
pluralism
political culture
referendum
republic
socialism
totalitarian regime
universal suffrage

KEY CONCEPTS

■ Democracy is one possible form of government. All democracies have shared core principles such as universal suffrage, free and fair elections, majority rule, and limited government.

■ Majoritarianism, elitism, and pluralism are three political theories that explain how democracy in the United States works. .American political culture is dominated by the fundamental values of individual freedom, equality, order, and security.

■ American political culture is dominated by two moderate ideologies: conservatism and liberalism.

For a full discussion of the American democratic system, see the 2011–2012 and 2013–2014 editions of *American Government & Politics Today*, Chapter 1.

WHAT GOVERNMENT DOES

Most political scientists and philosophers believe that a government's most basic task is to provide security and order. Although this seems simple enough, there are many governments in the world today that fail at even these basic tasks.

However, democratic governments go beyond ensuring the security of their citizens. Democratic regimes also work to provide a high level of liberty, which can be defined as the most freedom a citizen can exercise before it interferes with another citizen's freedom. Liberty can work both for and against a democratic government. By ensuring a high level of liberty, a democracy can help make its citizens more content. But the same liberty allows citizens to speak out and demonstrate against the government if they are unhappy for some reason.

WHAT IS DEMOCRACY?

Several different forms of government can be implemented by a society. At one extreme are totalitarian regimes, governments in which the citizens have no practical influence or opportunities for independent action. A form of government with slightly less control is authoritarian government, which permits very limited citizen input and allows some private social and economic activity. On the other end of this spectrum is anarchy, or the absence of government. Democracy falls between these two extremes.

There are several different forms of democracy itself. One is direct democracy. In a direct democracy, citizens participate in making all decisions. The ancient Athenians sometimes practiced direct democracy. Direct democracy is practiced in the United States on the state and local levels in the form of initiative, which allows citizens to place a proposed law on the ballot for all citizens to vote for or against; referendum, which allows citizens to approve or disapprove of a legislative action; and recall, which allows citizens to vote elected officials out of office if dissatisfied with their performance.

However, on the national level, the United States is a democratic republic. In a democratic republic, citizens elect officials to represent their interests. In a country the size of ours, this is a much more efficient and practical form of democracy than direct democracy.

Electing representatives is not enough to make a country a democratic republic. To be democratic, a government must grant all adult citizens suffrage (the right to vote), protect minority rights, and protect civil liberties, such as freedom of speech and freedom of the press.

THEORIES ABOUT HOW AMERICAN DEMOCRACY WORKS

Political scientists have developed three theories to explain how democracy works in the United States:

- **Majoritarianism** This theory states simply that in a democracy, the government should do what the majority of its citizens wants it to do. One weakness in using this theory to describe how democracy works in the United States is low voter turnout. Some political scientists argue that majoritarianism cannot describe American democracy until more citizens actively participate in the political process.

- **Elitism** Elite theory holds that all the important decisions made by the U.S. government are actually made by a relatively small and elite minority. Elite theorists disagree on whether there is one cohesive group of elite decision makers or if there are competing elite groups. While this theory seems to be at odds with the idea of democracy, some research shows that American political elites are more attentive to civil liberties and democratic values than the general public.

- **Pluralism** Pluralist theory holds that U.S. policy arises from the conflicts among groups that compete with one another for power. Political scientists argue that even if many Americans don't participate in the political process, an organized group represents their interests. Competition among these groups results in a compromise in policy. This compromise, according to proponents of pluralist theory, leads to policies that enjoy widespread support from a broad population. One criticism of pluralist theory is that some groups in American society, such as the poor, have few, if any, groups advocating on their behalf. A second criticism is that some groups are too powerful and that too much policy is created to appease these powerful groups. A final criticism is that there is too much competition among groups, creating gridlock that prevents the government from accomplishing any significant policy work.

In addition to the theories about how democracy in America works, there are fundamental values that are part of the dominant political culture. Americans learn these values through a process called political socialization (discussed in greater detail in Chapter 4). These values are as follows:

- **Individual freedom** The Bill of Rights outlines the basic liberties Americans enjoy, such as the freedoms of speech, religion, and the press. Many Americans are willing to limit speech they don't agree with, and most are willing to limit freedom in the name of security, although some are hesitant to go too far in protecting liberties. The USA PATRIOT Act, passed in the aftermath of the 9/11 attacks, limited American civil liberties, such as protection from unreasonable searches.

- **Equality** Americans have a fundamental attachment to the idea of equality. Over the course of American history, the treatment of women, African Americans, and other minorities has become more equitable and fair. However, many Americans stop short of wanting to guarantee equal economic outcomes to all citizens.

- **Order** American citizens expect their government to create policies that help establish and maintain order.

- **Property** Americans believe that the government should work to protect their right to acquire and maintain property or wealth. This is one reason why most Americans oppose the idea of economic equality. Sometimes American property rights come into conflict with the needs of society at large. The government does have the right to use the power of eminent domain to take property, with compensation, from citizens for public projects such as roads and parks. In *Kelo v. City of New London* (2005), the Supreme Court ruled that a government (a city government, in this case) can use the right of eminent domain to take private property for the benefit of private corporations if the goal is economic stimulation, rather than strictly for building roads or some other public good. This was an extremely unpopular decision, and as a result many states passed laws prohibiting the use of eminent domain for the benefit of private corporations.

POLITICAL IDEOLOGY IN THE UNITED STATES

Our two major political parties are the Democrats and the Republicans. Both of these political parties are fairly moderate, for most Americans are moderate in their political beliefs. Many political scientists argue that this indicates that a greater number of Americans are becoming less ideological in their approaches to politics and government. However, the Tea Party movement, which arose after the 2008 election, proved that some independents are more ideological than members of the two major parties.

The Democratic Party is the liberal party in American politics. In general, American liberals advocate for greater government action to improve the welfare and equality of citizens, including greater support for anti-poverty programs and civil rights.

The Republican Party is the conservative party in American politics. In general, American conservatives favor a limited role for government in the economy and society. They do not generally support government efforts to provide relief to needy Americans and are wary of government efforts to create equality through civil rights programs. American conservatism can often be subdivided into economic conservatism, which favors less government interference in the economy and lower taxes, and social conservatism, which supports so-called traditional values and opposes same-sex marriage and abortion.

A third ideology, libertarianism, has recently seen an increase in its popularity in the United States. Libertarians believe in the least possible amount of government interference in all aspects of society, both economic and social.

A note of caution about these party descriptions: remember that the range of political belief is impossible to categorize in just three groups. However, these labels can help you understand some of the basic ideas of the two major parties and other important influences on American political beliefs.

POSSIBLE SHIFTS AND CHALLENGES TO AMERICAN DEMOCRACY

There have been several challenges to American democracy in the 21st century, including the following:

- **Demographic change** Americans are growing older and becoming more ethnically diverse. As more Americans live longer, there will be a greater need for social services, perhaps at the expense of younger Americans, who will have to foot the bill and may also lose their own programs as a result. Also, as Americans become more ethnically diverse, there may be a significant impact on voting behavior. The largest immigrant group in America today is Hispanics, and on the whole they tend to vote more often for Democrats than for Republicans.

- **Globalization** The United States is a significant actor on the world stage, and what happens here is often felt globally. Economic and political decisions made by the U.S. government—even those concerning domestic policy—can have not only a national impact but an international impact as well.

AP Tip

Understanding the views of how political elites behave is a basic tenet of political science and is applicable to many aspects of the U.S. government. These views could appear on AP exam questions relating to democracy, political parties, interest groups, the bureaucracy, and others.

MULTIPLE-CHOICE QUESTIONS

1. What is the term for a widely shared set of beliefs and attitudes toward government and the political process held by a community or nation?
   (A) pluralism
   (B) political socialization
   (C) dominant culture
   (D) political culture
   (E) political ideology

2. Alexander Hamilton believed that the United States should be run by the wealthy and well-educated. Which theory best describes this belief system?
   (A) pluralism
   (B) majoritarianism
   (C) elitism
   (D) Republicanism
   (E) popular sovereignty

3. The graphs below best support which of the following conclusions?
   (A) Blacks are the fastest-growing ethnic group.
   (B) Asians are the slowest-growing ethnic group.
   (C) White birth rates have dropped every year since 1980.
   (D) By the year 2075, the United States will have a minority majority.
   (E) Most of the increase in the Hispanic population is due to immigration.

4. Which of the following is the best description of a political ideology?
   (A) the means by which people develop their political beliefs
   (B) a changing set of political values, depending on the circumstances
   (C) a consistent set of values and beliefs about government
   (D) the methods by which citizens participate in politics
   (E) the value system held by the government, as demonstrated by its policies

5. Which term best describes the process by which a person acquires his or her political beliefs and behaviors?
   (A) political socialization
   (B) political culture
   (C) indoctrination
   (D) political acquisition
   (E) political ideology

6. Which term best describes a system of government that favors private ownership of wealth and free enterprise?
   (A) totalitarian
   (B) socialist
   (C) libertarian
   (D) capitalist
   (E) laissez-faire

7. The United States Constitution protects property rights. However, the government may take private property for public use under the condition that the owner be paid just compensation. This is called
   (A) capital reconstruction
   (B) eminent domain
   (C) public sovereignty
   (D) legitimate use
   (E) public domain

8. Which of the following statements best describes the term *liberals* as used in American political ideology?
   (A) They support government regulation of business and oppose environmental spending.
   (B) They support tax cuts for the wealthy and increased funding for social programs.
   (C) They support civil rights and government programs to improve social welfare.
   (D) They oppose generous government spending for education.
   (E) They support government regulation of abortion.

9. Conservatives favor all of the following EXCEPT
   (A) smaller government budgets
   (B) fewer government programs to redistribute wealth
   (C) fewer government regulations on business
   (D) fewer government restrictions on abortion
   (E) traditional values regarding individual behavior

10. The table below best supports which of the following conclusions?
    (A) Liberals place a high value on economic security and social order.
    (B) Conservatives favor policies supporting economic liberty and social order.
    (C) Libertarians do not value personal or economic freedom.
    (D) Conservatives do not favor government regulation of social and moral issues.
    (E) Liberals do not support a market economy.

11. In 2007, banks in Switzerland, Norway, and China lost billions of dollars because of the failure of the U.S. mortgage market. This is an example of
    (A) globalization
    (B) marketization
    (C) monetarism
    (D) federalism
    (E) currency exchange rate mechanisms

12. Which of the following is/are part of the definition of government?
    I. the legitimate use of force
    II. institutions
    III. political parties
    IV. interest groups
    (A) I and II
    (B) II only
    (C) I, II, and III
    (D) I and III
    (E) I, II, III, and IV

FREE-RESPONSE QUESTIONS

1. The composition of the United States population has changed over time; these changes have political consequences.
   a. Define demographic change.
   b. Identify one recent demographic change in the U.S. population and explain one political consequence of this change.
   c. Identify another recent demographic change in the U.S. population and explain one political consequence of this change.
2. The United States is a constitutional democracy that values majority rule while protecting minority rights.
   a. Define representative democracy.
   b. Explain one way in which the U.S. government has become more democratic over time.
   c. Explain one way in which the U.S. government protects the rights of minorities.

Answers

MULTIPLE-CHOICE QUESTIONS

1. **(D)** Political culture is the shared set of beliefs and attitudes about government and politics held by a community or a nation (*American Government, 2011–2012*, p. 14/ 2013–2014, p. 6).
2. **(C)** Elite theory is the perspective that society should be ruled by a small number of wealthy or well-educated people (*American Government, 2011–2012*, p. 12/ 2013–2014, p. 15).
3. **(D)** It is projected that whites will make up 45.6 percent of the population in 2075. This means that while whites will still make up the largest percentage of ethnic groups, they will be in the minority of the overall population (*American Government, 2011–2012*, p. 24/ 2013–2014, p. 23)
4. **(C)** Political ideology is a consistent set of values and beliefs about government and politics (*American Government, 2011–2012*, p. 18/ 2013–2014, p. 17).
5. **(A)** Political socialization is the process through which individuals learn a set of political attitudes and form opinions about issues (*American Government, 2011–2012*, p. 14/ 2013–2014, p. 6).
6. **(D)** Capitalism is a system characterized by the private ownership of wealth-creating assets, free markets, and freedom of contract. Because the United States regulates business, it is not a pure capitalist system (*American Government, 2011–2012*, p. 17/ 2013–2014, p. 10).
7. **(B)** Although the Constitution protects property rights, the power of eminent domain allows the government to take private property as long as the owner is paid just compensation (*American Government, 2011–2012*, pp. 17–18/ 2013–2014, p. 10).
8. **(C)** Liberals support government action to improve social welfare and civil rights. They are tolerant of political and social change (*American Government, 2011–2012*, pp. 19– 20/ 2013–2014, pp. 18–19).

9. **(D)** Conservatives oppose abortion rights. They believe that government should have a limited role in providing social programs and favor individual and business initiatives. Many conservatives favor traditional family values (*American Government, 2011–2012*, p. 20/ 2013–2014, pp. 18–19).

10. **(B)** According to the table, conservatives value economic liberty and believe the government should promote social order (*American Government, 2011–2012*, p. 18/ 2013–2014, p. 17).

11. Globalization is the increasing interdependence of citizens and nations across the world. The impact of the mortgage failure demonstrates this interdependence (*American Government, 2011–2012*, p. 25–26/ 2013–2014, p. 23).

12. **(A)** The government is made up of institutions (executive, legislative, and judicial). Governments have ultimate authority within society and may legitimately use force. Interest groups and political parties are outside actors that try to influence the government (*American Government, 2011–2012*, p. 5/ 2013–2014, p. 5).

FREE-RESPONSE QUESTIONS

1. (a) Demographic change describes trends in the characteristics of a population, including age, regional distribution, and ethnic composition.

   (b) One recent change in the U.S. population is the growing percentage of Hispanics. Hispanic voters are diverse, but most vote for the Democratic Party. This means more Democrats might be elected in the future. In addition, more Hispanic candidates might be elected. Furthermore, the Republican Party will make efforts to appeal to Hispanic voters.

   (c) Another recent change is the "aging of America." Birth rates are declining, and people are living longer. The political consequences are that there will be an increased need for pensions and health care, and candidates and the government will need to address these issues (*American Government, 2011–2012*, pp. 23–25/ 2013–2014, pp. 20–23).

2. (a) A representative democracy is a government based on popular sovereignty in which the government's power is limited by a document or by widely held beliefs. The United States and Great Britain are representative democracies.

   (b) The United States has become more democratic over time through the expansion of voting rights. Originally limited to property-owning white males, women, minorities, and 18-year-olds have been granted the right to vote. The United States now has universal suffrage.

   (c) One way the rights of minorities are protected is through the First Amendment's protection of the freedom of speech. This means that groups that do not control government can have their voices heard and may advocate for change (*American Government, 2011–2012*, pp. 10–11/ 2013–2014, pp. 13–15).

PUBLIC OPINION AND POLITICAL SOCIALIZATION

One common feature of American politics is opinion polls, which are conducted frequently on a wide variety of issues. Officials in government pay attention to opinion polls, but they don't necessarily act on the information the polls provide. Knowing where Americans' attitudes come from and how they can be classified explains a lot about how American politics works.

KEY TERMS

gender gap
generational effect
life cycle effect
media
opinion leader
opinion poll
political socialization
political trust
public opinion
sampling error
socioeconomic status

KEY CONCEPTS

■ Political attitudes are derived from many sources, including family, school, peers, the media, stage of life, and significant political events.

■ Education, income, race and ethnicity, region, religion, age, gender—all have an impact on voting behavior. .Public opinion polls are used to measure what Americans believe about politics in general, specific issues, and candidates.

- Research shows that public opinion has an important impact on government and policy making, but it is not the sole predictor of government or official action.

For a full discussion of public opinion and political socialization in the United States, see the 2011–2012 and 2013–2014 editions of *American Government & Politics Today*, Chapter 6.

Political Socialization

Opinion polls ultimately show Americans' underlying political values. These values are acquired through the process of political socialization. The places and people from whom we acquire these values are called agents of socialization. There are four primary sources of political socialization:

- **Family and social environment** Parents have a monopoly on time and attention early in the process of political socialization. Most Americans' political beliefs closely resemble those of their parents, especially if their parents were active and interested in political affairs and issues. In addition, it is through the family that individuals are introduced to politically important factors such as class, race, values about education, and religion.

- **School** From kindergarten through high school, Americans are taught everything from social norms and beliefs about democratic behavior to the importance of voting. During high school and post–high school education, individuals are often given an opportunity to become politically active in events such as campus elections. In addition, there is a clear link between educational attainment and political activity; the more educated one is, the more likely one is to engage in political behavior such as voting.

- **Peers** As Americans grow older, they encounter influences outside their family and school. Most peer influence is nonpolitical, but peer groups based on factors such as the "life cycle effect" and the "generational effect" can be significant agents of political socialization.

- **Media** Some political scientists contend that the media has become so influential that today it is equal to the family and schools in its impact on political socialization. Most high school–age students say they get their political information from the media rather than from their parents or peers.

- **The lifestyle effect** Older Americans are generally more conservative than younger Americans. That is because they are more likely to be concerned with their own economic position and want to maintain the social values they acquired when younger, which in many cases are more conservative than contemporary social values.

- **The generational effect** Generations of Americans have been influenced by political events that took place while they were coming of age. For example, Americans who came of age during the Great Depression identify strongly with the Democratic Party because of FDR and the New Deal. Americans who came of age during the 1980s tend to be more supportive of the Republican Party because of the influence of Ronald Reagan.

AP Tip

The measuring of public opinion and its impact on policy making are an important aspect of American politics and are likely to be included on the AP exam.

DEMOGRAPHICS AND VOTING BEHAVIOR

We acquire our political values and beliefs from agents of socialization, which are themselves influenced by a wide variety of factors, including education, income, region, race and ethnicity, religion, age, and gender. Remember that liberals tend to vote for Democrats, while conservatives tend to vote for Republicans. None of these factors is decisive. Combinations of these factors are much better predictors of political attitudes and activity than any single factor by itself.

- **Education** A shift in the way that college-educated Americans vote is underway. In the past, these voters tended to vote Republican; however, recent evidence shows that college-educated citizens, especially those who have received a post-graduate education, more often vote Democrat. Americans with degrees in law, medicine, or other professions tend to support the Democratic Party.

- **Income** Income provides a fair barometer of how someone will vote. Lower-income Americans tend to vote Democrat while higher-income Americans tend to vote Republican. Though there are some exceptions to this, as discussed above (under "education"), it is a fairly reliable indicator of voting behavior.

- **Religion.** Religious beliefs have a tremendous impact on political beliefs. Americans who are particularly religious (attending church at least once a week) and Protestant evangelicals tend to be more conservative and therefore vote Republican. Jewish voters tend to be more liberal than other Americans and vote Democrat.

- **Race and ethnicity** African Americans and Hispanics, the two largest racial minorities in the United States, tend to be more liberal than whites on economic and social-welfare issues (though they tend to be more conservative than most Democrats on such social issues as abortion). Among Asian Americans, the Democrats enjoy a slim margin of support over the Republicans.

- **Gender** Since the 1980s, a noticeable split has emerged in the voting behaviors of men and women. In that time, women have become more liberal. There are two possible explanations for this. First, women tend to have more liberal views on issues such as capital punishment and civil rights than men do. Secondly, women usually earn less than their male counterparts and therefore are more likely to support anti-poverty programs.

■ **Region** The area of the country in which one lives also profoundly affects political beliefs and values. The South, once a stronghold of the Democratic Party, has grown more conservative in recent decades and now is solidly Republican, although the election of 2008 showed some fissures. The Northeast and the West coast continue to be pockets of liberalism.

Public Opinion and the Political Process

In a democracy, it is important that government officials know what the citizens believe and which policies they support. American politicians in the United States keep up with the beliefs of their citizens mainly through the use of opinion polls. Opinion polling has been used for over 100 years, but it was only in the mid-20th century that these polls became fairly reliable predictors of political beliefs and behaviors.

Polling companies, such as Gallup, use random sampling to determine what the public believes about an issue or which candidate they are going to support in an election. In random sampling, a small number of people, chosen at random, are used to represent the views of the entire country. The usual size of a random sample is between 1,500 and 2,000 individual responses. There are three primary problems with opinion polling:

■ **Sample errors** Sometimes not enough people are polled, or were not chosen randomly enough to provide an accurate view of public opinion on an issue or a candidate.

■ **Poll questions** Polling questions are often very simple in their format, such as yes/no or agree/disagree. Because of this limitation, opinion polls fail to capture the intricacies of American opinion. Also, the way a poll question is worded or asked can influence the responses given.

■ **Access to technology** Opinion polls are most commonly conducted by telephone. Many Americans have only cell phones, which are not part of polling companies' databases.

■ Opinion polls in recent decades consistently show that the level of trust Americans have in the government and other societal institutions fluctuates depending on the circumstances. For example, during the 1970s, in the aftermath of the Watergate scandal, opinion polls showed Americans had a high level of distrust in the government. Today people are expressing historically high levels of mistrust in government.

Multiple-Choice Questions

1. Which of the following citizens is most likely to participate in politics?
   (A) a 65-year-old male high school graduate
   (B) a 35-year-old college-educated woman
   (C) a 70-year-old female college professor
   (D) a 40-year-old man with an associate's degree
   (E) an 18-year-old woman starting college

2. All of the following are characteristics of an accurate random sample EXCEPT
   (A) the questions must be asked in clear, unemotional language
   (B) people must have some knowledge of the issues
   (C) the sample must include at least 10 percent of the population
   (D) each person must have an equal chance of being interviewed
   (E) even the most accurate polls have some sampling error

3. What is political socialization?
   (A) a person's identification as a liberal or a conservative
   (B) the distribution of the public's beliefs about an issue over time
   (C) the process by which people acquire their political values
   (D) an informal meeting of people who share the same political ideology
   (E) the official position taken by the government on any important issue

4. Which of the following has the greatest impact on political socialization?
   (A) peers
   (B) the media
   (C) community
   (D) parents
   (E) college professors

5. Which of the following statements best describes the relationship between religion and ideology?
   (A) Evangelical Christians are more likely to vote for Republicans.
   (B) Voters who describe themselves as very religious are more likely to vote for Democrats.
   (C) Most Catholics vote for Republicans because of the party's stance on abortion.
   (D) Region is more important than religion in determining voting patterns.
   (E) There is no predictable link between religious views and voting patterns.

6. Which of the following best describes the relationship between ethnicity and voting?
   (A) Asian Americans are more likely to vote for a Republican.
   (B) Non–Cuban Hispanics are more likely to vote for a Republican.
   (C) African Americans are more likely to vote for a Democrat.
   (D) Voting patterns are more strongly correlated with gender than with ethnicity.
   (E) There is little correlation between ethnicity and voting patterns.

7. All of the following are true about the correlation between age and voting EXCEPT
   (A) Young people tend to vote for liberal candidates as a way of rebelling against their parents.
   (B) Older people tend to be more conservative.
   (C) A generational effect occurs when an important event affects political viewpoints over time.
   (D) Older Americans are concerned about their economic well-being, and that makes them more conservative.
   (E) Older Americans tend to retain their social values.

FREE-RESPONSE QUESTIONS

1. Americans have diverse political viewpoints, and there are a number of factors that influence political behavior.
   a. Define political socialization.
   b. Identify the most important factor influencing political socialization and explain why it has an impact.
   c. Identify another factor that influences political socialization and explain why it has an impact.
2. Public opinion polling is used to measure Americans' beliefs about a number of issues, and polling can be relatively accurate under certain conditions.
   a. Explain how one of the factors listed below can have an impact on the accuracy of a public opinion poll.
   b. Explain how another factor from the list below can impact the accuracy of a public opinion poll.
      random sample
      the way questions are worded
      sampling error
   c. Identify and explain one reason why it is more difficult to obtain an accurate public opinion poll than it was in the past.

Answers

MULTIPLE-CHOICE QUESTIONS

1. **(C)** Voter turnout increases with age and educational level. Women vote at slightly higher rates than men do (*American Government, 2011–2012*, pp. 218–224/ 2013–2014, pp. 188–193).
2. **(C)** Accurate polling requires a random sample with clear questions about understandable topics. Although larger samples are more accurate, they are expensive. A sample of between 1500 and 2,000 voters is sufficient (*American Government, 2011–2012*, pp. 226–229/ 2013–2014, pp. 196–198).
3. **(C)** Political socialization is the complex process by which people acquire their political beliefs (*American Government, 2011–2012*, pp. 214–215/ 2013–2014, p. 183).
4. **(D)** Parents shape their children's ideology. Because children have a strong need for parental approval, they are very receptive to their parents' views (*American Government, 2011–2012*, p. 215/ 2013–2014, p. 184).
5. **(A)** Evangelical Christians, and those who are very devout, tend to vote for Republicans (*American Government, 2011–2012*, pp. 220–222/ 2013–2014, pp. 191–192).
6. **(C)** Since the New Deal, African Americans have largely identified with the Democratic Party (*American Government, 2011–2012*, p. 222/ 2013–2014, p. 192).
7. **(A)** Older people are concerned about their economic well-being while retaining their social values. A generational effect means that important events shape a cohort's worldview. Older people tend to be more conservative (*American Government, 2011–2012*, pp. 213/ 2013–2014, p. 188).

FREE-RESPONSE QUESTIONS

1. (a) Political socialization is the process by which people acquire their political beliefs and attitudes.

   (b) The most important factor influencing political socialization is the family. Children learn a wide range of values from their parents. In some families, the dinner table is a political classroom, and this creates a favorable environment for studying political affairs. Parental influence on party identification is stronger when both parents identify with the same party.

   (c) Education also has influenced political socialization. In elementary school, children learn patriotic rituals, such as saying the Pledge of Allegiance. They also learn about the structure of government. In high schools, students learn about their rights and responsibilities as citizens, and this heightens political awareness. Students in high schools and colleges also develop their questioning and critical thinking skills. Other factors that impact political socialization are peers and the media. These factors, accurately and adequately explained, would also earn full credit (*American Government, 2011–2012*, pp. 214–216/ 2013–2014, pp. 183–186).

2. (a) Accurate polling requires a random sample of the entire adult population. This means that any voter or adult has an equal chance of being interviewed. Random sampling is essential to an accurate poll. This prevents one demographic group from having too much of a say, which would influence the poll's results.

   (b) The way questions are worded can affect a poll's accuracy. Loaded or emotional language can skew a poll's results by leading to the "right" answer. For example, a poll that asks whether innocent boys should die in foreign wars will generate many negative responses. A poll that asks whether American soldiers should defend freedom throughout the world might generate positive responses. The emotional wording of questions has a negative impact on a poll's accuracy.

   Sampling error is the percentage of error that is possible even though the poll is conducted according to sound methods. Pollsters need to make fewer than 2,000 calls to obtain a sampling error of plus or minus 3 percent. In close elections, this sampling error may make it difficult to predict a winner.

   (c) Technology is making it more difficult to conduct an accurate poll. Many people have caller ID and refuse to answer telephone polls. This increases the non-response rate, which undercuts the survey results, making polling less accurate than it was in the past. The increasing use of cell phones and the growing number of people who do not have landlines, when adequately explained, would also be factors that would earn full credit (*American Government, 2011–2012*, pp. 226–231/ 2013–2014, pp. 196–199).

5

POLITICAL PARTIES

The United States is a two-party system, meaning there are only two parties that have any realistic chance of winning elections at any level of government. Americans have a love-hate relationship with political parties—many are distrustful of political parties in this country, yet they decry the lack of parties in nondemocratic regimes around the world. Americans believe in democracy and see political parties as a part of democracy; however, they often see the two-party American system as an impediment to greater representation. Perhaps much of this relationship can be explained by the growing party dealignment that is currently taking place in American politics.

KEY TERMS

dealignment
divided government
electoral college
national committee
national convention
party identification
party-in-government
party-in-the-electorate
party organization
party platform
patronage
plurality
political party
realignment
safe seat
splinter party
straight-ticket voting
swing voters
third party
ticket splitting
tipping
two-party system

KEY CONCEPTS

- Parties are different from other types of interest groups and associations in that they concentrate on choosing and electing candidates to public office.

- The history of political parties in the United States can be divided into seven periods.

- The two major parties enjoy several electoral and psychological advantages over the minor parties.

- Although it may appear hierarchical, party organization in the United States is actually loose and can be chaotic.

- Despite the dominance of the two-party system in American political history, minor parties, sometimes called third parties, have played an important role in American politics.

- Many factors have played a role in the decline in party identification over the past 30 years.

For a full discussion of political parties, see the 2011–2012 and 2013–2014 editions of *American Government & Politics Today,* Chapter 8.

POLITICAL PARTIES AND AMERICAN POLITICS

Political parties differ from other political groups in American society in one simple respect: parties actually advance candidates for elections. Parties serve five basic functions in American politics:

- They recruit candidates for office. Through this recruitment, parties help minimize the number of uncontested seats, thus creating greater voter choice in each election.

- Parties help organize elections. Although elections are run by the state governments, parties provide election volunteers, help create interest in and provide information about the campaigns, and coordinate get-out-the-vote efforts.

- Parties develop competing platforms, or sets of ideas about public policy, from which voters can choose.

- When a party, or its candidates, wins an election, the party accepts responsibility for governing. This means that they have to create and implement policy, staff bureaucracies, and communicate with the electorate.

- The party that loses an election acts as the loyal opposition. The party out of power develops alternative policies to those being proposed or implemented by the party in power. By doing this, the party that is not in power helps create debate on public policy.

POLITICAL PARTIES IN AMERICAN HISTORY

Although the Constitution makes no mention of political parties—in fact, many of the Founding Fathers were wary of the influence of parties on the government—the United States has been a two-party system almost from the start. The party system began to develop even before the Constitution was adopted, and it then transformed during Washington's presidency into what most historians call the First Party System, with the Federalists and the Democratic-Republicans. The Federalist Party disappeared by 1820. The election of 1824 helped to create the Second Party System, with the Democrats and the Whigs. Eventually, the tension over slavery tore the Whig Party apart, and the Republican Party emerged in its place. This Third Party System, which came into being in 1860, is still in place today.

The Third Party System can be divided into four phases, each marked by a critical election:

- The first phase started with Lincoln's election in 1860 and was characterized by Republican domination of the White House; however, Congress was evenly contested between the two parties during this phase.

- The second phase started in 1896 with the election of William McKinley and was characterized by Republican domination of both the White House and Congress. The election of 1896 solidified the links between the Republican Party and business interests in the United States.

- The election of 1932 brought the second phase to a close and ushered in the New Deal coalition. This third phase lasted from 1932 through 1968; during that time the Democrats were the dominant party in both presidential and congressional elections.

- The New Deal coalition fell apart as the Democrats lost the support of Southern whites, mostly over the issue of civil rights for African Americans. This created the fourth and current phase of the Third Party System, which is sometimes referred to as the era of divided government. In recent elections, Americans have had a tendency to split their tickets in general elections: they vote for a candidate from one party for a particular office and a candidate from another party for a different office. Since 1968, the White House and Congress have rarely been controlled by the same party—between that year and 2012, there have only been 14 years in which the same party controlled the White House and both houses of Congress.

THE TWO MAJOR PARTIES TODAY

Critics of the two major parties today claim that there are no significant differences between them. That is not true. There are several important differences between the Republican Party and the Democratic Party:

- **Core constituents** Democrats draw much of their support from ethnic minorities; the well-educated; and Americans living in cities, in the Northeast, and on the East and West coasts. In contrast, Republicans draw much of their support from lower-income whites; evangelical Christians; businesspeople; rural Americans; and the Southern, Great Plains, and Rocky Mountain regions of the country.

■ **Economic beliefs** The Democratic Party is usually viewed as more supportive of social welfare policies and greater government intervention in the economy in the form of government regulation and oversight. Republicans, on the other hand, are usually viewed as strong believers in limited government intervention in the economy and a greater emphasis on self-reliance.

■ **Cultural politics** In recent years the two parties have increasingly diverged on cultural issues. The Democratic Party is more supportive of abortion rights and gay marriage, while the Republican Party usually opposes these issues. The greater emphasis on cultural issues has resulted in a partial shift in each party's constituency. Lower-income Americans, who in the past have typically supported the Democratic Party, are more culturally conservative. This has drawn them to the Republican Party in greater numbers in recent elections. The same is happening on the other end of the income scale, as wealthy Americans are being drawn to the Democratic Party because of their more liberal cultural positions.

PARTY ORGANIZATION

Political parties in the United States, unlike their European counterparts, are loosely organized. Party organization, membership, and influence are reflected in each of the following ways:

■ **Party-in-the-electorate** This refers to all the individuals who claim to favor a particular party, whether or not they actually do anything to support that party. This attachment may be more emotional or psychological, rather than based on a rational evaluation of the issues. Party leaders, however, pay close attention to the affiliation of the electorate.

■ **Party organization** This refers to how each party is organized. While on paper parties appear to be hierarchical, with power flowing down from the national organization, in reality the two major parties in the United States are fairly decentralized. Party organization can be broken into three components:

■ **National party organization** The most visible component of the national party organization is the national party convention. At the convention, the party's choice for president (and vice president) is nominated and the party platform is written. A platform is an explanation of the party's position on issues and how the party will address each issue if elected. Between conventions, the national committee, which is chosen at the convention, oversees the day-to-day operation of each party at the national level. The final component of the national party organization is the national chairperson, who serves as a spokesperson, fundraiser, and executive for the party.

■ **State party organization** Each state has at least two party organizations (one for the Democrats and one for the Republicans), so it is difficult to make generalizations for more than 100 different organizations. However, each state organization engages in many of the same types of activities as the national organization, such as voter education, formulating policy, and supporting candidates for election.

▪ **Local party machinery** At the lowest level, parties are organized by city, township or county. These local parties used to operate on the basis of patronage, meaning that faithful party supporters were rewarded with government jobs and contracts. However, because of political reform, patronage is no longer an important factor in how local parties work. Today, local party organizations provide the volunteers who pass out campaign literature and canvass door-to-door.

▪ **The party-in-government** After an election, the emphasis for the winning party shifts from campaigning to governing. Party membership is an important factor in how Congress operates, how a bureaucracy is staffed, and which policies are introduced and implemented. However, a party's ability to implement its policies is restricted by the checks and balances found in the Constitution and, as discussed above, Americans' more recent preference for divided government. Also, party unity in the United States is tenuous at best. American political parties have a hard time ensuring that all their members support their platform because, unlike European parties, they have little control over who runs for office. American parties usually just provide support for a candidate from their party rather than choose which party member they want to represent them. However, in recent years, party unity has grown because of the increase in the number of safe seats each party has in Congress. A safe seat is one that can reliably be counted in a party's favor, regardless of the current popularity of the party as a whole. This allows the members of Congress who hold these seats to be more ideological in their policies. One effect of this increased party unity is a rise in partisanship, which has made governing more difficult on both the national and the state levels.

WHY THE TWO-PARTY SYSTEM ENDURES

Four factors explain the dominance of the two-party system in American politics:

▪ **Historical foundation** Political arguments in America have often been seen as black and white. The major issues that American politics have historically revolved around, such as slavery in the 1800s, have lent themselves to opposing viewpoints and, therefore, two parties.

▪ **Political socialization** The longevity of the Democratic and Republican parties in American politics has created a persistence that is reinforced by political socialization.

▪ **The winner-take-all system** Most elections in the United States are decided by plurality voting: the winning candidate doesn't need a majority of the vote to win, just the greatest number of votes. This is especially true in presidential elections, where all but two states allocate their electoral college votes to the candidate with the most votes in their state. This winner-take-all system makes it difficult for minor parties to win elections—voters often feel that a vote for a minor party candidate is a wasted vote, even if they agree with the minor party's platform.

- ▪ **State and federal law** Officials in office write the rules for elections. As members of one or the other of the two major parties, these officials often write in legal roadblocks to impede minor parties from enjoying any measure of electoral success.

The Role of Minor Parties in U.S. Politics

Minor parties, often called third parties, do exist, and they can have considerable influence on American politics. There are three basic types of minor parties in American politics:

- ▪ **Ideological parties** These minor parties are created to advocate for a particular issue or ideology. Examples of this type of party are the Libertarian Party and the Green Party.
- ▪ **Splinter parties** These are parties that break away from one of the two major parties over some policy or ideological disagreement. The Bull Moose Party, formed by Theodore Roosevelt who left the Republican Party, is an example of a splinter party.
- ▪ **Individual parties** Sometimes a party is created to support an individual's political candidacy. For example, Ross Perot helped create the Reform Party to support his presidential bids in 1992 and 1996.

The influence of these parties does not come from electoral success; their candidates rarely win elections. But minor parties play important roles in American politics. First, citizens who don't believe they are being heard by the two major parties can turn to minor parties to push certain policies. Minor parties initiated many major reforms, such as women's suffrage and the direct election of senators. The two major parties often embrace the issues of minor parties in an effort to expand their appeal to a greater number of voters. Minor parties can also affect the outcome of an election. In the 2000 election, Al Gore might have won Florida had it not been for the 100,000 votes that were cast for Ralph Nader.

The Future of the Democratic and the Republican Parties

When considering the future of the two major parties in American politics, political scientists often discuss the ideas of realignment, dealignment, and tipping.

- ▪ **Realignment** The ideological and party preference of American voters can shift from one party to another over time. When a long-lasting shift takes place, political scientists and observers say that the electorate has realigned. This change in the electorate's party preference is usually signaled by what is called a realigning election. For example, the election of Franklin Roosevelt in 1932, which showed that the electorate's party identification had shifted to the Democrats, was a critical election. After 1932 the Democrats were the majority party for most of the next 35 years.

◼ **Dealignment** In recent decades, the number of voters who haven't expressed a strong party identification has grown. This rise in the number of independent voters, according to some political scientists, may lead to a period of increased voter volatility, when neither party will be able to create a long-lasting majority. One weakness with this theory is that the number of truly independent voters may be as small as 10 percent.

◼ **Tipping** Realignment can also occur through demographic changes. When this occurs, it is called tipping. For example, California has consistently voted Democratic in recent presidential elections. One reason for this may be that the minority population in California, which tends to vote Democratic, has grown steadily in recent decades.

AP Tip

The factors that determine party identification and the results of declining party identification are likely to appear on the AP exam.

MULTIPLE-CHOICE QUESTIONS

1. All of the following statements accurately describe American political parties EXCEPT
    (A) they recruit candidates for political office
    (B) they coordinate election campaigns
    (C) they run government when their party is in the majority
    (D) they link people with government
    (E) they are able to enforce strict party discipline among their members

2. Which of the following statements best describes why the Federalists and the Anti-Federalists cannot accurately be described as political parties?
    (A) They did not have differing positions on the issues.
    (B) They did not nominate candidates for office.
    (C) They did not have national leaders.
    (D) They were not official organizations.
    (E) They were not able to convey their ideas to most citizens.

3. Which of the following statements best describes party control of the government over time?
    (A) Since the post–Civil War period, the Democrats and the Republicans have alternated in power, with each party enjoying a long period of dominance.
    (B) The two-party system began with Lincoln's election in 1860.
    (C) Parties tend to alternate in power every other term.
    (D) The Democrats have been more successful than the Republicans in maintaining power.
    (E) Third parties rarely form, because most voters identify with the Democrats or Republicans.

4. All of the following are reasons for the dominance of a two-party system EXCEPT
    (A) most states use a winner-take-all system in awarding electoral college votes
    (B) states use a plurality system in electing governors
    (C) third-party campaigns are centered around a popular figure and do not articulate a clear ideology
    (D) members of the House of Representatives are elected using a first-past-the post, single-member district system
    (E) Federal Election Commission rules place restrictions on campaign financing by third-party candidates

5. Which term best describes a gathering of delegates of a single political party from across the country to choose candidates for president and vice president?
    (A) national caucus
    (B) national primary
    (C) national convention
    (D) party platform
    (E) general election

6. Which of the following best describes a realigning election?
    (A) a presidential election with a very close vote that causes citizens to be skeptical of the result
    (B) an election marked by a realignment among certain groups of voters
    (C) an election in which the candidate wins by a large margin, with a mandate to pursue his or her policies or issues
    (D) an election in which the incumbent is defeated because most of the public is dissatisfied with his or her policies or votes
    (E) an election in which a third party emerges, causing an important split in one of the major parties

7. Which of the following statements explains why the United States is described as having a two-party system?
    (A) The Constitution specifically provides that there will be two major parties.
    (B) Third parties tend to represent specific racial and ethnic groups that don't have enough members to win an election.
    (C) While third parties often have candidates in state and local elections, they rarely nominate candidates for the presidency.
    (D) Third parties tend to represent certain regions of the country, such as the South.
    (E) Although third parties compete in elections, they rarely win.

8. When one party controls one or both houses of Congress and the president is from another party, what is this called?
    (A) electoral realignment
    (B) bipartisanship
    (C) divided government
    (D) realignment
    (E) party polarization

9. All of the following are types of minor parties in the United States EXCEPT
   (A) splinter parties
   (B) parties centered around a charismatic personality
   (C) ethnic minority parties
   (D) ideological parties
   (E) single-issue parties

10. Which of the following statements best describes the national committees of the major political parties?
   (A) They share power with state and local party organizations.
   (B) They are highly centralized and organized.
   (C) National party organizations are far more important than state party organizations.
   (D) They are fragmented, disorganized, and ineffective.
   (E) They have little impact on state-level elections.

11. What is a party machine?
   (A) a machine for counting votes accurately
   (B) a bandwagon used by candidates to rally supporters
   (C) a centralized party organization that uses patronage to reward loyal voters
   (D) a coalition of interest groups that ban together to support a political party
   (E) an effective and democratic means of distributing government contracts and jobs

12. How do delegates to national party conventions differ from the voters who identify with their party?
   (A) Democratic delegates tend to be more moderate than Republican delegates.
   (B) Delegates are more likely than voters to support their party's frontrunner.
   (C) Delegates tend to be younger than the average party member.
   (D) Republican delegates tend to be more conservative than Republican voters.
   (E) Republican delegates are more ethnically diverse than Democratic delegates.

FREE-RESPONSE QUESTIONS

1. Although the American political parties have changed over time, the United States remains a two-party system.
   a. Explain the winner-take-all feature of the electoral college.
   b. Explain how the winner-take-all feature contributes to a two-party system.
   c. Explain how members of the House of Representatives are elected.
   d. Explain how the election system for members of the House of Representatives contributes to a two-party system.
   e. Explain one informal reason that the United States has a two-party system.

2. The number of Americans identifying with a political party fluctuates over time. This change in party identification impacts government and politics.
   a. Define party dealignment.
   b. Identify and explain one way in which the two major political parties might react to dealignment.
   c. Identify and explain one way in which dealignment impacts the functioning of government.
   d. Identify one type of third party and explain how a third party might impact an election.

Answers

MULTIPLE-CHOICE QUESTIONS

1. **(E)** Parties link people with government by sponsoring candidates, coordinating campaigns, and running the government when they are in the majority. Unlike political parties in many other countries, discipline in American political parties is weak (*American Government, 2011–2012*, pp. 277–279/ 2013–2014, pp. 244–245).

2. **(B)** Although they were partisan, the Federalists and the Anti-Federalists were not political parties because they did not offer candidates for office. They can best be described as factions (*American Government, 2011–2012*, pp. 279–280/ 2013–2014, pp. 246–247).

3. **(A)** Since the post–Civil War period, power has alternated between parties, with each party maintaining power for long periods of time. These are called party eras (*American Government, 2011–2012*, pp. 281–283/ 2013–2014, pp. 248–250).

4. **(C)** Third parties are at a disadvantage in the methods for electing the president, members of Congress, and state governors. Furthermore, Federal Election Commission rules make it more difficult for them to raise funds (*American Government, 2011–2012*, pp. 298–299/ 2013–2014, pp. 264–267).

5. **(C)** A national convention is a gathering of party delegates from all over to select the presidential and vice-presidential candidates and draft a party platform (*American Government, 2011–2012*, pp. 291–293/ 2013–2014, pp. 258–260).

6. **(B)** A realigning election occurs when groups of voters, such as African Americans, shift their loyalty and voting patterns over the long term. This is known as party realignment (*American Government, 2011–2012*, pp. 304–305/ 2013–2014, p. 271).

7. **(E)** Two major parties have dominated government, alternating control. Third parties rarely win elections (*American Government, 2011–2012*, p. 300/ 2013–2014, pp. 267–269).

8. **(C)** Divided government occurs when the president is from one party and one or both houses of Congress are controlled by the opposing party. This has been the general pattern—with some exceptions—since 1969 (*American Government, 2011–2012*, pp. 283, 285/ 2013–2014, p. 263).

9. **(C)** Third parties may be ideological, single issue, splinter, or charismatic (*American Government, 2011–2012*, p. 300/ 2013-2014, pp. 267–269).

10. **(A)** American national party committees have gained strength, but the system is decentralized, and state and local party committees play important roles in election campaigns (*American Government, 2011–2012,* pp. 291–296/ 2013–2014, pp. 258–262).

11. **(C)** Political machines are large and well-coordinated party organizations that offer people favors, such as government contracts, in exchange for votes (*American Government, 2011–2012,* p. 295/ 2013–2014, p. 261).

12. **(D)** Republican delegates are more conservative and Democratic delegates are more liberal than their respective party members (*American Government, 2011–2012,* p. 293/ 2013–2014, pp. 258, 264).

FREE-RESPONSE QUESTIONS

1. (a) The winner-take-all feature means that the candidate who wins the majority of the vote in a state is awarded all of that state's electoral college votes.

    (b) It is unlikely that a third-party candidate would receive a plurality of votes in many states. Because third parties have a hard time winning votes in the electoral college, the system favors the two major parties.

    (c) Members of the House of Representatives are elected using a first-past-the-post, single-member district system. This means that the candidate with the plurality of votes in a district wins the seat.

    (d) Unlike some countries that have a proportional system, which allows smaller parties to win a percentage of seats in the legislature, the system for electing members of the House of Representatives favors the two major parties because it is difficult for a candidate to win a plurality of the votes.

    (e) One informal reason for the two-party system is political socialization. Children learn at a fairly young age to think of themselves as a Republican or a Democrat. As a result, the two-party system is perpetuated through the family (*American Government, 2011– 2012,* pp. 298–299/ 2013–2014, pp. 264–267).

2. (a) Party dealignment is a decline in party loyalties that reduces voters' long-term commitment to a particular political party.

    (b) One way in which Republicans and Democrats might react to dealignment is to find issues that will resonate with a certain group of voters and encourage them to support their party in the long run. For example, the Republicans might try to appeal to the conservatism of many Hispanic Americans. The Democrats might target younger voters who are interested in social issues, such as gay rights.

    (c) Dealignment may result in divided government, when voters support a candidate from one party for the presidency and candidates from the opposing party for Congress. This is called ticket-splitting. Divided government may cause gridlock in policymaking.

    (d) One type of third party is a splinter party in which a candidate splits from a major party because of some kind of disagreement. Sometimes splinter parties divide the votes of the party they left, allowing the opposing party to win the election. This happened when Woodrow Wilson became president.

There are other possible answers. Sometimes third parties are started by an individual or group committed to a particular issue, interest, or ideology. Third parties can also be organized around a charismatic person who wants to run for office (*American Government, 2011–2012*, pp. 300–308/ *2013–2014*, pp. 267–269, 272–273).

CAMPAIGNING FOR OFFICE

Voting is the most recognizable and fundamental form of political participation. Campaigns are extremely complicated and expensive endeavors for the candidates, who must consider a host of issues when deciding whether to run for office. Once a candidate chooses to run, fundraising often becomes the primary focus of the campaign. While money does not buy an election, it does allow a candidate to get his or her message out to the public. In choosing among two or more candidates, voters rely on party identification and an assessment of the issues and policies and the candidates' attributes.

KEY TERMS

battleground state
communications
director
corrupt practices acts
finance chairperson
focus group
front-loading
Hatch Act
independent
expenditures
issue advocacy
advertising
political action
committee (PAC)
political consultant
pollster
presidential primary
press secretary
soft money
superdelegate
tracking poll

Key Concepts

- The nature of campaigning has changed since the early 20th century because of both efforts to make the process more transparent and the evolution of the media-driven campaign, which has increased the cost of campaigns.

- Campaigns are long and expensive, and candidates are increasingly relying on electronic media to communicate with voters.

- Campaign finance is a continual source of controversy and reform.

- For a full discussion of elections and campaigns, see the 2011–2012 and 2013–2014 editions of *American Government & Politics Today,* Chapter 10.

Candidates

Candidates for local, state, and national office often don't match the demographic makeup of the United States in general. Throughout most of the 20th century, the overwhelming majority of candidates for office were male, of Anglo descent, and Protestant. Additionally, most office seekers were professionals, and many were lawyers. However, with the passage of the civil rights legislation in the 1960s more African Americans began holding office. By 2007, there were over 9,500 African American officeholders, and in 2008, the United States elected its first African American president, Barack Obama.

There has also been a significant increase in the number of women running for offices of all types. In 2012, 182 women ran for Congress, and 81 of these candidates were successful..

The Modern Campaign

Campaigns have changed significantly since the mid-20th century. At one time, political campaigns were almost entirely organized and run by political parties. An effective party organization was key to electoral victory. With the decline of party identification (see *American Government & Politics Today,* Chapter 8) and the advent of campaign finance laws, the ability of political parties to organize and run campaigns was hampered. Today, campaigns are mostly the effort of the candidates themselves, with some assistance from the party.

A modern campaign is run, in large part, by paid professionals. Volunteers help with simple tasks, but paid consultants make the crucial decisions. Some of the roles that every campaign needs to fill in order to be successful include the following:

- **Political consultant** This person, perhaps the most important in any campaign, devises the overall campaign strategy and theme.

- **Finance chairperson** As the costs of campaigns have become higher and higher, especially those for national office, every campaign hires a professional fundraiser.

- **Pollster** Every campaign hires a person or professional polling company to conduct polls on the issues and how to sell the candidate's message (see *American Government & Politics Today*, Chapter 6, for more on polling).

- **Communications director** This person helps shape the message for the campaign and the response to attacks from opposing candidates.

- **Press secretary** Because the media plays a tremendous role in the success of any campaign, the press secretary is an important part of the campaign. The press secretary deals directly with the press..

In most elections in the United States, and all at the national level, a candidate does not need a majority to win office; he or she just needs the *most* votes, even if it is less than a majority of the total votes cast. This is called a plurality system. To win, a candidate tries to capture most of the voters that belong to his or her party and enough independent voters to ensure a plurality of votes. Candidates use several approaches to accomplish this:

- **Candidate visibility and appeal** Candidates who are well known enjoy greater electoral success. Incumbents, for example, have a tremendous advantage over their usually less well-known opponents. Candidates who aren't very visible or well known generally have to devise a strategy to raise their visibility in an election.

- **Opinion polls** Candidates use polls as a source of information about voter beliefs and preferences. A special type of poll, a tracking poll, is used by candidates to determine how well they are doing against their opponent(s).

- **Focus groups** Campaigns conduct interviews with small groups of people called focus groups. These interviews are used to help craft the candidate's image and message. Often, members of focus groups include members of specific target so the campaign can gauge how its message is being received by a variety of people.

CAMPAIGN FINANCE

The importance of money in a modern election campaign cannot be denied.. Salaries for campaign professionals and the costs of conducting polls and purchasing advertising are all significant. In the latter half of the 20th century and into the early part of the 21st century, the cost of political campaigns at all levels increased tremendously. Nearly $6 billion was spent during the 2011–2012 election cycle. Campaign finance is subject to a series of federal laws that has developed over the course of nearly a century.

In the early 20th century, Congress passed a series of corrupt practices acts that were an effort to regulate both the amount of money a campaign could accept in contributions, and how much money campaigns could spend. In 1939, Congress also passed the Hatch Act. This law placed limits on political activities in which government employees could engage. The act also included limits on campaign contributions and expenditures. However, these laws were mostly ineffective, so Congress updated campaign finance regulation in the 1970s.

The Federal Election Campaign Act (FECA), passed in 1971 and amended in 1974, created the Federal Election Commission (FEC). The FEC is a nonpartisan committee charged with the implementation and oversight of campaign finance law. FECA also created the basic rules for campaign finance, including these:

- **Public financing of presidential campaigns** FECA provides public funds for a presidential candidate during the primary season and general election campaign. By raising a given minimum, a candidate becomes eligible to receive matching federal funds. Once a candidate meets the minimum threshold, the FEC matches further contributions up to a preset limit. After the nominees are chosen, the FEC provides each candidate and party with a preset amount of money he or she can spend on the campaign.

- **Limited presidential campaign expenditures** Candidates who accept federal funding for presidential campaigns agree to federal spending limits. The Bush-Kerry race in 2004 was the last time both candidates accepted public money for the general election campaign.

- **Contribution limits** FECA put a $1,000 cap on hard money donations—money given directly to a candidate's campaign. The Supreme Court narrowed this limit in the case *Buckley v. Valeo* (1976), ruling that candidates could spend as much of their *own* money on their *own* campaigns as they wanted.

- **Reporting requirements** Candidates are required to file reports detailing how much money their campaigns have taken in, from what sources, and in what amounts.

- **Creation of Political Action Committees (PACs)** FECA created a mechanism, called the political action committee, or PAC, to allow unions, corporations, and other special interest groups to make campaign donations to candidates. PACs must receive funds from 50 volunteer donors, give money to at least five candidates, and be limited to $5,000 per candidate each election cycle. Since their creation, both the number of PACs and the money they contribute to political campaigns has grown significantly. In 1976, there were about 1,000 PACs; today, there are more than 4,600. PAC spending has grown from $19 million to over $1 billion in recent campaigns.

There is no public financing for congressional campaigns. However, any funds raised for a congressional campaign are subject to the same limits created by FECA and BCRA (McCain-Feingold, discussed below).

It wasn't long before parties, candidates, and interest groups found loopholes in FECA's requirements. There were three main loopholes exploited by these groups:

- **Soft money** Hard money is defined as money given directly to political campaigns, and FECA limited hard money contributions to $1,000. Soft money—that is, money given directly to a political party—was not so limited. Parties used these soft money contributions on their conventions, voter registration drives, and other political activities that supported their candidates. The amount of soft money donated to parties increased dramatically during the 1990s and the early part of the 21st century.

- **Independent expenditures and issue advocacy** Interest groups, unions, and corporations are allowed to spend money on advertising and other campaign activities as long as they are not coordinated with a particular campaign. The Supreme Court has allowed the government to restrict this type of spending when done to endorse a specific candidate, but the Court has also allowed unlimited independent expenditures on issue advocacy. For example, the Christian Coalition can spend as much money as it likes on television commercials to promote its agenda.

In 2002, as a result of weaknesses in FECA, Congress passed the Bipartisan Campaign Reform Act (BCRA), commonly referred to as McCain-Feingold, after its Senate sponsors, John McCain and Russ Feingold. BCRA created the following requirements:

- **A ban on soft money contributions** McCain-Feingold eliminated soft money contributions to national party organizations altogether. It also placed a $10,000 limit on contributions to state and local party organizations.

- **A higher limit on hard money contributions** McCain-Feingold raised the limit on hard money contributions to $2,000 and indexed it to inflation to allow it to increase naturally over time. However, it left the $5,000 PAC limit in place.

- **Advertisement limits** BCRA restricted the airing of ads that mention a candidate for federal office. These types of ads cannot be aired within 30 days of a primary election or within 60 days of a general election. A recent Supreme Court decision, *Citizens United v. FEC* (2010), held that these restrictions violate the First Amendment. . The Court's decision allows corporations and unions to spend an unlimited amount of money in a campaign and run political advertisements without restriction.

Despite the efforts to limit the influence of money, significant loopholes that allow campaigns to circumvent these limits remain. Under the Internal Revenue Service tax codes, 527 and 501(c) groups (so called in reference to the section number of the tax code that allows them to operate) are allowed to raise unlimited funds for campaigns as long as their advocacy is for issues, rather than for specific candidates.

RUNNING FOR PRESIDENT

Presidential candidates are chosen every four years at a national party convention. There, the candidate who has a majority of the pledged delegates at the convention is nominated. Until 1972, the selection of the presidential candidate was made at the convention. Today, the national convention serves to confirm the results of a long nomination process made up of 50 individual state primaries and caucuses.

Party conventions lost much of their importance in the wake of the 1968 Democratic National Convention in Chicago. Anti-war protestors, upset at having been locked out of the nomination process, rioted outside the convention hall. These riots were broken up by use of extreme violence on the part of the Chicago police. The McGovern-

Fraser Commission, created to make the nomination process more open and democratic, proposed reforms that placed greater emphasis on diversity in the selection of convention delegates. However, a few years after those reforms were implemented, the Democratic Party introduced the idea of super delegates, party officials who are meant to help balance the nomination process

Today, most states use presidential primaries to allocate delegates among different presidential candidates. Citizens cast a vote for the candidate they prefer; the Democratic Party allocates delegates to candidates proportionally (one of the McGovern-Fraser reforms), while the Republican Party uses a winner-take-all system, allocating all of the delegates for a state to the candidate with the most votes. There are three types of presidential primaries:

A recent trend in the presidential nomination process is front-loading. In an effort to get greater media attention and play a more important role in the nomination process, many states have moved their primaries or caucuses to earlier dates.. Front-loading makes it even more important to do well early on if a candidate is to have a chance at winning a party's nomination for president.

A candidate seeking the nomination of his or her party goes through a long and grueling process. Often the discussions about running for president begin soon after a presidential election. Official announcements are made months before the first caucuses and primaries. Historically, Iowa has held the first caucuses, and New Hampshire has held the first primary in the campaign season. These two small, quite unrepresentative states have a disproportionate influence in presidential nominating. Because they are the first contests, Iowa and New Hampshire serve to whittle the field of candidates down. From there, the surviving candidates move on to the rest of the primaries and caucuses. The party's choice is officially nominated at the national convention.

AP Tip

Campaign finance continues to be a hotly contested political issue. Knowledge of FECA and McCain-Feingold is essential to understanding recent reforms and will likely be part of the AP exam.

MULTIPLE-CHOICE QUESTIONS

1. Which of the following statements best explains the impact of the primary election system on political parties?
   (A) Primary elections have strengthened the power of parties, because more people are involved in the process.
   (B) Primary elections have weakened the power of political parties, because they cost the parties a great deal of money.
   (C) Primary elections have weakened the ability of national parties to choose their own candidates for office.
   (D) Primary elections weaken political parties because candidates may not follow the party's platform.
   (E) Primary elections have had no significant impact on the power of political parties.

2. Which of the following best describes the Hatch Act?
   (A) It expanded the civil service system.
   (B) It restricted the amounts an individual may spend on his or her own campaign.
   (C) It created the Federal Election Commission.
   (D) It restricts the political activities of government employees.
   (E) It reduced total spending on presidential campaigns.

3. Which of the following statements best explains the role of presidential nominating conventions today?
   (A) Conventions are dramatic because the party's choice for the nomination is not announced until the final day of the convention.
   (B) Conventions are more likely to be deadlocked over a candidate now than they were 80 years ago.
   (C) Conventions do not play in important role in determining the party's platform.
   (D) Conventions ratify the results of a long nomination process in which the nominee is chosen prior to the convention.
   (E) The presidential nominee chooses a vice president on the last day of the convention.

4. What is the purpose of states scheduling earlier primaries and caucuses (front-loading)?
   (A) to move a party's convention to a date that is earlier than the other party's convention in order to gain national attention first
   (B) for a particular state or region to hold an early primary to gain attention from the media and candidates
   (C) to move a state's primary late in the process because a candidate has already been selected; this relieves the state of the cost of holding an election
   (D) in close races, to hold a primary election right before the national convention so that a state may choose the nominee
   (E) to hold primary elections on different days for Republicans and Democrats so undecided voters can vote in both party primaries

5. All of the following are part of the Bipartisan Campaign Finance Reform Act of 2002 EXCEPT
   (A) soft money contributions to national political parties from corporations were banned
   (B) money given to national parties must be in the form of individual donations and PACs
   (C) independent organizations cannot use their own money in ads that refer to a clearly identified federal candidate within the 60 days before an election
   (D) individuals can no longer spend unlimited amounts of their own money on their campaigns
   (E) soft money contributions to national political parties from unions were banned

6. What is a political action committee?
   (A) a group organized for the specific purpose of donating money to political campaigns
   (B) an interest group that advocates for a particular issue
   (C) an independent organization that runs "issue ads"
   (D) an organization that donates money to charities in order to claim a tax deduction
   (E) a group that nominates and endorses candidates for office

7. What are 527 organizations?
   (A) groups that provide soft money for presidential campaigns
   (B) informal groups that raise money on behalf of a particular candidate
   (C) organizations formed for the purpose of raising and donating funds to a political party
   (D) groups that provide hard money to congressional candidates
   (E) tax-exempt organizations outside of political parties that attempt to influence elections

8. How is a 21st-century campaign different from campaigns in the past?
   (A) Campaigns cost less, because the Internet is a low-cost method of reaching voters.
   (B) It is more difficult to raise campaign funds due to finance reform legislation.
   (C) Campaigns are less dependent on political parties.
   (D) Campaigns are more focused on loyal party voters than they were in the past.
   (E) Campaigns are more focused on the party's ideas than on a particular candidate.

Free-Response Questions

1. Presidential campaigns have changed over time, and national conventions now confirm the nomination rather than select the candidate.
   a. Describe both of the following:
      presidential primaries
      front-loading
   b. Explain how each of the items you described in (a) is important to the process of nominating a candidate.
   c. Identify and explain one way the national convention process has changed over time.

2. The role of money in elections is controversial and several attempts have been made to limit the influence of campaign contributions on the political process.
   a. Identify one item from the list below and explain one way in which it impacted campaign contributions.
   b. Identify another item from the list below and explain one way in which it impacted campaign contributions.
      Federal Election Campaign Act
      Buckley v. Valeo (1976)
      Bipartisan Campaign Finance Reform Act of 2002
   c. Explain one way in which organizations have been able to circumvent limits on campaign contributions.

Answers

MULTIPLE-CHOICE QUESTIONS

1. **(C)** Primary elections allow voters, instead of national party leaders, to choose the candidate (*American Government, 2011–2012*, pp. 359–360/ 2013–2014, p. 328).

2. **(D)** The Hatch Act restricted political activities by government employees. It also set spending limits, but there were many loopholes, and the law was ineffective at reducing spending (*American Government, 2011–2012*, p. 348/ 2013–2014, pp. 318–319).

3. **(D)** National party conventions today serve as pep rallies to confirm the candidate predetermined by a long nominating process (*American Government, 2011–2012*, pp. 362–363/ 2013–2014, p. 332–334).

4. **(B)** Front-loading is holding a state's primary or caucus early in the year so that the state maximizes attention from the media and the candidates (*American Government, 2011–2012*, pp. 360–361/ 2013–2014, p. 329).

5. **(D)** In *Buckley v. Valeo*, the Supreme Court ruled that it is unconstitutional to restrict the amount of money congressional candidates can spend on their own campaigns (*American Government, 2011–2012*, pp. 349– 353/ 2013–2014, p. 320).

6. **(A)** Political action committees (PACs) are committees set up by and representing a corporation, labor union, or special interest group for the purpose of raising campaign donations (*American Government, 2011–2012*, pp. 349–351/ 2013–2014, pp. 320–321).

7. **(E)** 527 organizations are groups that focus on encouraging voter registration and supporting particular issues. They are not part of political parties and often create ads on behalf of their causes (*American Government, 2011–2012*, p. 354/ 2013–2014, pp. 323-326).

8. **(C)** Campaigns rely less on political parties than they did in the past, in part because fewer people identify with a political party (*American Government, 2011–2012*, p. 343/ 2013–2014, p. 311).

FREE-RESPONSE QUESTIONS

1. (a) A presidential primary is a statewide vote to select delegates. Party supporters vote for the candidate they favor, and the candidates win delegates according to a specific formula. These delegates then attend the national convention.
    Front-loading is a state or region's practice of scheduling primaries or caucuses early in the year.

    (b) Primaries allow party members to express their preferences through a simple vote. This weakens party control over the nominating process, because the rank-and-file members—not the party leaders—make the decisions.
    Front-loading brings more media and candidate attention to a state or region. This means that the area may receive a disproportionate amount of attention, especially if the state has a small population.

    (c) One change in the national convention process is that the nominee has usually been selected well before the convention takes place. This means that there is less drama, and less media coverage, than in the past. Conventions are now well-scripted pep rallies (*American Government, 2011–2012*, pp. 357–363/ 2013–2014, pp. 328–329, 333).

2. (a) The Federal Election Campaign Act was an attempt to set limits on the amount of money that could be contributed to political campaigns. The law set a limit of $1,000 for individual contributions and $5,000 for political action committees. PACs were new legal entities created by the law, and they were required to register with a new agency, the Federal Election Commission. The law was not very effective, however, because there was no limit on the amount individuals and PACs could give to political parties. This became known as the "soft money" loophole.

   (b) In *Buckley v. Valeo*, the United States Supreme Court ruled that the government could not place limits on the amount an individual could contribute to his or her own campaign, that such spending was a constitutionally protected form of free speech. This overturned the limits set in the 1973 law as they applied to an individual's own campaign.

   The Bipartisan Campaign Finance Reform Act of 2002, also known as the McCain-Feingold Act, bans soft money. The limit on individual contributions was raised to $2,000, indexed for inflation. "Independent expenditures" by corporations, labor unions, and other associations are restricted.

   (c) 527 organizations are one way of avoiding limits on campaign spending. 527s are tax-exempt entities that raise soft money independent of a political party and do not contribute directly to individual campaigns. Instead, they encourage voter registration and run ads advocating for certain issues (*American Government, 2011–2012*, pp. 348–349, 353–356/ 2013–2014, pp. 319–326).

VOTING AND ELECTIONS

Voting is the most basic and most measurable activity in a democracy. Americans have the opportunity to vote in a wide variety of national, state, and local elections. Some have speculated that for just this reason, Americans suffer from voter fatigue, one possible explanation for low voter turnout in the United States.

KEY TERMS

Australian ballot
Indiana/party-column ballot
Massachusetts/office-block ballot
rational ignorance effect
registration
voter turnout

KEY CONCEPTS

■ Voter turnout is an important measure of democratic health. Since the 1960s, voter turnout in the United States has declined.

■ Over the course of American history, the right to vote and the ability to exercise that right have been won by groups originally denied voting privileges.

■ The method by which elections are conducted has changed over the past century.

■ The method of choosing the president using the electoral college is unique. However, it does have its critics because of its undemocratic nature.

For a full discussion of voting and elections, see the 2011–2012 and 2013–2014 editions of *American Government & Politics Today*, Chapter 9.

101

VOTER TURNOUT

In recent decades, voter turnout in U.S. elections has declined. In so-called off-year or midterm elections for federal and state representatives, voter turnout rarely reaches 50 percent, and local election turnout is even lower, with voter turnout rates commonly around 25 percent. Although turnout in presidential elections is usually high, even these elections have seen a decline in voter turnout—in fact, it was just over 50 percent for the 2012 presidential election. This has caused many to wonder about the health and vitality of American democracy.

Some political scientists argue that low voter turnout is a sign of apathy and discontent, and that it allows decision making to be held by too few Americans. On the other hand, others argue that low voter turnout is not a problem at all. These political scientists see low voter turnout as a sign of happiness with the current state of affairs, and that even with low turnout, representative democracy can work.

Still other political scientists argue that turnout is not declining at all. They point to the fact that there is an important difference between the voting-age population (all Americans over the age of 18, which includes adults who are ineligible to vote, such as convicted felons and noncitizens) and the eligible voter population (those Americans who are actually eligible to vote). When looking at voter turnout from the perspective of percentage of eligible voters, voter turnout does not seem as low as some critics contend.

Political scientists have identified several factors that increase the likelihood that someone will actually vote:

- **Age** Voter turnout increases with age. In fact, 65–74-year-olds have the highest voter turnout of any age group (over 74 percent in 2008). On the opposite end of the spectrum, voter turnout among 18–24-year-olds is the lowest (just under 49 percent in 2008). However, voter turnout among young Americans has increased in recent presidential elections, partly because both parties are putting in a lot of time and effort to get young Americans to vote.

- **Educational attainment** Voter turnout and educational attainment are closely related. Americans with some college education have 30 percent higher voter turnout than those with no high school education.

- **Minority status** Whites have a higher voter turnout than African Americans, Hispanics, and Asians. There are a few factors that help account for this. With Hispanics and Asians, voter turnout is lower because not all Hispanics and Asians are citizens. Also, lower voter turnout among these groups may be a product of factors other than being a minority, such as educational attainment, age (minority groups are younger than the white population), and income level.

- **Income level** Wealthy and middle-class Americans vote in greater numbers than poor Americans. In 2008, wealthy Americans were almost twice as likely to vote as Americans with low incomes.

- **Competitive elections** Voter turnout is generally high in states in which there are genuinely competitive elections.

- **Uninformative media coverage and negative campaigning** Media coverage of modern election campaigns is mostly superficial. Coverage fails to inform voters about the important issues and the candidates' policies to deal with these issues. Because of this, voters don't have the information needed to make informed decisions at the polls, and so they don't vote. In addition, modern campaigns are highly negative. By the time election day comes, voters have heard nothing but negative information about both candidates, which creates a reluctance to vote at all.

- **The rational ignorance effect** Some Americans feel their vote won't make any difference. Because they lack political efficacy, they do not seek out political information or vote. They avoid learning about politics and voting because the effort to do so is greater than the reward.

Congress and various activists have addressed the issue of low voter turnout. In 1993, for example, Congress passed the "Motor Voter" law, which allowed people to register to vote when they applied for or renewed their driver's licenses. Two other tactics, early voting and absentee/mail-in ballots, have been tried, but none of these efforts has had a positive impact on voter turnout. In fact, one study shows that states that allow early voting or the widespread use of absentee/mail-in ballots actually had lower voter turnout than states that didn't use either of these methods.

EXPANDING THE RIGHT TO VOTE

The Constitution originally left the question of who could vote in the hands of each state, and early on most states restricted the right to vote to white property-holding males. In the early to mid-1800s, most states did away with property qualifications. (North Carolina was the last to do so in 1856.)

Despite this expansion of suffrage (the right to vote), most Americans were still not allowed to vote. Only after the Civil War, when the federal government began to get involved, was suffrage expanded to more and more sectors of American society. Ratified in 1870, the Fifteenth Amendment extended suffrage to all males regardless of race. This allowed former slaves the technical right to vote, though most Southern states created ways to prevent them from exercising this right. It was not until 1920, when the Nineteenth Amendment took effect, that women nationwide were granted the right to vote. The last major expansion of the right to vote was the Twenty-sixth Amendment (1971), which lowered the voting age to 18.

The federal government also has helped minority groups exercise their right to vote through the Voting Rights Act of 1965 (see the 2011–2012 and 2013–2014 editions of *American Government & Politics Today*, Chapter 5, for more information on both how the right to vote had been denied to African Americans and the Voting Rights Act). This law has made it easier for minorities to vote because it requires federal approval of changes in electoral law in states with a past history of voter discrimination. The law also makes ballots available in languages other than English for citizens who have limited English proficiency. Congress and President Bush extended this law in 2006.

Today, the United States has near universal adult suffrage. Very few groups are not allowed to vote—among them are convicted felons (in most states), noncitizens, and individuals who have been found mentally incompetent. One factor, however, continues to inhibit the right to vote: registration requirements. In the United States, you must be registered to vote, often weeks before an election. In essence, this turns voting into a two-step process. Despite the 1993 passage of the "motor voter" law, which was designed to make registration easier, critics contend that voter registration drives voter turnout down. Supporters of voter registration claim that it helps prevent fraud.

PRIMARY AND GENERAL ELECTIONS

Voters select office holders in a general election. Prior to the general election, parties select candidates through primary elections. There are three types of primaries:

- **Closed primary** In a closed primary, only registered members of a particular political party can vote. For example, only registered Republicans can vote in the Republican primary in Colorado.

- **Open primary** An open primary allows registered voters to participate in one party's primary in an open primary state. However, voters are limited to choosing candidates from just one party.

- **Blanket primary** In this type of primary, each voter is given a ballot that lists the names of all the candidates for all offices. This allows the voter to choose candidates from different parties for different offices. For example, a voter could choose a Republican for president and a Democrat for Senate. A Supreme Court decision handed down in 2000 struck down blanket primaries as unconstitutional. Currently, only Louisiana uses the blanket primary, and only for state and local elections, which are nonpartisan according to Louisiana law

- A small number of states use caucuses or conventions to allocate delegates. Caucuses consist of a series of meetings, starting at the local level and culminating in a convention at the state level, where delegates to the national convention are allocated.

HOW ELECTIONS ARE CONDUCTED

Elections in the United States were once marred by high levels of corruption and fraud. In the late 1800s, each political party printed its own ballots, which were then distributed by the fistful to supporters, who then stuffed them in ballot boxes. To combat voter fraud, states created registration requirements and adopted the Australian, or secret, ballot. Ballots are now printed, collected, and counted by state officials, thereby reducing the likelihood of electoral fraud.

The Australian ballot can be printed in two different formats. The first format is called the office-block, or Massachusetts, ballot. In this type of ballot, candidates are listed by office. In the second format—the party-column, or Indiana, ballot—all of a party's candidates are listed in a single column under the party heading. Parties prefer the party-column because it encourages party-line voting and may increase the impact, called the coattail effect, of a popular candidate on the party's other candidates.

Despite the use of voter registration and the Australian ballot, voting mistakes and fraud still occur in the United States today. The election of 2000 in Florida was marred by these mistakes and fraud. There, thousands of voters, mostly African Americans, were improperly purged from voter rolls because Florida's secretary of state gave election officials poor instructions prior to the election. Studies also found that two voting precincts in Florida had more ballots cast than people who voted.

The 2000 election also brought attention to the antiquated voting technology that many poor counties in Florida, as well as other states, were using. This outdated technology is more prone to mistakes and fraud and helped contribute to the confusion in the 2000 election. In response, Congress passed the Help America Vote Act in 2002. This law created minimum standards for voting machine technology and provided funds for counties to upgrade their voting machines.

THE ELECTORAL COLLEGE

Presidential elections are unique because they are the one election in the United States in which the people do not directly elect the person to fill the office. A voter casting his or her vote in a presidential election is actually choosing an elector, someone who will cast a vote in the electoral college. The framers of the Constitution chose this system because they believed that a small group of informed electors would be better qualified to choose the president than the people as a whole.

The method of choosing an elector is left to each individual state. Most states allow the party to choose a group of electors to represent their state's preference for president. Each state has a number of electors equal to its congressional delegation, plus three electors for Washington D.C., for a total of 538 electors.

All but two states allocate their electors in a winner-take-all system, which means whichever candidate won the most votes in those states gets all the electors, regardless of the actual percentage of the vote they won (Maine and Nebraska make proportional allocations). The Constitution does not legally require an elector to vote for the party's candidate, but the instances of an elector's vote not reflecting his or her state's popular vote are rare and have never impacted an election.

To win the presidential election, a candidate must receive a majority of the electoral votes (currently 270). Because of the distribution of votes in the electoral college, it is actually possible for a candidate to become president when the opposing candidate wins the popular vote. This has happened four times in U.S. history, most recently in 2000, when George W. Bush won a majority in the electoral college, despite the fact that Al Gore had more popular votes.

Critics of the electoral college argue that the system has several flaws. In addition to the fact that someone who did not win the popular vote can win the election, critics contend that the electoral college over-represents small states thanks to the guarantee of at least three electors to each state, and that the winner-take-all system of allocating electors does not accurately reflect the actual results of the election.

AP Tip

Factors that influence voter turnout, both positively and negatively, are important and likely to be on the AP exam.

MULTIPLE-CHOICE QUESTIONS

1. All of the following are reasons for low voter turnout in the United States EXCEPT
   (A) media coverage of campaigns is superficial and uninformative
   (B) negative ads make candidates unappealing to voters
   (C) citizens feel that their votes are unlikely to affect the outcome of an election
   (D) states are making it more difficult for voters to register and vote
   (E) voting in person takes time and can be inconvenient

2. Which of the following citizens is most likely to vote?
   (A) a 65-year-old Asian American with a high school diploma
   (B) a 35-year-old African American with a bachelor's degree
   (C) a 70-year-old non-Hispanic white college professor
   (D) a 40-year-old Hispanic American with an associate's degree
   (E) an 18-year-old non-Hispanic white starting college

3. Which of the following statements best describes why voter turnout in the 2010 midterm elections was lower than voter turnout in the 2008 presidential elections?
   (A) Voter turnout is always lower for midterm congressional elections than it is for presidential elections.
   (B) Voter turnout rates decline in periods of economic recession.
   (C) Voter turnout rates are higher during wartime.
   (D) Voter turnout rates decline when there are a large number of state and local ballot issues.
   (E) Voter turnout rates decline where campaigns are very negative.

4. Which of the following populations provides the most accurate prediction of voter turnout?
   (A) the voting age population
   (B) the number of eligible voters
   (C) voters who are registered to a political party
   (D) citizens between the ages of 18 and 80
   (E) the number of people who voted in the last presidential election

5. All of the following statements about elections are true EXCEPT
   (A) the United States holds elections for federal offices every two years
   (B) elections are frequent in the United States because of federalism
   (C) many states conduct yearly elections on ballot issues
   (D) some states allow citizens to elect judges
   (E) voting fraud is prevalent

6. Colorado has nine electoral college votes and follows the system used by the overwhelming majority of states in allocating them. If Candidate A receives 45 percent of the popular vote, Candidate B receives 40 percent of the popular vote, and Candidate C receives 15 percent, how will Colorado's electoral college votes be distributed?

   (A) Candidate A will receive five votes, and candidate B will receive four votes.

   (B) It is impossible to determine, because electors may vote as they please.

   (C) Candidate C will receive one vote and may use it to break a tie between candidates A and B.

   (D) Candidate B will receive nine votes.

   (E) Candidate A will receive nine votes.

7. All of the following statements about the electoral college are true EXCEPT

   (A) if no candidate wins 270 electoral college votes, the election is decided by the House of Representatives, with one vote per state

   (B) candidates who win the popular vote win the presidential election most of the time

   (C) a candidate may win the popular vote and lose in the electoral college

   (D) a candidate must win a majority of the total electoral votes to win in the electoral college

   (E) the major political parties are in favor of eliminating the electoral college

8. Which of the following groups may be legally prohibited from voting?

   (A) noncitizens

   (B) convicted felons

   (C) those who have declared bankruptcy

   (D) election law violators

   (E) I and II

   (F) II and III

   (G) I, II, and IV

   (H) I, II, and III

   (I) II, III, and IV

9. Which of the following statements about voter registration is true?

   (A) Registration requirements increase voter turnout.

   (B) Registration requirements decrease voter turnout.

   (C) Registration requirements increase voter turnout among Democrats.

   (D) There is no direct correlation between voter registration requirements and turnout.

   (E) Registration requirements have a greater impact on state and local elections than on national elections.

10. The electorate has expanded to include all of the following EXCEPT

    (A) the mentally incompetent

    (B) women

    (C) nonproperty–holding white men

    (D) African Americans

    (E) those who are 18 and older

11. What was the primary purpose of the 2002 Help America Vote Act?
    (A) increase voter registration
    (B) increase voter turnout
    (C) provide free transportation to the polls
    (D) increase the use of mail in ballots
    (E) improve the accuracy of voting machines

FREE-RESPONSE QUESTIONS

1. Voter turnout in the United States is lower than in many countries.
   a. Identify and explain one formal requirement that reduces voter turnout.
   b. Identify and explain another formal requirement that reduces voter turnout.
   c. Identify and explain one reason—other than the formal requirements for voting—why citizens might choose not to vote.
   d. Describe one proposal for raising the level of voter turnout and explain why it might be effective.

Answers

MULTIPLE-CHOICE QUESTIONS

1. **(D)** Citizens can register to vote when they apply for a driver's license, and most states offer mail-in ballots. This makes registration and voting easier (American Government, 2011–2012, p. 321/ 2013–2014, p. 289).

2. **(C)** Voter turnout increases with age and educational level. Non-Hispanic whites vote at higher rates than other groups (American Government, 2011–2012, pp. 317–319/ 2013–2014, p. 284–285).

3. **(A)** Voter turnout rates are consistently lower during congressional midterm elections than they are for the following presidential election (American Government, 2011–2012, p. 316/ 2013–2014, p. 283).

4. **(B)** Eligible voters are those who meet the legal requirement for voting. This is the most accurate way to measure voter turnout because it excludes those who are not allowed to vote (American Government, 2011–2012, p. 317/ 2013–2014, pp. 283–284).

5. **(E)** Americans vote more often than citizens of most other countries because our federal system provides a wide range of elections at the national, state, and local level. While there have been instances of voting fraud, they are difficult to prove (American Government, 2011–2012, pp. 315–317, 326–327/ 2013–2014, pp. 281–282, 295–297).

6. **(E)** Like 48 other states, Colorado uses a winner-take-all system. Candidate A, having received the plurality vote, will be awarded all nine of the state's electoral college votes (American Government, 2011–2012, p. 331/ 2013–2014, pp. 298–300).

7. **(E)** Usually the winner of the popular vote wins in the electoral college, although this result is not guaranteed. If there is no majority winner in the electoral college, the election is decided by the House of Representatives, with one vote per state. The major

political parties do not want to eliminate the electoral college because it benefits them (*American Government, 2011–2012*, pp. 329– 332/ 2013–2014, pp. 298–300).

8. **(C)** Certain persons may be legally disqualified from voting, including noncitizens, convicted felons, and those who have violated election laws (American Government, 2011–2012, pp. 322– 323/ 2013–2014, p. 289).

9. **(B)** Registration decreases participation in the political process (American Government, 2011–2012, p. 323/ 2013–2014, p. 290).

10. **(A)** The electorate has been expanded to include non-property owners, African Americans, women, and those 18 and over. The mentally incompetent may be excluded from voting (American Government, 2011–2012, pp. 322–323/ 2013–2014, pp. 288–289).

11. **(E)** The 2002 Help America Vote Act distributed funds to help communities acquire new, easier-to-use, more accurate voting machines (*American Government, 2011–2012*, p. 329/ 2013–2014, p. 298).

FREE RESPONSE QUESTIONS

1. (a) One formal requirement is that voters must register. In most states this must be done prior to the election. This means that voters must decide well ahead of time whether they plan to vote on election day, which decreases voter turnout.

    (b) Another formal requirement for voting is that a citizen must not be a convicted felon. Many countries allow people to vote after they have served their sentences, but the United States prevents these persons from voting long after they have paid their debt to society. This eliminates convicted felons from the voter rolls, decreasing turnout.

    (c) People might choose not to vote because of negative campaigning. After weeks of viewing negative ads, voters may be turned off by both candidates and choose to stay home on Election Day.

    (d) One proposal to raise voter turnout is to eliminate the requirement that voters register before the election. Some states allow voters to register on election day, and North Dakota has no voter registration requirement. This would encourage people to vote even if they decided to do so at the last minute (American Government, 2011–2012, pp. 321–323/ 2013–2014, pp. 285–290).

INTEREST GROUPS

Policy making in the United States is often the result of pluralist competition between two or more interests. Interest groups exist in order to advance and advocate for citizens' beliefs and political values. There is an interest group for nearly every major issue in American politics. However, interest groups are often criticized. Critics contend that the money provided by interest groups and the familiar relationships between lobbyists and government officials result in policy that favors narrow interests rather than the good of the larger community.

KEY TERMS

boycott
climate control
direct technique
free rider problem
indirect technique
interest group
labor movement
latent interests
lobbyist
material incentive
public interest
purposive incentive
service sector
social movement
solidary incentive

KEY CONCEPTS

■ Interest groups perform important tasks that can strengthen the connection between citizens and the government.

■ Americans join a wide variety of interest groups for different reasons.

111

- Because of differences in resources and focus, not all interest groups are equally successful in meeting their goals.

- Interest groups use a variety of tools, both direct and indirect, to accomplish their policy goals.

- Interest groups draw heavy criticism from many citizens and political scientists, who believe they are detrimental to politics. Recent efforts to reform and limit their influence have come about as a result of scandals and criticism about the role interest groups play in the policy-making process.

For a full discussion of interest groups, see the 2011– 2012 and 2013–2014 editions of *American Government & Politics Today*, Chapter 7.

WHY INTEREST GROUPS EXIST

Americans have always been "joiners." Alexis de Tocqueville, a French historian who traveled in the United States during the early 1800s, was astounded by the number of groups and associations to which most Americans belonged. James Madison declared in *Federalist* No. 10 that multiple groups competing for influence would protect the interests of all Americans. Interest groups are important to any democracy, but in the United States there are over 100,000 associations, ranging from parent-teacher associations to powerful interest groups such as the National Rifle Association (NRA). There are several reasons the United States has so many groups:

- **The First Amendment** The right to establish and join associations is protected in the First Amendment. Two clauses, in particular, protect and encourage interest group formation: the right to assembly, and the right to petition the government for a redress of grievances.

- **Federalism** The existence of different levels of government (national, state, local) encourages the formation of groups to address issues at different levels of government. In addition to the better-known national groups, there are thousands of neighborhood associations in the United States that strive to influence local governments.

- **Social movements** Many interest groups were originally created in response to a demand for change. For example, the women's rights movement and the civil rights movement were created to help address the inequalities faced by women and African Americans.

However, a climate conducive to interest groups does not explain why so many exist. Individual Americans need a reason or incentive to join. There are several different types of incentives that might convince Americans to join an interest group:

- **Solidary incentives** Americans often join interest groups for friendship and because of shared interests. People join groups such as the National Audubon Society to learn more about birds, rather than some overt political reason, even though the Audubon Society does have a political agenda.

■ **Material incentives** Some interest groups offer people a tangible incentive to join. AARP (American Association of Retired Persons), for example, offers members a discount on a wide variety of products and services, including insurance and travel opportunities. Sometimes these incentives are indirect, like protection from too much government regulation or policies that protect subsidies for a variety of activities.

■ **Purposive incentives** Americans also join interest groups to accomplish a specific political, economic, or social purpose. Interest groups such as the NRA or Planned Parenthood have very specific and overt political goals, which is why people often join these groups.

Although it could be argued that everyone has interests that might be advanced by political action, not everyone is part of an interest group. Many issues can be considered latent, including those issues that have not reached a level of concern among enough people to cause action. Other times, those who are interested in a particular cause are too disorganized to form a group. Another reason many Americans do not join interest groups is the free rider problem. Some policies that interest groups are able to convince the government to enact benefit a large group of people, regardless of whether they belong to the interest group. For example, when the NAACP was able to get the government to desegregate schools, all African Americans benefited, whether they belonged to the NAACP or not. Environmental groups often encounter the free rider problem. Everyone benefits from cleaner air or water, but few Americans actually belong to an environmental interest group that works for these policy goals.

TYPES OF INTEREST GROUPS

The thousands of interest groups can be broken into several different categories:

■ **Economic interests** The largest single category of interest groups is economic interest groups. These groups can be broken into several subcategories:

■ **Business interests** Perhaps the most numerous type of interest groups are those representing business interests. Often these groups are umbrella groups, meaning they represent certain types of businesses or companies—for example, the American Pet Products Manufacturers Association or the better-known U.S. Chamber of Commerce. These groups are likely to agree on policy that reduces taxation or government regulation, but they often have little else in common because of the wide diversity of American business.

■ **Agricultural interests** Despite the fact that less than 2 percent of Americans are engaged in agriculture, agricultural interest groups wield great influence in shaping public policy. These interest groups have been successful in protecting and expanding farm subsidies in the United States.

■ **Labor interests** Labor unions were once much more powerful in shaping public policy than they are today. Over the past several decades, labor union membership has declined in the United States. Part of the reason for this is the decline in industrial jobs and the increase in service sector jobs, which tend to have lower rates of union membership. Despite their decline in influence, groups such as the AFL-CIO still exert some influence in shaping public policy.

■ **Public employee unions** Although traditional labor unions have declined in membership and influence in recent years, public employee unions have increased in numbers and influence. These unions are made up of government workers, including teachers or police officers.

■ **Professional interests** These interest groups represent trained professionals such as doctors, lawyers, and architects, among others. While the influence of these groups varies, some—for example, the American Medical Association and the Association of Trial Lawyers of America—are tremendously influential in shaping public policy.

■ **Environmental interests** Environmental interest groups have experienced rapid growth in the numbers of groups and in their membership since the 1970s. Among the more prominent environmental interest groups are the National Wildlife Federation and the Environmental Defense Fund.

■ **Public-interest groups** These interest groups' memberships are diverse, because they work for policies that they believe would benefit the nation or community as a whole, rather than a particular segment of the population. Some public interest groups include:

■ **Ralph Nader** While Ralph Nader himself is not an interest group, he is responsible for the organization of several consumer and public interest groups dealing with a number of issues, including automobile safety.

■ **Common Cause** This is a group committed to reforming the political process to make it more democratic and open.

■ **Other public-interest groups** include League of Women Voters (educating women voters), Consumer Federation of America (consumer protection), and American Civil Liberties Union (protecting civil rights)

■ **Single issue groups** One important subcategory of interest groups is single issue groups. These focus their time, effort, and money on a single issue such as abortion, gun rights, or support of Israel. This singular focus often gives these groups an advantage over interest groups with a broader focus.

■ **Foreign governments** Foreign governments lobby the U.S. government on a wide range of issues, including trade, research, and defense issues.

INTEREST GROUP SUCCESS

The success of an interest group depends on three primary factors:

- **Size and resources** To accomplish their goals, interest groups need to influence how elected officials vote on policies that are important to them. This makes the number of members and the amount of money an interest group has important factors in the success the interest group enjoys. The greater its membership, the more votes the group may be able to deliver for elected officials; money increases the group's ability to make campaign contributions to officials who support its goals. Greater funds also help pay for advertising, mailings to members, and other resources that help the group get its message to elected officials.

- **Leadership** Interest group success is often improved by quality leadership. Good leadership can help the interest group negotiate with members of Congress and sell its message to the public.

- **Cohesiveness** The dedication and effort of an interest group's members are perhaps the most important key to the group's success. The more dedicated a group's members are, the more likely they are to engage in letter-writing campaigns, contact their representatives, donate money to the group, or contribute to any number of efforts that can help the interest group achieve its goals.

INTEREST GROUP STRATEGIES

Interest groups use many tools and strategies to meet their goals. Although they are rarely successful in getting Congress or the president to completely endorse their causes, they often manage to get parts of their wish lists adopted, or soften the impact a piece of legislation would have on their interests.

There are two forms of interest group strategies—direct techniques and indirect techniques.

DIRECT TECHNIQUES

Direct techniques involve applying direct pressure or influence on policymakers; for example:

- **Lobbying** The term lobbying refers to a host of different activities in which a lobbyist, usually a paid professional, attempts to persuade a government official to support an interest group's goals. Lobbying often includes some or all of the following activities:

- **Private meetings** Lobbyists meet with members of Congress, government bureaucrats, and presidential aides to furnish information and pitch their interest group's cause.

- **Testimony** Lobbyists often provide expert testimony in congressional committee hearings or before bureaucratic agencies, such as the Federal Trade Commission, on issues that are important to the interest group.

- **Drafting of legislation and regulations** Lobbyists often assist members of Congress and bureaucrats in drafting legislation or rules for the implementation of laws.

- **Social perks** Lobbyists often invite government officials to fancy dinners, to parties, or on trips. They use these occasions to discuss issues important to their interest groups in a relaxed setting.

- **Political information** Lobbyists can provide polling numbers on specific issues or information on what other officials believe about an issue and how they are likely to vote.

- **Nominations** Lobbyists often provide lists or help vet candidates to be nominated to executive agencies that are important to them.

- **Ratings** Interest groups often publish a rating of every member of Congress, usually on a scale from 0 to 100, indicating how often that member supports issues important to the group. For example, environmental groups issue ratings on each member of Congress's environmental voting record.

- **Building alliances**. Interest groups will work with other interest groups that share their goals. This allows these groups to pool resources and create a greater pool of potential members to influence policy making.

- **Campaign assistance** Interest groups can offer candidates election support. They help provide campaign volunteers, endorse candidates, and provide financial support in the form of campaign donations and independent expenditures.

INDIRECT TECHNIQUES

Interest groups also influence policymakers by using third parties, most often the public, in an effort to achieve favorable policy. These indirect techniques include the following:

- **Public pressure** Interest groups use public relations in an effort to create public sympathy or support for a position. If successful, the public then will help convince policy makers to develop policy favorable to the interest groups. This is sometimes called climate control.

- **Using constituents as lobbyists** Rather than create a general public mood in support of their goals, interest groups can also enlist their constituents. They can encourage their members to engage in a letter-writing, phone, or e-mail campaign to convince public officials to support the interest group's agenda, or they can ask influential members, such as businessmen or celebrities, to contact policy makers on the group's behalf.

- **Unconventional pressure**. Sometimes interest groups—especially those that may lack conventional forms of political power—may resort to activities such as protests and boycotts. The civil rights movement is one example of the successful use of unconventional pressure to meet a group's goals. One problem with unconventional pressure is that protests can sometimes turn violent and create a backlash against the group's goals.

AP Tip

Because interest groups are growing in influence and political parties are weakening, the tools that interest groups use are likely to be part of several questions on the AP exam.

REGULATING LOBBYISTS

Because interest groups have the potential to have a significant influence over the policies that are made and in the ways in which they are implemented, their lobbyists and activities are subject to federal regulation. The basic regulations on lobbyists are as follows:

- Federal regulation defines a lobbyist as anyone who spends at least 20 percent of his or her time lobbying members of Congress, their staffs, or members of the executive branch.
- All lobbyists must register with both the House and the Senate.
- Lobbyists must file quarterly reports detailing which bills they have lobbied on, how much money was spent, and the branch of government contacted. Lobbyists do not need to provide the names of individuals they contacted.
- Representatives of foreign-owned firms are required to register with both the House and the Senate.
- The House adopted a ban on gifts, while the Senate adopted a $50 limit on gifts.

Both houses outlawed all-expenses-paid trips or junkets.

The Campaign Finance Reform Act (McCain-Feingold), passed in 2002, was an effort to regulate lobbying by banning soft money contributions. Prior to 2002, corporations, unions, and other organizations could make unlimited contributions to political parties, which gave them a way around limits on contributions to individual candidates. However, the new law did not address 527 organizations and the money spent by these groups has increased dramatically.

Despite these regulations, abuses still occur. In 2006, lobbyist Jack Abramoff pled guilty to three counts of fraud in relation to his lobbying activities on behalf of Native American gaming interests. This scandal resulted in tighter restrictions on lobbyists, including tightened reporting requirements and an extension of the period before a former member of Congress can take a job as a lobbyist.

In 2010 the Supreme Court ruled in *Citizens United v. FEC* that corporations could spend unlimited amounts of money in election campaigns. The 2012 election demonstrated the impact of the *Citizens United* decision. Corporations spent millions of dollars funding issue ads.

Interest groups are a source of controversy in American politics. Most interest group membership is skewed toward the wealthier and better-educated segments of American society. Rarely do members of poor or undereducated classes join interest groups. Also, leaders of interest groups often have different social or economic backgrounds than the average member, which causes some critics to question how well they can represent their members' interests.

MULTIPLE-CHOICE QUESTIONS

1. All of the following are arguments made by James Madison in *Federalist* No. 10 EXCEPT
   (A) factions are dangerous and should be destroyed
   (B) factions are an inherent part of humanity
   (C) it is inevitable that strong differences will develop among factions
   (D) each faction in society will try to influence government policies
   (E) representative democracy helps control the problems caused by factions

2. Interest groups do all of the following EXCEPT
   (A) hire lobbyists to represent them in talking with members of Congress
   (B) attempt to influence the government to enact policies they favor
   (C) back candidates for state and federal office
   (D) educate the public about issues
   (E) monitor government activities

3. Lobbyists do all of the following EXCEPT
   (A) engage in private meetings with public officials
   (B) testify before congressional committees
   (C) assist legislators in drafting legislation
   (D) rally public support on behalf of a particular piece of legislation
   (E) provide important information to senators and representatives

4. Which of the following is an unconventional means of political participation?
   (A) grassroots lobbying
   (B) providing assistance to a political campaign
   (C) forming a coalition with other groups
   (D) boycotting a product, business, or state
   (E) asking individuals to contact their representatives in Congress

5. Why are lobbyists useful to members of Congress as they consider legislation?
   (A) Most lobbyists are Washington outsiders.
   (B) Lobbyists have bigger research staffs than members of Congress do.
   (C) Lobbyists are policy generalists who have knowledge about a broad range of topics.
   (D) Members of Congress must listen to lobbyists in order to get electoral support.
   (E) Lobbyists can provide much needed data and expert knowledge in their area to members of Congress.

6. An interest group would use grassroots lobbying on all of the following issues EXCEPT
   (A) abortion
   (B) Medicare
   (C) Social Security
   (D) complex tax legislation affecting a few people
   (E) immigration

7. An interest group has many members but lacks financial resources. Which lobbying method would it most likely use?
   (A) encouraging members to write letters to members of Congress
   (B) forming a third party to support a candidate for office
   (C) forming a PAC
   (D) forming a 527 group and airing an advertisement on television
   (E) staging a violent protest to garner national media attention

8. There is an old saying that "politics makes strange bedfellows." For example, environmental groups and business groups have worked to strengthen government policies to clean up hazardous-waste dumps. This is an example of
   (A) political action committees
   (B) 527 organizations.
   (C) grassroots lobbying.
   (D) building alliances.
   (E) direct lobbying.

9. Some organizations focus on the best interests of the overall community rather than the narrow interests of a particular group. Which of the following are examples of these issues?
   I. government responsiveness
   II. Medicare
   III. consumer protection
   IV. abortion
   (A) I and II
   (B) I, II, and III
   (C) I and III
   (D) I, III, and IV
   (E) III and IV

10. How have interest groups managed to avoid the spending limitations set forth in the Campaign Finance Reform Act of 2002?
    (A) by forming 527 organizations, which run TV ads without donating directly to a campaign or candidate
    (B) by giving hard money directly to a candidate
    (C) by giving soft money to political parties in unlimited amounts
    (D) by giving money to other interest groups, which then donate the funds to political campaigns
    (E) through lobbyists, who often gave tax-free money to candidates directly in cash

11. A scandal involving Jack Abramoff put pressure on Congress to tighten its rules on lobbyists. Which of the following are lobbyists still allowed to do?
    (A) pay for "fact-finding" trips to exotic locations
    (B) give advice about how to write a key piece of legislation
    (C) give a member of Congress a new set of golf clubs
    (D) buy dinner for a member of Congress and his or her family, as long as official business is discussed
    (E) give a $10,000 campaign contribution to a member of Congress to help with election expenses

FREE-RESPONSE QUESTIONS

1. Interest groups attempt to influence the policy-making process in a number of ways and through multiple access points.
   a. Define one technique from the list below and explain how interest groups can use this technique to advance a cause.
   b. Define another technique from the list below and explain how interest groups can use this technique to advance a cause.
      campaign assistance
      hiring a lobbyist
      grassroots lobbying/public pressure
2. Social movements and interest groups bring together people who share common goals and seek to have their voices heard in the political process.
   a. Define social movement.
   b. Describe one type of interest group from the list below and give a specific example.
      public interest groups
      economic interest groups
      environmental groups
   c. Describe one type of policy that the interest group you identified in (b) would attempt to influence.
   d. Describe another type of interest group from the list below and give a specific example.
   e. Describe one type of policy that the interest group you identified in (d) would attempt to influence.

Answers

MULTIPLE-CHOICE QUESTIONS

1. **(A)** James Madison defined factions as self-interested groups adverse to the community as a whole. He believed that factions were inevitable but that representative democracy could control them. The only way to destroy factions, he believed, would be to destroy liberty (*American Government, 2011–2012*, p. 248, Appendix B/ 2013–2014, p. 212, Appendix C).
2. **(C)** Interest groups educate the public, monitor government policy making, and attempt to get favorable policies enacted. They do not run candidates for office. (*American Government, 2011–2012*, pp. 263–265/ 2013–2014, p. 212).
3. **(D)** Lobbyists meet personally with members of Congress, provide important information, assist in drafting legislation, and testify before committees (*American Government,, 2011–2012*, pp. 262–263/ 2013–2014, pp. 229–230).
4. **(D)** A boycott is an unconventional means of political participation. To be effective, boycotts must gain widespread support (*American Government, 2011–2012*, p. 266/ 2013–2014, p. 234).
5. **(E)** Members of Congress are policy generalists who must make decisions on a broad range of issues. Lobbyists have expertise in specific fields. Members of Congress need credible information and often rely on lobbyists to provide it (*American Government, 2011–2012*, pp. 262–263/ 2013–2014, pp. 229–230).

6. **(D)** Not every issue lends itself to grassroots lobbying, which encourages individual interest group members to contact members of Congress. Interest groups are more likely to use grassroots lobbying when a large number of people will be affected by a policy (*American Government, 2011–2012,* pp. 265–266/ 2013–2014, pp. 232–233).

7. **(A)** Writing letters is an inexpensive form of grassroots lobbying. While protesting also gains the public's attention, in most cases that attention is short-lived (*American Government, 2011–2012,* pp. 265–266/ 2013–2014, pp. 233–234).

8. **(D)** Groups that are concerned about the same piece of legislation build alliances to represent their joint concerns (*American Government, 2011–2012,* p. 264/ 2013–2014, pp. 230–231).

9. **(C)** Public interest groups include Nader's consumer protection group and Common Cause, which advocates for government responsiveness and political reform. Single-issue groups like those who support or oppose abortion, or AARP, which is concerned with the issues facing older Americans, are more narrowly focused (*American Government, 2011–2012,* pp. 256–257/ 2013–2014, pp. 224–225).

10. **(A)** The Campaign Finance Reform Act barred the contribution of unlimited amounts of soft money to parties. To avoid these spending limits, interest groups have formed tax-exempt 527 organizations that run ads independent of a party or candidate (*American Government, 2011–2012,* pp. 353–356/ 2013–2014, p. 232).

11. **(B)** Lobbyists may offer advice to members of Congress. Giving financial incentives, such as gifts, travel, and meals, is generally prohibited (*American Government, 2011–2012,* pp. 267–268/ 2013–2014, p. 236).

FREE-RESPONSE QUESTIONS

1. (a) Interest groups hope to see elected people who will support their issues, so they help campaign on such candidates' behalf. Interest groups may provide people to help work on a campaign, including precinct works to get out the vote, volunteers to put up posters and pass out literature, and people to make phone calls. Sometimes an official endorsement from an interest group helps attract support from voters who care about a particular issue.

   (b) A lobbyist is a person who attempts to influence legislation and other types of policy-making. Interest groups hire lobbyists so that a trained professional will advance their cause. Lobbyists meet with members of Congress and government bureaucrats. They provide necessary information about particular issues and help draft legislation. Lobbyists also testify before committees to provide support for political campaigns.

   Alternate (b): Grassroots lobbying/public pressure is designed to generate public pressure directly on government officials. Interest groups contact their members, asking that they contact the members of Congress representing their district or state. Modern technology has made this even easier with e-mail. No one enjoys dealing with people who are upset, and members of Congress want to satisfy their constituents. An example of this is the American Association of Retired Persons and its use of grassroots lobbying in support of a prescription drug benefit (*American Government, 2011–2012,* pp. 262–265/ 2013–2014, 229–234).

2. (a) A social movement represents the demands of a large segment of the public for political, economic, or social change. The women's rights movement is an example of a social movement.

(b) Public interest groups focus on what is best for the overall community, rather than a narrow subgroup. Ralph Nader's consumer rights organization is an example of a public interest group.

(c) One type of policy that a public interest group would advocate is public safety. These groups want to ensure the public is made aware of unsafe products and they pressure manufacturers to adopt stricter safety standards.

(d) Economic interest groups are formed to promote the interests of businesses and labor. An example is the National Education Association, which is a union for teachers.

Alternate (d) Environmental groups seek to protect air, soil and water quality, to preserve natural areas, and to protect animals. The Sierra Club is an example of an environmental group.

(e) Labor unions seek policies that benefit workers, such as regulation of working hours and the protection of pension benefits.

Alternate (e) Environmental groups advocate for policies that protect land from development. Some groups purchase threatened natural areas and then donate the land for management by state and local authorities (*American Government, 2011–2012,* pp. 246–247, 249–258/ 2013–2014, pp. 213–214, 217–225).

9

THE CONGRESS

The founders of the United States believed that the legislative branch should be the most powerful of the three branches. To that end, Congress was given a host of important powers in the Constitution. While today's Congress has been overshadowed by the presidency, it's still important to understand its powers.

KEY TERMS

bicameralism
casework/ombudsperson
conference committee
direct primary
discharge petition
earmarks
enumerated powers
filibuster
franking
gerrymandering
House majority leader
House minority leader
instructed delegate
joint committee
lawmaking
logrolling
oversight
pork
president pro tempore
reapportionment
redistricting
representation
Rule
Rules Committee
select committee
Senate majority leader
Senate minority leader

seniority system
Speaker of the House
standing committee
trustee
whip

KEY CONCEPTS

■ Congress serves several functions: legislative, representative, constituent service, and oversight.

■ Most congressional powers are explained in Article I of the Constitution. Perhaps the most important source of congressional power has been the "necessary and proper" or "elastic" clause.

■ There are several important differences between the House and the Senate.

■ Congressional elections are a decentralized process. Incumbents usually enjoy a significant advantage in elections.

■ After every census, the seats in the House of Representatives are reapportioned to reflect changes in state populations. Reapportionment is an extremely important political activity and is subject to immense partisan pressure.

■ Most congressional work is done in committees and subcommittees. The committee system speeds up the legislative process and allows members of Congress to become specialists in a few policy areas.

■ Congressional leadership plays an important part in how Congress works. Congressional leaders have a key role in maintaining party discipline and working out compromises with members of the opposition party.

■ The legislative process in the United States is difficult and there are several points at which a bill can be killed.

For a full discussion of Congress, see the 2011–2012 and 2013–2014 editions of *American Government & Politics Today,* Chapter 11.

CONGRESSIONAL BASICS

The U.S. Congress is a bicameral legislature—it has two separate and distinct chambers, called houses. The lower house is the House of Representatives; the upper house is the Senate. At the Constitutional Convention, states with large populations favored a legislature based on state populations, while the smaller states wanted equal representation. This disagreement was solved by the Great Compromise, which created the House of Representatives, in which membership is based on each state's population, and the Senate, in which each state has two members.

The House was also designed to represent the interests of the people through frequent direct elections (House members are elected every two years). The House of Representatives currently has 435 members divided among the 50 states. Because populations change over time, the Constitution calls for a census to be taken every 10 years. Once a census is complete, the seats in the House are re-divided among the states, a process called reapportionment.

The Senate, on the other hand, was designed to represent elite interests in American society. Originally, the legislature in each state chose senators, but as a result of the Seventeenth Amendment, U.S. senators are now chosen by popular vote. Senators serve six-year terms, and the terms are staggered so that only one-third of the Senate stands for election every two years.

Members of Congress do not do all their work on their own, however, but are aided by a variety of professionals and assistants. Each member has a personal staff, most of which is usually dedicated to casework (discussed below). In addition to a personal staff, members of Congress have access to staff services provided by the Congressional Research Service, the Government Accountability Office, and the Congressional Budget Office.

THE FUNCTIONS OF CONGRESS

Congress serves four primary functions:

- **Lawmaking** This is the most basic function of any legislature. Congress makes laws on a wide variety of issues, including the federal budget, health care, military spending, and gun control.

- **Representation** Members of Congress have to act on behalf of their constituents and the nation as a whole. Sometimes these interests come into conflict and a member has to choose which to support. There are two views on how members of Congress should act when faced with such a conflict:

- One view, called the trustee view, holds that members should act to protect the broad interests of society, even those counter to their constituents' interests.

- The other view holds that members of Congress should act as instructed delegates and follow the wishes of those who elected them to Congress in the first place.

- Most members of Congress blend these two styles, sometimes referred to as a "politico" style.

- **Constituent service** One of the most important jobs a member of Congress has is constituent service. Constituents often contact their congressional representatives about difficulties with the bureaucracy, such as trouble receiving a Social Security check. In this capacity, the member of Congress is acting as an ombudsperson, a person who helps solve problems with public officials or agencies.

- **Oversight** Once a bill becomes a law, congressional committees hold meetings and hearings to assess how the legislation is being implemented by the bureaucratic agency in charge of that policy area. Oversight is important because it allows Congress to assess the success of a program, and it offers a check on the executive branch.

THE POWERS OF CONGRESS

Most congressional powers are listed in Article I, Section 8, of the Constitution. These enumerated powers include the abilities to declare war, tax, regulate interstate commerce, coin and print money, and spend. Although the houses have the same basic legislative function, some powers are particular to one or the other. For example, the House of Representatives has the exclusive power to introduce all revenue-generating bills. It also has the power of impeachment—that is, charging the president, vice president, or certain other government officials with crimes.

The Senate's particular powers include the powers of confirmation and ratification. The Senate must approve presidential appointments of Cabinet secretaries, ambassadors, and justices. It must also approve by a two-thirds majority any treaty negotiated by the president, and it holds the trial for any official impeached by the House of Representatives.

Congress has also gained additional powers through several constitutional amendments. For example, Congress gained the power to levy an income tax through the Sixteenth Amendment.

However, the most important source of congressional power may be the "necessary and proper" or "elastic" clause. This clause has allowed Congress to expand its power into areas not mentioned specifically in the Constitution.

The powers of Congress are subject to the system of checks and balances. For example, the president can veto a bill passed by Congress, or the Supreme Court can strike it down as unconstitutional.

CONGRESSIONAL ELECTIONS

Most candidates for congressional office are chosen by direct primary. Elections give voters an opportunity to voice approval or disapproval of their representatives, but one significant fact regarding congressional elections is that incumbents enjoy a tremendous advantage over their challengers. This is especially true of members of the House of Representatives. House incumbents have had a 90 percent reelection rate. Incumbents' advantages include the following:

- **Redistricting** After reapportionment, House districts in the states are redrawn to reflect changes, if any, in population. This is called redistricting. Each district in a state must contain an approximately equal number of people, but the boundaries can be drawn to favor one party over another—a tactic called gerrymandering. Lines can be drawn to make a district more likely to favor either a Democratic or a Republican candidate. The Supreme Court has consistently refused to interfere in cases brought against political gerrymandering. The court has taken a different stand on race, however. So-called "minority-majority" districts, districts that are more likely to elect minority representatives, were struck down by the Supreme Court in 1995; the Court decided that race could not be the dominant factor in drawing congressional districts. While gerrymandering has helped create safe seats for certain members of the House, it has also increased partisanship in Congress.

- **Name recognition** Incumbent members of Congress have an advantage in winning reelection because most of the voters already know who they are. Through speeches, media coverage, and the franking privilege (the ability to mail information to their constituents for free), members of Congress create a larger public awareness of who they are and what they are doing in Congress.

- **Casework** Members of Congress have staff members devoted to casework, including helping constituents cut through red tape and fielding complaints about issues. Good casework builds constituent loyalty.

AP Tip

The advantages of being an incumbent are important in understanding the dynamics of Congress. Incumbency is likely to appear on the AP exam in some form.

THE CONGRESSIONAL COMMITTEE SYSTEM

Almost all of the work in Congress is done in committees. Because of the complex nature of the legislative process and the issues Congress must deal with, the committee system allows members to specialize in a few policy areas. This speeds up the policy-making process and allows for the writing of better legislation. Committees wield a lot of power over the legislative process. Most bills introduced in Congress rarely make it out of committee to the full house for debate. In the House a discharge petition can be used to bring a bill out of committee, but this is rarely successful because to do so requires 218 votes. Every member of Congress will eventually vote on every bill that makes it out of committee, but the specialists in the individual committees write the legislation. There are four types of committees in Congress, and one committee of particular note in the House:

- **Standing committees** The most important and most common type of committee, standing committees are permanent and deal with broad areas of legislation—for example, defense, taxes, and foreign affairs. The Senate has 20 standing committees and the House has 19. The majority party in each house controls the party breakdown between Democrats and Republicans on every committee. Most standing committees are further broken down into several subcommittees, allowing for even further policy specialization. (For a list of the standing committees in both houses of Congress, see *American Government and Politics Today, 2011–2012*, Table 12-5, p. 426 and 2013–2014, Table 11-5, p. 362.)

- **Select committees** These are temporary committees created in either house to investigate a particular issue.

- **Joint committees** Composed of members from both houses, joint committees deal with a particular policy area, such as taxation.

- **Conference committees** When the House and the Senate pass different versions of the same bill, a conference committee is convened. Members from both houses of Congress meet to hammer out the differences between the two versions.

- ■ **House Rules Committee** Because of the number of representatives in the House, debate on the House floor is limited. The House Rules Committee creates a "rule" for each bill that is to be debated. This rule sets the time allowed for debate, the time the debate will take place, and what type of amendments, if any, can be offered on the bill. The House Rules Committee exerts great influence over the legislative process in the House.

Committee leadership is usually awarded on the basis of seniority—that is, which member has been on that committee the longest. The senior member of the majority party usually becomes the committee chair, and other senior members of the majority party head up the subcommittees. When Newt Gingrich became Speaker of the House, he instituted term limits for committee chairs.

Committee organization and leadership are important because this is where the bulk of congressional work is done.

CONGRESSIONAL LEADERSHIP

Each party in Congress has a set of leaders in each house charged with managing the legislative process, dealing with the media, overseeing the rules of each house, and fundraising. Other than the president, these are often the most visible leaders of each party. Because of the size of the House of Representatives and therefore the importance of organization, House leaders wield more power than their Senate counterparts do.

HOUSE LEADERSHIP

- ■ **Speaker of the House** In the House of Representatives, the majority party's leader is called the Speaker of the House. The Speaker presides over House meetings, appoints members of joint and conference committees, schedules legislation for action, and assigns bills to committees to start the legislative process.

- ■ **House majority leader** The House majority leader is elected by the majority party in the House, assisting the Speaker in carrying out his or her duties, as well as helping formulate party policies and strategy.

- ■ **House minority leader** The House minority leader works to maintain party discipline and cohesion, formulate policy alternatives to those proposed by the majority party, and, though lacking real power in these areas, consults with the Speaker on committee assignments, scheduling legislation, and recognizing speakers on the House floor.

- ■ **Party whips** Republican and Democratic whips assist the leadership of their respective parties by channeling information from leadership to members and vice versa. Whips help take polls among party membership to determine support of a given issue and round up members when important votes are being held.

SENATE LEADERSHIP

- **President pro tempore** The Constitution put the vice president in charge of the Senate. In reality, the vice president attends Senate votes only when there is a possibility of a tie, ready to vote to break it. The majority elects a president pro tempore to chair the Senate in the vice president's absence; even so, the real power in the Senate lies with the Senate majority leader.

- **Senate majority leader/minority leader** The Senate majority leader schedules debates and makes committee assignments with the cooperation of the minority leader. Since a single senator can stop all floor action, the two leaders most often work closely together to keep the Senate functioning. The Senate majority and minority leaders also rely on assistants, called whips, to organize their members and persuade them to vote in desired ways.

The most basic job of congressional leaders is to meet with members of their own parties, as well as leaders of the opposition party, in an effort to make the legislative process work. Party discipline in Congress is not high, so many times party leaders have to exert pressure on their members in order to usher their party's legislative programs through Congress. The whips play an important role in this process.

THE CONGRESSIONAL LEGISLATIVE PROCESS

The legislative agenda in Congress is large and complex. During any given session, thousands of bills covering a wide range of topics, from the important to the mundane, are introduced. Congress has developed a system to reduce the traffic, and most bills never make it past the initial stages.

Once a bill is introduced in either house, it is assigned to an appropriate committee, which often sends it to a subcommittee for hearings and discussion. The original bill is frequently revised and changed by the subcommittee before the entire committee votes on it. If a bill survives committee—and most do not—it is then forwarded to the entire house for what is called a floor vote. In the House of Representatives, a bill coming out of committee is sent to the Rules Committee before it goes to the entire House. The Rules Committee attaches to every bill a rule that sets the guidelines for the floor debate, detailing the length of debate and the types of amendments that can be added during the debate.

The Senate has no counterpart to the Rules Committee. This means senators can use the filibuster to prevent a vote on a bill. Because there is no limit on how long a senator may speak once he or she has the floor, a senator can refuse to yield the floor and literally talk a bill to death. A filibuster can be brought to a close only through a cloture vote, a vote by 60 or more senators to bring the debate to an end.

To speed the legislative process, or to help guarantee the passage of a particular piece of legislation, leadership in either house will sometimes offer incentives to wavering party members, or even to members from the opposing party. One example of this process is logrolling. In logrolling, a member of Congress will support a colleague's bill in exchange for that colleague's support on a later bill. A second method of drumming up support for a bill is through the use of earmarks, often called "pork." Earmarks are funds placed in a bill for special projects in a congressperson's state or district. By doing this, supporters of a bill are able to increase the number of supporters.

Once a bill is approved, it moves on to the other house, where it goes through the same process. If there are differences between the Senate-passed and House-passed versions of a bill, a conference committee made up of both senators and representatives meets to work out a compromise. Once a compromise is worked out, the revised bill goes back to both houses for another floor vote.

If a bill has survived this far, it has one final step to go through: it is sent to the president. The president can either sign the bill into law or veto it. A presidential veto can be overridden by a two-thirds vote in both houses of Congress, though this rarely happens. If a president does not sign or veto a bill within 10 days, one of two things can happen: the bill becomes law without his signature or, if Congress adjourns within the 10-day window, the bill dies. This is referred to as a pocket veto.

This legislative process offers dozens of opportunities for a bill to either die or be altered. (For a diagram showing how a bill becomes law, see *American Government & Politics Today, 2011–2012,* Figure 12-5, p. 435 and 2013–2014, Figure 11-5, p. 369.)

MULTIPLE-CHOICE QUESTIONS

1. Of the following members of Congress, who will most likely be chosen to head the House Appropriations Committee when the majority is Republican?

Rep.	Party	Years in Congress	Years on Appropriations Committee
Smith	R	18	2
Jones	R	15	6
Gonzales	D	22	8
Wilson	D	26	4
Jefferson	I	12	12

   (A) Smith
   (B) Jones
   (C) Gonzales
   (D) Wilson
   (E) Jefferson

2. A congressional committee was created to investigate the 2010 oil spill in the Gulf of Mexico. What kind of committee would this be?
   (A) standing
   (B) joint
   (C) select
   (D) conference
   (E) oversight

3. The House Rules Committee does all of the following EXCEPT
   (A) adopt procedures under which the House will consider a bill
   (B) set time limits on debate
   (C) permit or forbid certain amendments on the floor
   (D) review bills and place them on a calendar
   (E) establish the number of votes needed for a bill to pass in the House

4. A filibuster in the Senate can be used to talk a bill to death. A cloture vote can end a filibuster. Taken together, what is the impact of these practices?
   (A) Neither political party can control the Senate unless it has at least 60 votes.
   (B) A party with 51 votes can get most of its legislative agenda passed.
   (C) The Senate rarely passes legislation on controversial issues.
   (D) Most important decisions are made in committees because it is difficult to pass a bill in the Senate as a whole.
   (E) The president's party has a significant advantage because the vice president can vote to break a tie in the Senate.

5. Which of the following statements best describes reapportionment?
   (A) Seats in the Senate are redistributed every 10 years, according to population shifts.
   (B) The boundary lines for congressional districts are redrawn every 10 years, according to population shifts.
   (C) Seats in the House of Representatives are reallocated every 10 years, according to population shifts.
   (D) Every 10 years, there is an official count of the population.
   (E) Committee assignments in Congress are redistributed every two years, according to each party's representation in Congress.

6. All of the following are powers of the Senate EXCEPT
   (A) approving the appointment of Cabinet heads
   (B) initiating all revenue bills
   (C) approving treaties with foreign nations
   (D) holding impeachment trials
   (E) approving appointments to the federal judiciary

7. Incumbents have certain advantages over challengers. These include all of the following EXCEPT
   (A) casework
   (B) franking privileges
   (C) name recognition
   (D) the public's generally positive view of Congress
   (E) the ability to run for reelection in a "safe district"

8. Where does most of the work of Congress take place?
   (A) on the floor of the House of Representatives
   (B) on the floor of the Senate
   (C) in committees
   (D) in oversight hearings
   (E) in the White House, where members of Congress meet with the president

9. When it is most likely that Congress will override a presidential veto?
   (A) when there is divided government
   (B) when the president is a lame duck
   (C) when the overwhelming majority of both houses of Congress is from the party that is not the president's
   (D) when the president uses a pocket veto
   (E) when the president sends a strong veto message to Congress

10. Congress held hearings to investigate the Federal Emergency Management Agency's (FEMA) response to Hurricane Katrina. This is an example of
    (A) legislative review
    (B) committee work
    (C) administrative review
    (D) special investigation
    (E) congressional oversight

11. How does party leadership differ in the House of Representatives from party leadership in the Senate?
    (A) Because the Senate has more powers than the House, its leaders also have more power.
    (B) Leaders in the House have more control over the agenda and over their own party's members.
    (C) Leadership is more centralized in the Senate.
    (D) Party discipline is stronger in the Senate.
    (E) There is no significant difference in leadership positions in the House and Senate.

12. The "bridge to nowhere" was an approximately $400 million proposal to build a bridge to an island in Alaska with about 50 residents. What is the term for this type of congressional spending?
    (A) pork
    (B) discretionary spending
    (C) logrolling
    (D) authorization
    (E) deficit

FREE-RESPONSE QUESTIONS

1. Party leaders in Congress attempt to influence party members' votes. However, there are limits to this influence.
   a. Identify one formal leadership position in either the House of Representatives or the Senate and explain how the individual in that position influences members of his or her party in Congress.
   b. Identify another formal leadership position in the House of Representatives or Senate, and explain how the individual in that position attempts to influence members of his or her party in Congress.
   c. Identify and explain one factor that makes it difficult for party leadership to influence members of their party in Congress.

2. The Founding Fathers created a bicameral Congress and gave the houses of Congress different and sometimes overlapping powers.
   a. Identify and explain two formal powers that are unique to the House of Representatives.

b. Identify and explain two formal powers that are unique to the Senate.

c. Identify and explain two ways in which the committee system requires the House and Senate to work together in policy making.

Answers

MULTIPLE-CHOICE QUESTIONS

1. **(B)** Although this rule is not always followed, the chairman of the committee is usually the member from the majority party who has served the longest on that committee (*American Government, 2011–2012*, p. 427 /*2013–2014*, p. 363).

2. **(C)** A select committee is established for a limited time period and for a specific purpose (*American Government, 2011–2012*, p. 426 /*2013-2014*, p, 362).

3. **(E)** The House Rules Committee reviews bills and puts them on the agenda. It sets time limits and can restrict the kinds of amendments allowed. Bills must pass the House of Representatives by majority vote (*American Government, 2011–2012*, p. 427 /*2013–2014*, pp. 348 and 363).

4. **(A)** It takes 60 votes to end a filibuster. This means that neither party can control the Senate unless it has 60 votes. Otherwise, the minority party can use the filibuster to block legislation sponsored by the majority party (*American Government, 2009–2010*, p. 423 / *2011–2012*, pp. 411–412 /*2013–2014*, p.p. 348–349).

5. **(C)** Reapportionment is the redistribution of seats in the House of Representatives after each census to reflect population shifts. The redrawing of district boundaries is called redistricting (*American Government, 2011–2012*, p. 417 /*2013–2014*, p. 354).

6. **(B)** The Senate approves treaties and major presidential appointments. It holds impeachment trials. Revenue bills must be initiated in the House (*American Government, 2011–2012*, pp. 409–410 /*2013–2014*, p. 347).

7. **(D)** Incumbents have several advantages, including casework to help constituents, name recognition, franking privileges (free mail service, but not for campaign literature), and living in safe districts. This gives incumbents an advantage, despite low approval ratings for Congress as a whole (*American Government, 2011–2012*, pp. 415–416 /*2013–2014*, pp. 353, 359).

8. **(C)** Most of the work of Congress takes place in committees (*American Government, 2011–2012*, p. 424 /*2013–2014*, p. 361).

9. **(C)** It takes a two-thirds vote in both houses of Congress to override a presidential veto. This is more likely to occur when the party opposing the president overwhelmingly controls each house (*American Government, 2011–2012*, p. 435 /*2013–2014*, p. 348,).

10. **(E)** Oversight is the process of following up on the laws Congress has enacted. Congress reviews the operations of an agency to determine whether the agency is effectively carrying out policies as Congress intended (*American Government, 2011–2012*, p. 407 /*2013–2014*, pp. 344–345).

11. **(B)** The House of Representatives is larger than the Senate and harder to manage. As a result, leaders in the House exercise more control over the agenda and party discipline is stronger (*American Government, 2011–2012,* pp. 428–432 /2013–2014, p. 364–366).

12. **(A)** Pork, also known as earmarks, refers to special projects that are intended to benefit a member's district (*American Government, 2011–2012,* p. 434 /2013–2014, p. 368).

FREE-RESPONSE QUESTIONS

1. (a) One leadership position in Congress is the Speaker of the House. The Speaker is the most important person in the House. He or she is elected by the majority party and presides over all House meetings. The Speaker assigns members to committees and decides which bills will be handled by which committees. This is one way he or she can use party leadership to influence members of his or her party in Congress; if a wayward member is sponsoring a bill, the Speaker can assign that bill to a committee, where the bill is likely to get an unfavorable reception and be killed. Conversely, the Speaker can assign the bill to a safe committee, where it will receive a favorable reception in exchange for the sponsor's party loyalty.

   (b) Another leadership position in Congress is whip. A whip is a member of Congress who aids the majority or minority leader in getting legislation passed. Whips ensure that party members show up for floor debate and cast their votes on important issues. Whips conduct polls among party members about their views on legislation and put pressure on wavering members to support the party's legislation.

      You might also discuss the roles of the majority and minority leaders, which would earn points with an adequate explanation.

   (c) Despite the importance of party leadership, members of Congress represent their states or districts, and they want to be reelected by their constituents. This means that they do not always act in accordance with their party's platform. As a result, they are independent actors, and it is difficult for their parties to control their votes on particular issues. In addition, sometimes members of Congress simply do not agree with a piece of legislation, and they vote their conscience. Furthermore, members of Congress will vote against legislation sponsored by their party if the bill goes against the interests of their home state (*American Government, 2011–2012,* pp. 404–405, 428–32 /2013–2014, pp. 341–342, 363–367).

2. (a) One constitutional power of the House of Representatives is to vote on articles of impeachment—the power to formally charge the president, vice president, or other high-ranking government official with serious crimes. A majority vote of the House is required to impeach the president. Another formal power of the House of Representatives is the ability to initiate revenue bills. These are bills that provide income for the federal government, through such methods as the income tax. Although the Senate must also approve revenue bills, they start in the House, because the Founding Fathers considered the House to be closer to the people.

(b) The Senate is the upper house of Congress, and the Constitution gives it several specific powers. One of these is to confirm important officials, such as Supreme Court justices and Cabinet secretaries. This gives the Senate a check on the president's decisions. Another formal power is the authority to ratify treaties. Although the president negotiates treaties with foreign nations, the Senate must approve them before they become law. The Senate also holds impeachment hearings. This means the Senate has the final say over whether a president should be removed from office before the end of his term. A two-thirds vote of the Senate is required for removal.

(c) The committee system in Congress allows the House and Senate to work together on policy making. One example is conference committees. In order for a bill to become law, it must pass both houses of Congress with the same language. Conference committees allow members of the House and Senate to work out the differences in legislation each house has approved. Another way the committee system allows both houses to make policy together is through joint committees, which are composed of members of both the House and the Senate. These committees consider important topics, such as the country's economic policies (*American Government, 2011–2012,* pp. 407–410, 424–428, 467 /2013–2014, pp. 345–346, 360–363).

10

THE PRESIDENT

The executive branch, headed by the president, is the dominant branch of government in the United States today. Presidential power has grown tremendously since the beginning of the twentieth century. Part of this growth in power is the result of domestic changes in how government operates in the United States. But this growth is also the result of the United States' role as an international power and the fact that the Constitution gives the president the lead in foreign affairs.

KEY TERMS

advice and consent
appointment power
Cabinet
chief executive
chief legislator
chief of staff
civil service
commander in chief
constitutional powers
diplomatic recognition
executive agreement
Executive Office of the President
executive order
executive privilege
expressed powers
head of state
inherent power
line-item veto
National Security Council
Office of Management and Budget
pardon
patronage
pocket veto
reprieve
signing statement

State of the Union message
statutory powers
Twelfth Amendment
Twenty-fifth Amendment
Veto message
War Powers Resolution
White House Office

KEY CONCEPTS

■ The powers of the president, while originally quite limited, have grown significantly over the past 200-plus years.

■ The modern president has several roles, including head of state, chief executive, commander in chief, chief diplomat, and chief legislator.

■ Presidents bring to office legislative programs they hope to enact during their terms.

■ Presidential power often rests on the president's ability to persuade and gain public approval.

■ The executive branch includes the president's personal staff, the Cabinet, the vice president, and many other agencies that report to him.

For a full discussion of the presidency, see *American Government & Politics Today*, 2011– 2012 edition, Chapter 13, and 2013–2014 edition, Chapter 12..

PRESIDENTIAL BASICS

The president is the head of the executive branch of the government. As such, he or she is in charge of the implementation of policy created by Congress. The formal requirements to be president are rather simple: the president must be at least 35 years old, be a natural-born citizen, and have resided in the United States for at least the preceding 14 years. In addition to these formal requirements, most U.S. presidents have shared several similar demographic characteristics, including being male, being fairly wealthy, being Protestant (except for Kennedy), and (with a few exceptions) having political experience. Until 2008, all had been white.

Because the president has to win a majority of the electoral college in order to win the election, there have been a few instances when the winner of the election actually lost the popular vote, most recently in 2000, when George W. Bush won the election despite having fewer popular votes than Al Gore. Two times—in 1800 and 1824—no candidate won a majority in the electoral college, so the House of Representatives had to decide the election. To help prevent this, the Twelfth Amendment, adopted in 1804, set up separate elections for president and vice president, since some of the confusion had arisen from the fact that it wasn't clear which electoral college votes went to the president and which to the vice president.

THE ROLES OF THE PRESIDENT

Presidential power can be classified in one of two groups: expressed or inherent. The expressed powers are either constitutional—they can be found in Article II—or statutory—those powers given to the president by congressional legislation. Inherent powers can be inferred from the Constitution. Once a president acts to create a new inherent power, later presidents have that precedent on their side. These inherent powers are often exercised in the form of executive orders, which have the force of law unless overturned by Congress or the courts. Presidential power is exercised in five distinct roles. The president exercises expressed powers in most of these roles, but in modern times all of them include inherent powers.

- **Head of state** This category includes all the ceremonial functions for which the president is responsible, such as receiving visiting heads of state at the White House, bestowing awards on war heroes, throwing out the first pitch of the baseball season, and representing the United States at times of national mourning, such as 9/11.

- **Chief executive.** The Constitution makes the president the chief executive of the United States, responsible for the enforcement of policies created by Congress, the decisions reached by federal courts, and treaties to which the United States is party. For this, the president was endowed with several specific powers:

- **Appointment and removal** To help implement and enforce policy, the president controls a bureaucracy with over 2.7 million employees. Most of these employees are members of the civil service, meaning they gained their jobs through a merit system and cannot be fired for political reasons. However, there are several thousand jobs that the president can appoint anyone to fill. Some of these include the heads of the Cabinet departments, federal judges (when there is a vacancy), and other important policy positions. With the exception of judges and a few other positions, the president can remove any of these appointments for either poor performance or policy disagreements.

- **Reprieves and pardons** One executive power given to the president by the Constitution is the power to grant reprieves and pardons for crimes against the United States. Most presidents have used this power. For example, President Carter gave a blanket pardon to all Vietnam War draft dodgers in 1977. Perhaps the most famous presidential pardon was President Gerald Ford's pardon of former President Richard Nixon for any crimes he may have committed while in office.

- **Signing statements** A recent controversy regarding the president's enforcement powers is the use of presidential signing statements. When Congress passes a bill, the president must sign it into law. Often presidents include a statement in this process, usually adding instructions to the law's implementation. However, President George W. Bush issued 800 such signing statements— more than all by previous presidents combined—which made clear that he would not enforce some aspects of the laws he had just signed.

- **Commander in chief** The president serves as overall commander of American military forces. He makes the decisions regarding when and where to use military force and what the objectives for the use of force should be. This power has become the source of much tension between the president and Congress over the past 50 years, as presidents have often exercised it without an official declaration of war from Congress. In an effort to limit the president's power to deploy troops without congressional approval, Congress passed the War Powers Resolution in 1973. That law requires that the president consult with Congress before sending troops into combat; troop deployments are to be limited to 60 days unless Congress approves an extension. Most presidents have ignored the War Powers Resolution as unconstitutional, and Congress has never tried to use it to force troops to return home. Despite this, the president's powers as commander in chief have expanded, especially in the wake of the 9/11 attacks.

- **Chief diplomat** The Constitution provides the president with several powers that make him the chief diplomat of the United States, a role that gives the president the lead position in formulating foreign policy.

- **Diplomatic recognition** The president has the authority to grant or withdraw formal recognition of a foreign government. For example, the United States had no formal diplomatic relationship with the People's Republic of China between 1949 and 1978 because of the communist government established there in 1949. President Clinton extended diplomatic recognition to Vietnam in 1995, more than 20 years after the end of the Vietnam War.

- **Treaties** The Constitution gives the president sole authority to negotiate treaties with foreign governments. However, before a treaty can take effect, the Senate must ratify it by a two-thirds majority. During the ratification process, the Senate can add amendments to the treaty that may require the president to renegotiate with other signatories to it.

- **Executive agreements** These are agreements between the president and the head of state of another government. They have the force of law, but do not require Senate approval. However, Congress can refuse to appropriate funds to support the agreement if they so choose. Executive agreements do not bind future presidents; as a consequence, they require the new president's consent to remain in effect.

- **Chief legislator** Every president in the modern era has sought to implement a legislative agenda by recommending that Congress pass certain pieces of legislation. Usually a president uses the annual State of the Union address to help create a legislative agenda in Congress. In that speech, the president calls for Congress to create or support particular policy initiatives that he believes to be in the best interest of the country. However, getting Congress to pass the recommended legislation can be difficult. The president has to use persuasion to push Congress to act on his agenda, sometimes bringing to bear public pressure, called "going public," through a televised address or a series of speeches given while touring the country. The president also works closely with congressional leadership, especially those leaders in the president's party, to help push the passage of his legislative agenda.

When a bill does make it through Congress, the president has several choices in how to proceed:

- He can sign the bill into law.

- He can veto the bill if he does not support it. When the president vetoes a bill, he must explain why in a veto message sent to Congress. (The president may not exercise a line-item veto; he must veto the entire bill. In 1996, Congress gave the president the power to exercise a line-item veto over the appropriation section of a bill, but in 1998 the Supreme Court struck this power down as unconstitutional.) Congress can override a veto with a two-thirds vote in both houses, but that is extremely difficult to do. Only 7 percent of vetoes have ever been overridden.

- He can do nothing and allow the bill to become law after 10 days without his signature.

- If Congress adjourns within 10 days of the bill being sent to the president and he has not signed it, the bill then dies. This is called a pocket veto. A pocket veto cannot be overridden. However, Congress may reintroduce the bill in the next session.

THE PRESIDENT AS PARTY CHIEF AND POLITICIAN

Although the Constitution does not address party politics, a sixth role the U.S. president plays is that of party leader. As such, he is the face of the party and its chief spokesperson. The president helps shape his party through the use of patronage, appointing supporters to key party or government jobs. For example, the president is also a key fundraiser for his party. He often campaigns in support of fellow party members running for office.

Despite all of the resources at his disposal, the president must rely on others for his success, much of which depends on his ability to persuade. A president usually can't persuade large majorities in the House and the Senate to support his programs, so his influence is felt more clearly when legislation is closely contested and a few votes here or there will swing it in the president's favor. The president must decide on his priorities; because he has a limited amount of political capital, he must choose when to spend that capital and when to save it. If legislation the president cares strongly about and has actively supported fails to make its way through Congress, his prestige is damaged, making it harder for him to persuade others to support him on the next issue.

Closely related to a president's power to persuade is his ability to use the media and public appearances to get his message out. By mobilizing public opinion, he can strengthen his position when dealing with Congress. A key indicator of a president's success in this area is his approval rating. Introduced during the Truman administration, an approval rating is determined by asking the same question periodically to a random sampling of people: "Do you approve or disapprove of the way President ——— is handling his job as president?" Presidents with a high approval rating usually have greater success in mobilizing public support for their legislative programs. Approval ratings fluctuate based on economic and international conditions, major events (referred to as rally events), and time in office.

Special Uses of Presidential Power

Presidents have three special powers at their disposal, each of which has helped to expand presidential power:

- **Emergency powers** In times of national crisis, the president may exercise powers not found in the Constitution. For example, Abraham Lincoln suspended civil liberties during the Civil War; more recently, President George W. Bush authorized warrantless wiretapping in an effort to fight terrorism. The Supreme Court has usually, but not always, upheld these emergency actions.

- **Executive orders** The president can issue executive orders to enforce existing laws, enforce the Constitution or treaties, and establish or modify rules for administrative agencies. Executive orders have been used to accomplish a wide variety of goals—for example, rationing during wartime and the creation of affirmative action programs. Executive orders have the force of law but may be rescinded by future presidents.

- **Executive privilege** Presidents have claimed the right to withhold certain information or prevent executive officials from testifying in court or before Congress, arguing that being forced to testify would violate the separation of powers. The Supreme Court has limited the application of executive privilege, most notably in the Watergate scandal under President Nixon and the Lewinsky affair under President Clinton.

The Executive Branch

The president has hundreds of advisers and staffers to help execute his duties. As the presidency has grown in power, the executive branch has expanded in order to carry out new duties. Among the most important advisers are the following:

- **The Cabinet** The Cabinet is made up of the heads of the executive agencies and other important officials, such as the National Security Adviser. Cabinet members today usually have little influence for two reasons. First, presidents have become increasingly reliant on the White House Office, whose members often have more personal loyalty to the president than do Cabinet members. Second, Cabinet heads can be more concerned with gaining resources for their respective departments rather than executing the president's agenda.

- **The Executive Office of the President** The Executive Office is a collection of various advisory boards and groups. The following are the most important:

- **The White House Office** The aides closest to the president make up the White House Office. They include his chief of staff, press secretary, and chief legislative liaison. Members of the White House Office are personally loyal to the president, often having known and worked with the president for a long time.

■ **The Office of Management and Budget** This office is in charge of developing the budget that the president submits to Congress.

■ **The National Security Council** This council is made up of the president's most important defense and foreign relations advisers.

■ **The vice president** The only formal constitutional power the vice president has is to preside over the Senate. However, in recent years, the vice president has served several important political and executive functions.

■ **Strengthening the ticket** The choice of a vice presidential running mate is often made to address some perceived weakness on the part of the presidential candidate. For example, Barack Obama chose Joe Biden as his running mate to counter arguments regarding his lack of experience—Biden had many years' experience as a senator.

■ **Supporting the president** Recent vice presidents have been given important policy initiatives to lead in support of the president's agenda. For example, Al Gore oversaw environmental issues while serving as President Clinton's vice president, and Dick Cheney wielded tremendous influence in shaping President George W. Bush's policies on the war of terror and in Iraq.

■ **Presidential succession** The vice president takes over as president if the president dies in office or resigns. The Twenty-fifth Amendment allows the president to temporarily turn power over to the vice president, as President George W. Bush did before undergoing a surgical procedure.

AP Tip

The president's powers in creating foreign policy, as commander in chief, and as chief diplomat, are likely to be covered on the exam.

MULTIPLE-CHOICE QUESTIONS

1. Which of the following best describes why Arizona Senator John McCain chose Alaska Governor Sarah Palin as his running mate in the 2008 presidential election?
   (A) She was from the West, and Senator McCain wanted to sway more voters in that region.
   (B) She was well-versed in foreign affairs, and Senator McCain wanted someone to round out the ticket in international matters.
   (C) She was a moderate who McCain thought might attract more Democratic voters to the ticket.
   (D) She was a conservative Republican placed on the ticket to energize the Christian right, as well as offer an alternative to Hillary Clinton to appeal to women voters.
   (E) She was a well-known national figure and was chosen because of her name recognition.

2. Which of the following statements most accurately describes the president's power to get his programs enacted?
   (A) Presidents often rule by decree and executive order; as a result, much of their program becomes law.
   (B) Presidents often have a majority in both houses of Congress; as a result, many of their proposals are adopted.
   (C) The president must rely heavily on persuasion to get things done.
   (D) Because the president can always call a press conference, he often uses the media to his advantage to get his program passed.
   (E) The president has more power to get things done in the second half of his term because by then he has established himself in office.

3. Why are signing statements controversial?
   (A) They represent an assertion by the president that part of a bill passed by Congress is unconstitutional.
   (B) They serve the same purpose as a pocket veto.
   (C) The Supreme Court has ruled that they are unconstitutional.
   (D) They encroach on the powers of the states.
   (E) They encroach on the power of the bureaucracy.

4. All of the following are formal powers of the president EXCEPT
   (A) to serve as commander in chief of the armed forces
   (B) to declare war
   (C) to make treaties
   (D) to grant pardons
   (E) to appoint Cabinet heads

5. How does an executive order differ from legislation?
   (A) Congress can issue an order requiring executive action without the president's approval.
   (B) Executive orders require only a one-third vote by Congress.
   (C) Executive orders can be issued only for routine matters.
   (D) Executive orders cannot be modified by congressional legislation.
   (E) Executive orders have the impact of law and do not require congressional approval.

6. Under what conditions would a Democratic president find it easiest to get legislation passed?
   (A) When moderate Republicans control Congress and are more likely to favor bipartisanship.
   (B) When the Senate is under Republican control, but the Democrats control the House of Representatives by a large margin.
   (C) When neither political party has a strong majority in Congress, so they are likely to turn to the president for guidance.
   (D) When the president does not face divided government.
   (E) When both Democrats and Republicans strongly favor the president in the most recent election.

7. Modern presidents do not rely much on Cabinet heads to make policy. All of the following are reasons for this EXCEPT
   (A) the Cabinet is large, with 15 members
   (B) Cabinet heads rarely share the president's political ideology
   (C) Cabinet heads are more responsive to their own staff than to the president

(D) Cabinet heads do not have much power over policy

(E) presidents rely more on a large White House staff to make policy

8. All of the following have resulted in the expansion of presidential power EXCEPT

(A) the president uses his televised State of the Union message as a tool to advance his policy agenda

(B) modern presidents have committed troops to foreign conflicts without congressional approval

(C) presidents have ordered agencies to conduct surveillance in order to prevent terrorist attacks

(D) presidents allocate money to federal agencies through the Office of Management and Budget, without congressional approval

(E) several recent presidents have used the threat of a veto to encourage Congress to modify legislation

9. Sometimes presidents claim authority that is not expressly spelled out in the Constitution. This is called

(A) historical power

(B) formal power

(C) expanded power

(D) necessary and proper power

(E) inherent power

10. The War Powers Resolution prevents the president from making long-term troop commitments without congressional approval. Which of the following statements best explains why the War Powers Resolution was passed?

(A) Congress believed the president needed more flexibility in responding to armed conflicts.

(B) Congress believed the president possessed national security intelligence that Congress lacked.

(C) Congress believed that too much power had accrued in the executive branch.

(D) Congress wanted to protect its power of the purse.

(E) Congress believed that national problems should be solved by the judicial branch rather than the executive.

11. All of the following are normally vice presidential duties EXCEPT

(A) attending the funeral of a third-world dictator

(B) presiding over the Senate each day as the leader of the majority party

(C) campaigning on behalf of his political party

(D) reviewing a key policy area, such as energy policy

(E) providing the president with a perspective from his region of the country

12. All of the following statements about executive agreements or treaties are true EXCEPT

(A) executive agreements are binding on future administrations

(B) treaties must be ratified by the Senate

(C) treaties and executive agreements reflect understandings between the United States and foreign governments

(D) treaties are binding on future administrations

(E) the president has the sole power to negotiate treaties

FREE-RESPONSE QUESTIONS

1. The president has several special powers and privileges.
   a. Identify and explain one presidential power from the list below, giving a specific example of how that power has been used.
   b. Identify and explain another presidential power from the list below, giving a specific example of how that power has been used.
      executive orders
      executive privilege
      emergency powers
   c. Explain one formal method Congress may use in checking executive power.
2. The president is the nation's leader in setting foreign policy. However, Congress has the power to limit the president's powers.
   a. Identify and explain two formal powers the president has over foreign policy.
   b. Identify and explain one informal power the president has over foreign policy.
   c. Identify and explain one formal power Congress has that limits the president's foreign policy powers.

Answers

MULTIPLE-CHOICE QUESTIONS

1. **(D)** Senator McCain is considered a moderate Republican. To strengthen the ticket, he chose Sarah Palin, a relatively unknown politician, because she is more socially conservative than he is. Senator McCain hoped Governor Palin would energize the conservative base of the Republican Party and appeal to female voters (*American Government, 2011–2012,* pp. 472–473/ *2013–2014,* pp. 405–406).
2. **(C)** The president does not have enough constitutional power to be a strong leader, and he must work with other institutions of government. He must rely predominantly on persuasion, rather than power, to get things done (*American Government, 2011–2012,* pp. 456–457/ *2013–2014,* p. 394).
3. **(A)** A signing statement is a written declaration that a president may make when signing a bill into law, pointing out that the president deems certain sections of the law to be unconstitutional. Some are concerned that this violates the principle of checks and balances (*American Government, 2011– 2012,* p. 450/ *2013–2014,* p. 383).
4. **(B)** The president is the commander in chief. He negotiates treaties, grants pardons, and appoints Cabinet heads (subject to Senate confirmation). But Congress has the formal power to declare war (*American Government, 2011–2012,* pp. 452–456/ *2013–2014,* pp. 383–388).
5. **(E)** An executive order is a rule or regulation issued by the president that has the effect of law without the direct approval of Congress (*American Government, 2011–2012,* pp. 465–467/ *2013–2014,* p. 398).

6. **(D)** Presidents who do not face divided government have an easier time getting legislation passed because their party controls both houses of Congress (*American Government, 2011–2012*, p. 456/ *2013–2014*, pp. 388–390).

7. **(B)** Cabinet heads are usually chosen from the president's party faithful. However, because the Cabinet is fairly large and the leaders are more responsive to the wishes of their staffs, presidents rely more on the White House staff in making policy (*American Government, 2011–2012*, p. 469/ *2013–2014*, pp. 403–404).

8. **(D)** The president gives the State of the Union address directly to Congress, outlining his policies. Recent presidents have committed troops and ordered surveillance without congressional approval. Congress controls the budget (*American Government, 2011–2012*, pp. 453, 456/ *2013–2014*, pp. 385–386, 389).

9. **(E)** Inherent power is authority claimed by the president that is implied, but not expressly granted, in the Constitution (*American Government, 2011–2012*, p. 461/ *2013–2014*, p. 393–394).

10. **(C)** The War Powers Resolution was passed to limit the president's power to commit U.S. troops to foreign conflicts (*American Government, 2011–2012*, p. 453/ *2013–2014*, p. 386).

11. **(B)** Although the vice president may be called on to break a tie vote in the Senate, he is not a member of the Senate and does not attend its proceedings (*American Government, 2011–2012*, p. 472/ *2013–2014*, p. 405).

12. **(A)** Executive agreements and treaties reflect negotiations between the United States and foreign governments. While treaties are binding on future administrations, executive agreements require each president's consent to remain in effect (*American Government, 2011–2012*, pp. 455–456/ *2013–2014*, pp. 387–388).

FREE-RESPONSE QUESTIONS

1. (a) An executive order is a regulation issued by the president that has the effect of law. Executive orders do not have to be approved by Congress, and this gives the president a sort of legislative power. Presidents have used executive orders to appoint administrators, to restructure the White House bureaucracy, to administer wage and price controls, and to classify government information as secret. One example of an executive order is when President George W. Bush banned foreign aid to countries that included abortion in their family-planning policies.

   (b) Executive privilege is the right of the president to keep some information secret or refuse to appear before Congress or the courts. It is based on the idea that the president has some powers separate from the watchful eye of Congress. This means that the president has the right to withhold information about meetings and documents related to the White House. For example, President George W. Bush claimed that meetings with Vice President Dick Cheney about energy policy were privileged.

   Alternate (b) Emergency powers are those inherent powers exercised by the president during a period of national crisis. The president is the most important actor in foreign affairs, and this allows him to make decisions quickly and without congressional approval, to safeguard the nation. One of the most famous examples of emergency powers is President Franklin Roosevelt's decision to intern Japanese-American citizens during World War II.

(c) Congress has the power to impeach the president. If the president has abused his executive power, the House of Representatives may approve articles of impeachment with a majority vote. The Senate holds an impeachment trial, and with a two-thirds vote, the president may be removed from office. Presidents Andrew Johnson and Bill Clinton were impeached, but neither was removed from office (*American Government, 2011–2012,* pp. 461, 464–469/ *2013–2014,* pp. 397–401).

2. (a) Under the Constitution, the president is the commander in chief. This makes him the highest-ranking officer in the armed forces. Presidents have used this power to commit troops to foreign conflicts. For example, presidents committed troops to the Vietnam conflict without an official declaration of war by Congress. Another formal presidential power is the authority to make treaties with foreign nations. For example, President Clinton supported NAFTA—the North American Free Trade Agreement. The Senate must ratify treaties.

(b) Presidents also have informal, inherent powers. For example, after the September 11 attacks, President Bush authorized surveillance to protect against terrorism. This included wiretaps against foreign nationals living in the United States.

(c) Congress has constitutional authority that limits the president's power over foreign affairs. Congress has the formal power to declare war. The War Powers Resolution is an attempt by Congress to limit the president's ability to commit troops for the long term without a formal declaration of war. Congress also controls the purse strings, through appropriations bills. It can reduce or eliminate spending on foreign policies it does not favor (*American Government, 2011–2012,* pp. 452–455/ *2013–2014,* pp. 386–388).

THE BUREAUCRACY

The federal bureaucracy is a complex web of federal agencies with overlapping jurisdictions. Most people think of it as wasteful, confusing, and rigid, and because the bureaucracy is such a large and complex organization, it is easy to find examples supporting this view. Many of these problems are the result of vague or contradictory policy goals articulated by the president or Congress. Reforming the bureaucracy is a stated goal of almost every elected official. However, little progress has been made, often because the federal bureaucracy administers programs that have many supporters among the American people.

KEY TERMS

administrative agency
bureaucracy
Cabinet department
capture
Civil Service Commission
enabling legislation
government corporation
Government in the Sunshine Act
independent executive agency
independent regulatory agency
iron triangle
issue network
line organization
merit system
Pendleton Act/Civil Service Reform Act
privatization
spoils system
sunset legislation
whistleblower

149

KEY CONCEPTS

- As a result of several factors, the size of the bureaucracy—and therefore the federal government itself—grew tremendously during the 20th century and continues to grow today.

- There are several different types of federal bureaucracies.

- Most bureaucrats are hired through a merit system and are protected from political pressures.

- The federal bureaucracy is a constant object of reform. Federal agencies have substantial power in setting policy.

- The president and Congress have at their disposal several tools to influence the bureaucracy.

For a full discussion of the bureaucracy, see Chapter 14 of the 2011–2012 edition of *American Government & Politics Today* and Chapter 13 of the 2013–2014 edition.

BUREAUCRATIC BASICS

A bureaucracy is a large organization that is structured hierarchically to carry out specific functions. A government bureaucracy is a group or agency that is in charge of implementing a law, program, or policy. In the United States, the bureaucracy is part of the executive branch. The bureaucracy is in charge of implementing acts of the legislature and decisions of the courts. Bureaucracies are large organizations with thousands of employees. The employees, called bureaucrats, are specialists who work in a specific policy area and are part of a hierarchical structure. Bureaucracies in the United States are organized in many ways—some are hierarchical, with directions and administrative decisions flowing down the chain of command, while others are more flexible in their approaches to administration.

There is no doubt that government grew tremendously at every level—federal, state, and local—during the 20th century. While the number of federal bureaucrats has remained fairly stable in recent years, the number of state and local employees has grown. Taken together, national, state, and local government employees account for 16 percent of all employment in the United States.

THE ORGANIZATION OF THE AMERICAN BUREAUCRACY

The four basic types of government bureaucracies, each with a different level of independence and relationship to the president, are as follows:

- **Departments** The largest bureaucratic agencies are Cabinet departments. They cover broad areas of policy responsibility. Except for the head of the Justice Department, who is called the attorney general, the heads of the departments are called secretaries. They are nominated by the president and must be confirmed by the Senate. This makes the department head directly responsible to the president. There are 15 different departments, including the Department of Defense and the newest, the Department of Homeland Security.

■ **Independent executive agencies** These agencies do not fall under one of the larger departments. Independent agencies are responsible for a wide variety of tasks, including intelligence gathering (Central Intelligence Agency) and running the government's museums and zoos (Smithsonian Institution). The president appoints directors of the independent executive agencies for a set term, though they still report directly to the president. Like the secretaries of departments, the heads of independent executive agencies need Senate confirmation.

■ **Independent regulatory agencies** These agencies are usually in charge of administering a specific policy, such as overseeing communications (e.g., Federal Communications Commission). Many agencies were created to oversee one or another aspect of the economy because Congress was concerned about its ability to keep up with the various technical aspects of the American economy. The heads of these agencies are nominated by the president and confirmed by the Senate. However, they do not report directly to the president and can be removed only for specific reasons set by law. Also, by law, the heads of all the agencies cannot come from the same party. These agencies have the power to create rules for their assigned area of supervision, enforce these rules, and resolve disputes regarding them. Critics often contend that rather than creating regulation in the interest of the greater community, many agencies create rules that are friendly to and for the benefit of the industries they are supposed to regulate. Critics refer to this as agency capture.

■ **Government corporations** These are bureaucratic agencies that offer services that could be provided by the private sector and sometimes are provided by private companies. Congress usually creates these corporations to supply services that are important but not very profitable, such as mail delivery and Amtrak train service.

STAFFING THE BUREAUCRACY

Bureaucrats can be divided into two broad categories—political appointments and civil servants.

■ **Political appointments** The president is responsible for making political appointments to the federal bureaucracy, including ambassadors and the heads of Cabinet departments, independent regulatory agencies, and independent executive agencies. These political appointments are listed in the so-called Plum Book. Political appointees often do not have much experience in the area to which they are appointed. Rather, these appointments are often used to reward political supporters (ambassadorships are often used this way) or increase diversity in the federal government. These political appointees often last less than two years on the job before they move back to the private sector. All political appointments are subject to Senate confirmation, which is another factor the president must take into account when making such appointments.

- **Civil servants** Until the late 1880s, government jobs were filled with supporters of the individual or party who won the presidential election. This was often referred to as the spoils system, or patronage. But the patronage system fostered corruption, and Congress passed the Pendleton Act (1883), which created a civil service commission, later called the Office of Personnel Management (OPM). The OPM fills federal jobs based on a merit system rather than political partisanship. The OPM recruits, interviews, and tests potential federal employees, then forwards the top candidates to the federal agency looking to hire someone. It also oversees promotions for civil servants. Additional civil service acts protect federal employees from being fired for political reasons, and prevent civil servants from taking part in many partisan political activities, especially while at work. Today, all but the very top positions in the bureaucracy are civil service positions, and therefore are protected from political interference.

One recent worry in regard to federal employees concerns their quality. Civil servants are extremely hard to dismiss—less than one-tenth of one percent of all civil servants are dismissed for incompetence.

REFORMING THE BUREAUCRACY

Given the considerable criticism of the bureaucracy as inefficient and ineffective, it is not surprising that many ways to reform the bureaucracy, including the following, have been suggested:

- **Deregulation** One way to reduce the influence of the bureaucracy is to reduce the role of the government in overseeing the economy. Republicans especially have long been champions of deregulation. During the 1970s and 1980s, the federal government weakened or eliminated regulations in the airline, banking, and telecommunications industries. Balancing deregulation with public safety and protection is a frequent conflict. For example, deregulation in the banking industry helped create the financial crisis of 2008.

- **Sunshine laws** In an effort to make bureaucratic decision making more transparent, Congress passed the Government in the Sunshine Act. This law required many government agencies to make their meetings open to the public. Also, the Freedom of Information Act requires government agencies to provide copies of reports and files to citizens that make a request for the information, though there are exceptions to this disclosure requirement for personnel issues and matters of national security. Since the 9/11 attacks, governments at all levels have made it more difficult to get certain types of information, such as blueprints for electrical stations and dams.

- **Privatization** More and more, services that used to be the exclusive job of the government are being opened up to competitive bids. In theory, competition should make the bureaucracy more efficient. Private companies have begun to provide government services such as constructing facilities and providing supplies for American troops stationed abroad.

■ **Incentives** The Government and Results Act requires each bureaucratic agency to create performance goals and publish a report detailing how it is attempting to meet these performance standards and if they are being met.

■ **Whistleblower protection** A whistleblower is someone who exposes governmental inefficiency or illegal activity. The 1978 Civil Service Reform Act protects whistleblowers from reprisals by their superiors, and the Whistleblower Protection Act, passed in 1989, provides further protection. However, most whistleblowers still face discipline or dismissal for exposing waste and corruption because the Supreme Court severely restricted the protection.

BUREAUCRATIC POLICY MAKING

Technically, bureaucratic agencies are administrative, not policy-making, institutions. In reality, however, bureaucratic agencies have important policy-making powers. Congress creates each agency and outlines its broad policy goals. The day-to-day implementation of programs is delegated to the agency's discretion through so-called enabling legislation. Congress does not have the expertise to oversee the daily application of its legislation, so it grants administrative discretion to the bureaucratic agency to implement a program within the broad guidelines created by Congress. Congress often intentionally creates vague mandates, thereby allowing the experts in the bureaucracy to handle the details of implementation.

Agencies use the discretion granted to them by Congress to issue rules or regulations to implement policies. Before a set of regulations can go into effect, the agency holds hearings, at which interested citizens and affected industries can voice their opinions. Rules and regulations can also be created through negotiated rulemaking. This means a bureaucratic agency and those interests that would be affected by proposed regulations can work together with a neutral party to help draft regulations. Often this method is used only with the agreement that none of the participants will challenge the rules and regulations in court.

The proposed rules also undergo a 60-day waiting period before they are implemented to allow for further hearings and lobbying by affected parties. These hearings allow the regulations to be modified, if need be. Also, rules and regulations can be challenged in court by an affected party after they're implemented.

Because bureaucratic agencies are created by acts of Congress, the regulations they issue carry the weight of law. The writing and enforcement of regulations frequently cause political disagreements among various interests in American society—for example, farmers and ranchers are often pitted against environmentalists when it comes to the writing of bureaucratic regulations. This competition can cause the bureaucratic process to bog down, which leads to still more criticism of bureaucracies as inefficient and ineffective. Rarely does policy shift in major or sudden ways.

The final step for a bureaucratic agency is implementation—putting policies and regulations into action. A number of factors, including vague or unclear legislation or the complexity of some government programs, can complicate implementation.

The result of this process is that bureaucrats make policy. The process of creating regulation and implementing those regulations gives the bureaucracy an important role in creating policy in the United States. There are two theories about how bureaucracy is influenced in creating policy:

- **Iron triangle** The term "iron triangle" is used to describe a three-way network among a bureaucratic agency, Congress, and interest groups. Policy is created by Congress, which controls the budget of the bureaucratic agency, to benefit an interest group. Since the bureaucratic agency is interested in protecting its budget, it will strive to please the relevant interest groups as it writes and implements the regulations. Favorable implementation pleases the interest group, which pours more support to its congressional supporters, starting the triangle all over again (See Figure 14-4 in *American Government & Politics Today, 2011– 2012*, p. 507/ 2013–2014, pp. 437–438).

- **Issue networks** Recently, critics have called the iron triangle model of policy making simplistic in its explanation of how policy is made. These critics argue that issue networks are a much better model to explain how the bureaucracy and other groups create policy. Issue networks include all possible parties interested in a particular issue, including individuals, interest groups, members of Congress, civil servants, scholars, and other experts and members of the media,. All of these parties work to influence the different policy-making institutions, Congress, the executive branch, the bureaucracy, and even the courts, to create policy that supports their positions. Because of the complexity of both these networks and the issues, conflicting policies may be created.

AP Tip

The power of Congress to oversee the bureaucracy is fundamental to the system of checks and balances and is likely to appear on the AP exam.

Congressional Control Over the Bureaucracy

Although some political pundits doubt whether Congress can exercise meaningful control over the bureaucracy, Congress does have some ways of exerting control.

- Many presidential appointments require confirmation. Usually confirmation is routine, but in rare cases, a presidential nominee withdraws from consideration because of senatorial scrutiny or fails to be confirmed, forcing the president to forward a new nominee.

- Another tool Congress can use is the federal budget. Congress can increase or decrease the appropriation an agency gets in the budget.

- Congress can exercise oversight of a bureaucratic agency by holding committee hearings to gather testimony from bureaucrats and citizens on the performance of a bureaucratic agency. Based on these hearings, Congress may take further budgetary or legislative action or pass legislation to create, abolish, or alter a bureaucratic agency.

- Congress can control the size and power of the bureaucracy by inserting sunset provisions into legislation that creates a program. A sunset provision places an expiration date on an agency unless specifically renewed by congressional action.

MULTIPLE-CHOICE QUESTIONS

1. Who exercises control over the bureaucracy?
   (A) There is very little control over the bureaucracy because agencies make regulations that have the force of law.
   (B) The executive branch controls the bureaucracy by appointing all federal employees.
   (C) Congress controls the bureaucracy because it has the power to fire agency heads after oversight hearings and for cause.
   (D) The judicial branch controls the bureaucracy by reviewing regulations to make sure they are constitutional before they go into effect.
   (E) Both Congress and the executive branch have some control over the bureaucracy.

2. An iron triangle is made up of which of the following?
   (A) the president, the Speaker of the House, and the Senate majority leader
   (B) the president, Cabinet heads, and the White House staff
   (C) House committees, Senate committees, and interest groups
   (D) congressional committees, agencies, and interest groups
   (E) Cabinet-level departments, agencies, and interest groups

3. How can Congress check the activities of the bureaucracy?
   I. through appropriations
   II. by appointing new agency heads
   III. through oversight hearings
   IV. through enabling legislation
   (A) I and II
   (B) I, II, and III
   (C) I, III, and IV
   (D) II, III, and IV
   (E) I and III

4. What was the purpose of the Hatch Act?
   (A) to create a merit system for most federal jobs
   (B) to limit the political activities of federal employees
   (C) to provide protection for whistleblowers
   (D) to deregulate rates in seven key industries
   (E) to prevent the president from appointing unqualified agency heads

5. Which of the following requires that all committee-directed federal agencies conduct their business regularly in public sessions?
   (A) Open Records Act
   (B) Pendleton Act
   (C) Government in the Sunshine Act
   (D) Freedom of Information Act
   (E) Political Activities Act

6. The Federal Communications Commission regulates the public airwaves. Although the president appoints commissioners, he does not have direct control over them. The FCC is an example of
   (A) a Cabinet department.
   (B) an independent regulatory agency.
   (C) a government corporation.
   (D) an oversight agency.
   (E) a regulatory agency.

7. Which of the following statements most accurately describes the federal civil service?
   (A) It is a nonpartisan merit system based on competitive examinations.
   (B) It employs nearly 10 percent of the American workforce.
   (C) Most jobs in the civil service are filled based on political affiliation and faithful service to a political party.
   (D) Most federal civil servants work in Washington, D.C.
   (E) Americans reject the stereotype of civil servants as faceless pencil pushers.

8. Which of the following factors make it difficult for Congress to control the bureaucracy?
   V. Agencies have substantial rule-making authority.
   VI. Agencies release studies about their own effectiveness.
   VII. Agency heads are difficult to criticize because they are appointed based on their expertise.
   VIII. Iron triangles protect agency interests.
   (A) I and II
   (B) II and III
   (C) I, II, and IV
   (D) I, II, and III
   (E) I, II, III, and IV

9. All of the following were demonstrated by FEMA's response to Hurricane Katrina EXCEPT
   (A) it is difficult to coordinate responses among local, state, and federal agencies
   (B) it is difficult to fire agency heads
   (C) one federal agency does not have direct control over other federal agencies
   (D) bureaucracies face complex problems and it is difficult to predict what will happen when a natural disaster strikes
   (E) political appointees are sometimes ill-equipped for their positions

10. Which of the following reports directly to the president?
    (A) Consumer Product Safety Commission
    (B) Interstate Commerce Commission
    (C) United States Postal Service
    (D) Central Intelligence Agency
    (E) Nuclear Regulatory Commission

11. The Department of Homeland Security was created after the terrorist attacks of September 11, 2001. What is the major bureaucratic challenge facing this department?
    (A) lack of public support
    (B) lack of congressional support
    (C) integrating agencies with different missions
    (D) inexperienced bureaucrats
    (E) lack of available information and resources

12. Which of the following is the best example of deregulation?
    (A) The Supreme Court reduced the fines of TV and radio stations that violated the FCC's obscenity rules.
    (B) The Transportation Security Administration imposed new rules, restricting the amount of liquids and gels allowed in carry-on luggage.
    (C) Consumers demanded that the FDA ban a drug that caused birth defects.
    (D) The Civil Aeronautics Board eliminated rules covering airline fares and routes.
    (E) The amount of air pollution has decreased due to strict standards requiring gasoline additives.

FREE-RESPONSE QUESTIONS

1. There are several types of bureaucratic agencies, and each is subject to oversight.
    (a) Pick one type of government agency or organization from the list below, and explain its role in policy making, giving a specific example.
    (b) Pick another type of government agency or organization from the list below and explain its role in policy making, giving a specific example.
    Cabinet departments
    independent executive agencies
    independent regulatory agencies
    (c) Explain one way in which the president exercises control over the bureaucracy.
    (d) Explain one way in which Congress exercises control over the bureaucracy.

2. The bureaucracy implements policies and goals set by Congress. Sometimes these policies are implemented effectively, and other times there are serious problems and obstacles in policy implementation.
    a. Identify one method the bureaucracy uses to ensure effective policy implementation.
    b. Give a specific example of effective policy implementation by the bureaucracy.
    c. Give a specific example of ineffective policy implementation by the bureaucracy.

Answers

Multiple-Choice Questions

1. **(E)** Both Congress and the executive branch have some control over the bureaucracy. The executive appoints agency heads and proposes agency budgets. Congress must approve budget proposals and can override regulations it does not like (*American Government, 2011–2012*, pp. 494– 495, 508–510, 522/ *2013–2014*, pp. 425–426, 438–440).

2. **(D)** An iron triangle is a mutually beneficial alliance among members of Congress, bureaucrats, and interest groups to make policies in a particular area, like agriculture (*American Government, 2011–2012*, p. 522/ *2013–2014*, pp. 437–438).

3. **(C)** Congress can check the bureaucracy by appropriating funds and holding oversight hearings. Enabling legislation sets the powers of the agency and the parameters within which it may operate (*American Government, 2011–2012*, pp. 508–509/ *2013–2014*, pp. 434, 437–440).

4. **(B)** The Hatch Act prohibited federal employees from actively participating in the political management of campaigns and prevented managers from pressuring their employees to donate to campaigns (*American Government, 2011–2012*, p. 497/ *2013–2014*, pp. 428, 429).

5. **(C)** The Government in the Sunshine Act requires that agencies headed by more than one person must hold meetings in public (*American Government, 2011–2012*, pp. 498–499/ *2013–2014*, p. 429).

6. **(E)** The FCC is an independent regulatory agency that operates without direct presidential control (*American Government, 2011–2012*, pp. 488–489/ *2013–2014*, p. 420).

7. **(A)** The federal civil service is based on a merit system where the selection, retention, and promotion of government employees is based on competitive examinations (*American Government, 2011–2012*, p. 497/ *2013–2014*, pp. 427–428).

8. **(C)** Bureaucracies are difficult to control because they have rule-making authority and Congress often relies on studies conducted by agencies. Iron triangles are mutually beneficial relationships that also protect agencies (*American Government, 2011–2012*, pp. 507, 510/ *2013–2014*, pp. 436–438).

9. **(B)** FEMA's response to Hurricane Katrina illustrated the difficulties in coordinating disaster relief efforts. Michael Brown, the head of FEMA, had no experience in emergency planning and disaster relief. He later resigned (*American Government, 2011–2012*, pp. 493–494/ *2013–2014*, pp. 423–425).

10. **(D)** The CIA is an independent executive agency and reports directly to the president (*American Government, 2011–2012*, pp. 487–488/ *2013–2014*, pp. 419–420, 424).

11. **(C)** The Department of Homeland Security merged 22 agencies into a single department. Integrating these different agencies posed a significant challenge (*American Government, 2011–2012*, pp. 492–493/ *2013–2014*, pp. 418, 423–424).

12. **(D)** Deregulation occurs when the government loosens or abandons its rules on an industry. The Civil Aeronautics Board deregulated airfares and routes (*American Government, 2011–2012*, pp. 489–491/ *2013–2014*, p. 422).

FREE-RESPONSE QUESTIONS

1. (a) Cabinet departments are the 15 major organizations in the bureaucracy that perform important functions in broad policy areas. Each department is headed by a secretary (except for the Department of Justice, which is led by the attorney general) appointed by the president and confirmed by the Senate. The Department of Homeland Security is a specific example. It coordinates intelligence information and tries to keep the county safe from terrorists.

   (b) Independent executive agencies are not located within a Cabinet department and report directly to the president. They are responsible for a specific area of policy that protects the public's interest. An example is the Environmental Protection Agency, which set rules about air, water, and soil quality.

   Alternate (b) An independent regulatory agency makes nonpartisan regulations about issues that impact the economy. An example of an independent regulatory agency is the Federal Communications Commission, which regulates the airwaves.

   (c) The president may control the bureaucracy through the appointment of Cabinet secretaries (subject to Senate confirmation). The president appoints people who share his philosophies in the hopes that this ideology will be translated into policy.

   (d) Congress controls the bureaucracy through oversight hearings. For example, hearings were held after Hurricane Katrina to investigate FEMA's response to the disaster (*American Government, 2011– 2012*, pp. 487–491, 508/ *2013–2014*, pp. 418–420, 424–426, 438–440).

2. (a) One way the bureaucracy makes sure that policy is implemented effectively is through developing a set of rules. For example, the Environmental Protection Agency sets rules on factory emissions.

   (b) An example of effective policy implementation occurred when the EPA issued new gas mileage requirements and new rules regulating tailpipe regulations for cars and trucks.

   (c) The response by the Federal Emergency Management Agency to Hurricane Katrina was ineffective. Not enough resources were sent to New Orleans immediately following the levee break. Furthermore, officials in Washington did not seem to have an accurate understanding of the extent of the devastation (*American Government, 2011–2012*, pp. 488–489 and general discussion pp. 492–494/ *2013–2014*, pp. 424–425, 434-437).

12

THE COURTS

The judicial branch is a source of great disagreement. Critics contend that it is undemocratic and has too much power. It is true that the power of the courts has grown tremendously through the use of judicial review (the power to determine if a law or action violates the Constitution) over the past 200-plus years. The courts, however, rarely deviate far from public opinion. They reflect the opinions of the officials who nominated and confirmed them; the officials, in turn, reflect the opinions of the American public. A final factor in keeping the courts in line with public opinion is judges' concerns about preserving the legitimacy of the courts.

KEY TERMS

    affirm
    appellate court
    broad constructionism
    case law
    class-action suit
    common law
    concurring opinion
    dissenting opinion
    diversity of citizenship
    federal question
    general jurisdiction
    judicial activism
    judicial implementation
    stare decisis
    strict constructionism
    trial court
    judicial restraint
    judicial review
    jurisdiction
    limited jurisdiction
    litigate
    majority opinion

opinion
oral arguments
political question
precedent
remand
reverse
rule of four
senatorial courtesy
unanimous opinion
writ of *certiorari*

Key Concepts

Law in America is derived from several sources, including the courts.

■ The federal court system consists of three layers: the district courts, the appellate courts, and, at the top, the Supreme Court.

■ The Supreme Court wields significant power in the choices it makes about which cases to hear, as well as in its opinions. The justices on the Supreme Court have a major influence on American society.

■ Because of the influence the justices have on policy, their nomination and confirmation process has become extremely partisan.

■ Through the use of judicial review, the federal courts have evolved into an institution that has a significant impact on public policy.

■ The other branches of government and the public have checks on the powers of the federal courts.

For a full discussion of the courts, see *American Government & Politics Today*, 2011–2012 edition, Chapter 15, and 2013–2014 edition, Chapter 14.

Sources of American Law

Law in the United States is created through several different processes:

■ **Common law** Judges may rely on common law to guide their decisions. Common law is the collection of legal precedents from previous decisions applied to a particular case.

■ **Constitutions** The U.S. Constitution is the supreme law of the land. Any law that violates the Constitution can be nullified through judicial action. State constitutions also help define the scope of what is legal in the United States.

■ **Statutory construction** Even though ours is a common law system, the legislation passed by Congress and state legislatures, along with the regulations created by the bureaucracy, are an increasingly important source of law in the United States. Even when there is legislation that deals with the issue before a court, it may be unclear. In such cases, the court's job is to interpret what the legislation means and how it should be applied in each case.

THE FEDERAL COURT SYSTEM

The court system in the United States is a dual system. There are independent court systems for each of the 50 states, plus Washington D.C., that operate alongside the federal system. Article III of the Constitution and congressional legislation created the federal system. Before any case can be heard by a state or federal court, two issues need to be resolved—jurisdiction and standing to sue.

■ **Jurisdiction** The authority of a court to hear a case, or jurisdiction, is determined by two primary factors: the location and the issue being brought to the court. If there is a federal question to a case— that is, a question about the Constitution, congressional legislation, executive action, or treaties—then the case will go to the federal court system rather than a state court system. Diversity of citizenship—if the parties to the case are from different states, or even a different country—is a second criterion that may send a case to federal court.

■ **Standing to sue** To have a court hear a case, the plaintiffs bringing the case must demonstrate that they have suffered or may suffer harm. The issue being heard by the court must be an actual situation that has a legal remedy, as courts will not consider hypotheticals. Sometimes a group of individuals who have all been impacted by an action will band together and file a single lawsuit. This is called a class-action suit. Groups like the NAACP used class-action suits to help desegregate public accommodations during the civil rights movement.

The national judicial branch is organized into two primary levels below the Supreme Court.

DISTRICT COURTS

U.S. district courts serve as the entry point for national jurisdiction. The district courts are trial courts that serve as the court of general jurisdiction, meaning there are very few types of cases that they cannot hear. Cases such as federal criminal cases, civil cases that allege a violation of national law, civil cases brought against the national government, and civil cases among citizens of different states (if the amount at issue exceeds $75,000) all fall under the district courts' general jurisdiction.

There are several specialized district courts that have limited jurisdiction. These courts hear cases about such technical issues as bankruptcy and tax issues. One specialized court that has been subject to recent scrutiny is the court created by the Foreign Intelligence Surveillance Act (FISA). The FISA court hears requests for special warrants to spy on terror and espionage suspects. The burden of proof to receive a FISA warrant is much lower than it is for a regular warrant. The judges of the FISA court meet in secret, and their decisions and opinions are not published. After 9/11, the standards to receive a warrant from the FISA court were lowered significantly.

Appellate Courts

Any case decided by a U.S. district court and decisions by federal agencies can be appealed to a U.S. court of appeals. There are 12 United States courts of appeals, each serving a specified geographic area, called a circuit.

Appellate courts operate differently from district courts: for district court decisions, the appellate court can review only the application of law and the procedures the district court used in reaching a decision; for federal agencies, the appellate court can review only rule making. If a three-judge panel determines that a mistake was made by the trial court, the original verdict is overturned and a new trial may be ordered. Appellate courts do not usually look at questions of fact; they focus on whether or not the law was applied correctly

Appellate court rulings often create precedents that influence other courts and cases in the future. Precedents are the basis of common law systems. When courts use a precedent as the basis for a decision, it is called *stare decisis*, a Latin term meaning "let the decision stand."

With the U.S. courts of appeals, the issue of uniformity occasionally arises. Because of the geographic organization of the appellate system, discrepancies from circuit to circuit are bound to appear. Laws are often applied differently across the United States because of different appellate court rulings.

The Supreme Court and How It Works

The highest court in the United States, the Supreme Court, plays a key role in bringing unity to national policy, clarifying it, and, in some cases, even creating such policy. Cases come to the Supreme Court in one of two ways:

- **Original jurisdiction** The Constitution gives the Supreme Court original jurisdiction in a small number of cases. Cases involving different states, ambassadors, and other public ministers go directly to the Supreme Court

- **Appellate jurisdiction** Nearly every case heard by the Supreme Court is heard on appeal. These are cases that have been heard, tried, and ruled on by lower courts. The Court's appellate jurisdiction is granted by Congress and can be changed or eliminated as part of the checks and balances system.

Because the Supreme Court controls its own docket, many cases that seem appropriate for the Supreme Court will not be accepted. When a litigant petitions the Court to hear a case, he or she is asking for a writ of *certiorari*. In what is called the rule of four, four justices must agree to issue a writ and place the case on the court's docket.

Several factors determine whether the Supreme Court will hear a case. Among them are whether appellate courts have reached conflicting decisions, whether a lower court's decision conflicts with an existing Supreme Court ruling, and whether the issue could have significance beyond the current case. The government's desires, presented by the solicitor general, also play a large role in setting the agenda for the Supreme Court.

Once the Court decides to hear a case, attorneys and other interested parties file briefs for the justices to read. The next step is oral argument before the Court. Each side's attorney gets to make his or her case before the justices. During this time, the justices may question the attorneys. After oral arguments, the justices meet in conference, during which the chief justice leads a discussion on the case and a vote is taken. After the vote, the case is assigned to one of the justices to write the Court's opinion on that case. The opinion includes the Court's judgment and reasoning for the decision. In the opinion, the Court can take one of several different actions. It can affirm, or agree, with the lower court's original ruling in the case; it can reverse or overturn the lower court's decision; or it can remand—or send back—the case to a lower court for a new trial.

The Court can also issue several different kinds of opinions:

- **Unanimous opinion** A unanimous opinion is issued when all of the justices agree on a case and for the same reasons.

- **Majority opinion** This type of opinion reflects the thinking and decision of a majority of the justices.

- **Dissenting opinion** A dissenting opinion is written by one or more justices who do not agree with the majority and explains the reasons for dissent. Dissenting opinions often provide an argument for overturning a decision in the future.

- **Concurring opinion** This type of opinion is written by one or more of the justices who agree with the judgment of the majority but have a different argument or reason for doing so.

JUDICIAL NOMINATIONS

Federal judges are appointed for a term of good behavior—in other words, they serve as long as they like unless they are impeached and removed for committing a crime. The duration of this term is meant to insulate judges from political pressures and to encourage them to be as impartial as possible. In appointing a judge, a president has an opportunity to influence policy long after he has left office. The president looks for candidates who are qualified and also share his ideology on important issues. Studies show that ideology is the driving factor when a president makes a nomination for the federal courts. The Rehnquist Court, chaired by a Reagan appointee, is generally considered to be the most conservative Court in American history.

The Senate checks this power because it has to confirm nominees for the federal courts. For an appointment to a district court, the practice of senatorial courtesy forces the president to nominate someone acceptable to the senator of the president's party from the state to which the judge will be assigned. Senatorial courtesy allows a senator to veto a judicial appointment from his or her home state by not returning the blue slip, a form on which they can make comments about the nominee. If senatorial courtesy is met, the nominee will be scheduled for a hearing before the Senate Judicial Committee. If the nominee receives a favorable vote from the committee, the entire Senate votes on the nominee.

Senatorial courtesy does not apply when it comes to nominations to the appellate courts or the Supreme Court. These appointments, however, receive much more scrutiny and public attention than do appointments to district courts. Almost 20 percent of presidential nominations to the Supreme Court have been either rejected or not acted on by the Senate. As a result, presidents have shown greater care and consideration in choosing Supreme Court nominees.

Partisan politics has been the primary reason for the failure of some nominees to be confirmed. Especially with district and appeals court nominees, the Senate has grown increasingly active in the scrutiny it gives to presidential appointments. Both Bill Clinton and George W. Bush had trouble securing Senate approval for their judicial nominations to the lower courts. However, President George W. Bush was able to nominate two new Supreme Court justices, including a new chief justice, John Roberts, during his administration, and both were confirmed fairly easily. To date, President Obama has also nominated, and the Senate has confirmed fairly easily, two new justices to the Supreme Court.

While Supreme Court nominees get the lion's share of media coverage, in recent years it has been at the appellate level that nominees have had a more difficult time getting confirmed.

JUDICIAL POLICY MAKING

The courts make policy through the use of judicial review. At the appellate level and especially the Supreme Court level, justices determine if actions or laws violate the Constitution, a process called judicial review. When the Supreme Court determines that something is unconstitutional, that decision affects the entire country. When looking at judicial review, legal scholars see four different philosophical approaches:

- **Judicial activism** This is a philosophical approach that sees judges using judicial review to play a co-equal role with the other two branches of government. Judicial activism holds that the judiciary should use its powers to check federal and state legislation and regulations that are excessive or discriminatory.

- **Judicial restraint** This philosophy, the opposite of activism, holds that judges should stick to precedents and legislation as closely as possible when making a decision. The thinking is that because judges are not elected, they should defer to the legislature, which more accurately reflects the will of the people; only when there is a clear and compelling reason for overturning a law or breaking with precedent should a judge do so.

- **Broad constructionism** This philosophy, which calls for judges to determine the context and purpose of a law when trying to interpret its constitutionality, is often associated with the idea that the Constitution is a "living" document that should change and adapt to the times.

- **Strict constructionism** Judges who hold this judicial philosophy believe that the Constitution is not open to interpretation, but rather that it should be read and applied in a literal manner. These judges try to apply what they believe was the original intent of the founders when making their judicial decisions.

CHECKS ON JUDICIAL POWER

The judicial branch, like the legislative and executive branches, is subject to the system of checks and balances. Perhaps the most important check is on its dependence on the other two branches for the implementation of its decisions. Without support from the president or Congress, a Supreme Court decision cannot be implemented—the courts have no enforcement tools. In addition, because all federal justices are nominated by the president and confirmed by the Senate, both the president and the Senate exert some control over the judicial branch.

Congress can also help check the judicial branch by proposing amendments to the Constitution or rewriting laws that have been struck down by the courts.

Public opinion and consent can also help check the judicial branch. Justices are not isolated from the opinions and pressures in American society. Most judicial decisions reflect important ideas discussed by the larger public. For example, in 2002, the Supreme Court ruled that executing prisoners who are mentally retarded violated the Eighth Amendment; it did so in part because of changes in public opinion regarding what is cruel and unusual punishment. Sometimes, as with school prayer in conservative areas of the country, some Supreme Court decisions are simply ignored by the people.

Finally, the courts often restrain themselves, giving deference to national laws and precedents. The courts often avoid issues that are viewed as political questions, refusing to hear cases that they believe should be resolved by either the legislative or the executive branch. For example, to date, the Court has not dealt with the issue of gays in the military, believing that this issue is better left to Congress or the president.

AP Tip

The nomination process, and the politics involved in it, is an important aspect of the judicial branch and a likely source of questions on the AP exam.

MULTIPLE-CHOICE QUESTIONS

1. Using the power of judicial review, the Supreme Court can do all of the following EXCEPT
   (A) declare a law passed by Congress unconstitutional
   (B) declare a law passed by a state unconstitutional
   (C) declare acts of the executive branch unconstitutional
   (D) determine the meaning and application of the Constitution
   (E) overturn a constitutional amendment as a violation of civil rights

2. Justice Antonin Scalia believes that the Supreme Court should defer to decisions made by the elected representatives. This judicial philosophy is usually described as
   (A) judicial restraint
   (B) judicial activism
   (C) conservatism
   (D) liberalism
   (E) constitutionalism

3. The federal courts have jurisdiction over the following cases EXCEPT
   (A) civil suits between citizens of different states in which the amount at issue exceeds $75,000
   (B) criminal cases involving violations of laws passed by Congress
   (C) civil cases brought against the national government
   (D) state appeals cases in which the defendant alleges his or her constitutional rights were violated
   (E) prosecutions under state criminal law

4. Which of the following statements best describes the practice of senatorial courtesy?
   (A) The Senate Judiciary Committee reviews all judicial nominees to make sure they do not have any scandals in their past.
   (B) The Senate will not confirm a nominee who is opposed by either senator from the nominee's state.
   (C) The Senate will not confirm a nominee who is opposed by the senior senator from the nominee's state if the senator is a member of the president's party.
   (D) The Senate will not confirm a nominee who is opposed by the senior senator from the nominee's state if the senator is a member of the majority party in the Senate.
   (E) The president is able to bypass Senate confirmation if one senator from the nominee's state approves of the appointment.

5. What is the role of judicial review in the system of checks and balances?
   (A) It undermines the Constitution by making the Supreme Court the final arbiter of the law.
   (B) It enhances the power of Congress by overturning the president's decisions.
   (C) It enhances the power of the president by overturning decisions of Congress.
   (D) It makes the courts a coequal branch with the president and Congress.
   (E) It enhances the power of the states by overturning national laws.

6. Judges make rulings that are written in the form of opinions that serve as precedents for future cases. This system is called
   (A) common law
   (B) statutory law
   (C) civil procedure
   (D) judicial review
   (E) judicial policy making

7. Which of the following statements best describes the jurisdiction of the Supreme Court?
   (A) The Court is exclusively a court of appellate jurisdiction.
   (B) The Court's jurisdiction is mostly appellate, but it has original jurisdiction in specified types of cases.
   (C) The Court is exclusively a court of original jurisdiction.
   (D) The Court can choose which cases of original jurisdiction to take.
   (E) Most of the Court's cases come directly from trial courts.

8. Litigants in state cases who wish to invoke the Supreme Court's jurisdiction must prove which of the following?
   I.   The case must raise an issue requiring immediate resolution.
   II. The case must have reached the highest state court.
   III. The case must be a criminal case.
   IV. The case must involve a federal question.
   (A) I and II
   (B) II and III
   (C) I, II, and IV
   (D) II and IV
   (E) I, II, III, and IV

9. What is required for the Supreme Court to grant a petition for a writ of *certiorari*?
   (A) The majority of the justices must vote to hear the case.
   (B) The justices from the majority party on the Court must agree to hear the case.
   (C) A circuit court of appeals must recommend that the justices hear the case.
   (D) The Constitution requires that four of the nine justices must vote to hear the case.
   (E) The unwritten "rule of four" means at least four justices must agree to hear the case.

10. What is the most important legal difference among majority, concurring, and dissenting opinions?
    (A) Majority opinions serve as precedent.
    (B) Concurring decisions rarely agree with the majority opinion.
    (C) Dissenting opinions do not serve as precedent, but concurring opinions do serve as precedent.
    (D) Dissenting opinions usually express political differences, while concurring opinions express different legal interpretations.
    (E) All three types of opinions serve as precedent, to varying degrees.

11. The Supreme Court refused to rule on the controversy regarding the rights of gays and lesbians in the military, preferring to defer to the executive branch. What is it called when the Supreme Court defers to other branches of government?
    (A) a hypothetical question
    (B) judicial restraint
    (C) a political question
    (D) judicial deference
    (E) judicial implementation

12. The Senate must confirm judicial appointments. Which of the following factors is the most frequent cause of the Senate rejecting a nominee?
    (A) the nominee's lack of judicial experience
    (B) partisan politics between the Senate and the president
    (C) the nominee's lack of experience as an attorney
    (D) the nominee's poor academic record
    (E) low presidential approval ratings

13. Which of the following statements about the Rehnquist Court is true?
    (A) The Court heard very few cases, and it is difficult to determine a trend in the Court's decisions.
    (B) Most of the justices were conservative when they were appointed, but their decisions became more liberal over time.
    (C) The Court's decisions were unpredictable, reflecting no clear ideology.
    (D) The Court's decisions reflected the conservative ideology of the presidents who nominated the majority of the justices.
    (E) The Court's decisions reflected the liberal ideology of the presidents who nominated the majority of the justices.

FREE-RESPONSE QUESTIONS

1. The federal courts are part of the system of checks and balances created by the Constitution. Considering the role of the courts, complete the following tasks:
    a. Identify and explain one check on judicial power held by Congress.
    b. Identify and explain one check on judicial power held by the executive branch.
    c. Identify and explain one check on the other branches held by the judiciary.

2. The Supreme Court is an independent branch of government. However, it is not completely immune from politics.
    a. Identify and explain two constitutional provisions that protect the Supreme Court's independence.
    b. Identify and explain one way the Supreme Court reflects the political viewpoints of American citizens.

Answers

MULTIPLE-CHOICE QUESTIONS

1. **(E)** Judicial review allows the Supreme Court to determine the meaning and application of the Constitution and overturn a law or regulation that violates the Constitution. Because amendments are part of the Constitution, they are, by definition, constitutional, and the Supreme Court may not overturn them (*American Government, 2011–2012*, pp. 520–522/ *2013–2014*, p. 446).

2. **(A)** Judicial restraint is the view that judges should avoid making new policy by closely following existing statutes and precedents (*American Government, 2011–2012*, p. 535/ *2013–2014*, p. 464).

3. **(E)** The federal courts do not have jurisdiction to hear criminal cases involving violations of state law unless there is an alleged violation of the defendant's constitutional rights (*American Government, 2011–2012*, p. 523/ *2013–2014*, p. 451).

4. **(C)** A senior senator from the president's party may veto a nominee from his or her state, killing the nomination (*American Government, 2011–2012*, p. 531/ *2013–2014*, p. 460).

5. **(D)** Judicial review gives the Supreme Court the power to check the president and Congress by overturning laws that are unconstitutional. This makes the Court a coequal branch of government (*American Government, 2011–2012*, pp. 520–522/ *2013–2014*, pp. 446, 449).

6. **(A)** Common law is a system by which court decisions serve as precedents for deciding similar cases in the future (*American Government, 2011–2012*, p. 517/ *2013–2014*, p. 446).

7. **(B)** Most of the Court's jurisdiction is appellate. The Court has original jurisdiction over cases involving ambassadors and other public ministers and cases in which a state is a party (*American Government, 2011–2012*, p. 525/ *2013–2014*, pp. 453–454).

8. **(D)** State court litigants who wish to have their appeals heard in the Supreme Court must prove both that they have exhausted all appeals in the state court system and that the case raises a federal question (*American Government, 2011–2012*, p. 525/ *2013–2014*, pp. 450–451).

9. **(E)** At least four justices must agree to hear a case. This is the unwritten "rule of four" (*American Government, 2011–2012*, p. 529/ *2013–2014*, p. 458).

10. **(A)** A majority opinion serves as precedent. Concurring and dissenting opinions do not serve as precedent, because they do not express the viewpoint of most of the justices (*American Government, 2011–2012*, pp. 529–530/ *2013–2014*, pp. 458–459).

11. **(C)** Sometimes the Court declares that the elected branches of government should decide an issue instead of the courts. This is called the political questions doctrine (*American Government, 2011–2012*, pp. 540–541/ *2013–2014*, p. 469).

12. **(B)** Partisan politics is an important factor in the rejection of a nominee by the Senate. This is especially true when the nominee is on either the far right or the far left (*American Government, 2011–2012*, pp. 533–534/ *2013–2014*, pp. 461–462).

13. **(D)** The majority of the justices on the Rehnquist Court were conservative, and the Court's decisions usually reflected a conservative ideology consistent with those of the presidents who nominated them (*American Government, 2011–2012*, pp. 536–537/ *2013–2014*, pp. 465–466).

FREE-RESPONSE QUESTIONS

1. (a) One check on the judiciary by the legislative branch is that the Senate must confirm the president's nominations of all federal judges. A growing proportion of nominees is not confirmed, or the process of confirming them has been delayed to the point where many have withdrawn their names from consideration. This is particularly true when a party that is not the president's controls the Senate and nominees are not confirmed due to partisan politics.

(b) The president also has a check on the judiciary. The president must nominate all candidates for the federal bench. While it is improper to ask candidates how they would rule in specific cases, the executive branch can inquire about their overall ideology. Of course, most judicial nominees are affiliated with the president's political party. Presidents consider many factors in making judicial nominations, including not only their political philosophy but also their race and gender. This gives the president significant power over who sits on the federal bench.

(c) The Supreme Court's most important power is judicial review. This is the power to determine the meaning of the Constitution and invalidate state and federal decisions if they violate it. For example, the Supreme Court determined that the Gun-Free School Zone Act exceeded Congress's power under the commerce clause. This was a check on Congress's power because it kept Congress from using powers that, in the Supreme Court's view, should be reserved for the states (*American Government, 2011–2012*, pp. 520–524, 530–534, 538–539/ *2013–2014*, pp. 446, 449, 459-463).

2. (a) One way the Constitution protects justices' independence is in allowing them to serve for life unless they engage in blatantly illegal behavior (which is rare). This means that judges do not have to run for reelection, and unlike elected officials, they do not have to please constituents. If the Court hands down an unpopular decision, the justices who wrote the majority opinion do not have to worry about losing their jobs for political reasons.

   Also, Supreme Court justices deliberate in secret. This means that they are not criticized in the media for the viewpoints they express while reviewing a case. Although interest groups might file *amicus curiae* briefs to try to influence a decision, justices can decide for themselves how to weigh these viewpoints. In addition, the legislature cannot reduce judges' salaries while they are in office.

(b) The Supreme Court is not completely isolated from politics, and studies show that it reflects public opinion as much as other government institutions do. One reason for this is the appointment process. The president appoints justices who share his ideology. Because the people select the president (indirectly through the electoral college), the viewpoints of the people are reflected in the president's nominees. Also, the Senate must confirm judicial appointments. Because the Senate is elected directly by the people, the confirmation process indirectly reflects the majority's will (*American Government, 2011–2012*, pp. 527–528, 531–534, 540/ *2013–2014*, p. 458, 459-463).

13

CIVIL RIGHTS

Civil rights are privileges and rights guaranteed to an individual and protected from arbitrary limitation by the government or another individual. The struggle for civil rights in the United States is about creating political and social equality. It began with African Americans but quickly spread to other racial minorities such as Latinos, then later to women, Americans with disabilities, and homosexuals. Of these, the African American struggle for civil rights is the best known and serves as a model for other groups in their struggle for equality in the United States.

KEY TERMS

affirmative action
busing
civil disobedience
civil rights
de facto segregation
de jure segregation
suffrage
grandfather clause
poll tax
separate-but-equal doctrine
sexual harassment
white primary

KEY CONCEPTS

- Progress for African Americans in receiving their civil rights was slow.

- African Americans initially used the federal courts to gain civil rights.

173

- Civil rights legislation came later as a result of public protest and a change in public opinion regarding the rights of African Americans.

- Women's rights are drawn from standards different from those used for race.

- Affirmative action to remedy past and present discrimination is controversial.

- Immigrants, people with disabilities, and homosexuals continue to raise political issues involving civil rights.

For a full discussion of civil rights, see Chapter 5 of the 2010-2011 and 2013–2014 editions of *American Government & Politics Today*.

CIVIL RIGHTS AND CIVIL LIBERTIES

The Bill of Rights is the primary source of our civil rights and liberties. Americans often use the terms *civil rights* and *civil liberties* interchangeably, but there is an important distinction between the two:

- **Civil rights** specify what the government must do to ensure equal protection and freedom from discrimination

- **Civil liberties** are limitations on government. They specify what the government cannot do.

AFRICAN AMERICANS AND CIVIL RIGHTS

Prior to adoption of the Thirteenth Amendment (1865), the Constitution left the issue of slavery to the individual states. The Thirteenth Amendment, which abolished slavery everywhere in the United States, was the first step toward guaranteeing civil rights for African Americans. The Fourteenth Amendment, adopted in 1868, was both an opportunity and a problem for African American activists: it seemed to guarantee equal rights for all, yet the Supreme Court limited the application of its equal protection clause. In *Civil Rights Cases* (1883), the Court ruled the equal protection clause did not apply to the actions of private individuals or groups. Later, in *Plessy v. Ferguson* (1896), the Court created the separate-but-equal doctrine, which legalized segregation.

The Fifteenth Amendment (1870) gave the right to vote (suffrage) to all adult males, regardless of race. However, many states erected legal barriers to prevent African Americans from exercising that right:

- **White primary** Southern states barred African Americans from voting in primary elections by arguing that political parties were private organizations. The Supreme Court overturned white primaries in 1944.

- **Grandfather clauses** These restricted the right to vote to individuals who could prove their grandfathers had voted before 1867, prior to the adoption of the Fifteenth Amendment.

- **Poll tax** To vote, a citizen had to pay a small tax. Because of widespread poverty among African Americans, the poll tax prevented many from voting.

- **Literacy tests** Before voting, voters had to pass a complicated literacy test. Illiteracy was higher among African Americans than among whites. In addition, white voting officials determined what was required to pass. African Americans were rarely allowed to pass these literacy tests.

If these judicial and legal means were not enough to prevent African Americans from enjoying equal treatment and protection, whites often resorted to extralegal means to deny African Americans their civil rights. African Americans were frequent targets of violence, intimidation, and murder.

THE AFRICAN-AMERICAN CIVIL RIGHTS MOVEMENT

The National Association for the Advancement of Colored People (NAACP) was established in 1909 to lobby in Washington and publicize black grievances, but its most influential role was played in the courtroom. The NAACP and other African-American groups began the fight for civil rights by attacking school segregation in the courts. In a series of court cases over nearly two decades, the NAACP implemented its strategy, culminating in *Brown v. Board of Education* (1954). In *Brown*, the Supreme Court ruled that separate schools were inherently unequal and overturned *Plessy* in a unanimous decision.

Brown was a landmark decision. The reasons for it and the means chosen to implement it were important and controversial. Three issues emerged from the decision:

- **Implementation** The *Brown* case was a class action suit that applied to all similarly situated African American students. The Court later ruled that integration should proceed in public schools "with all deliberate speed." In the South, this turned out to be at a snail's pace. In the late 1950s and early 1960s, the National Guard and U.S. army paratroopers were needed to escort black students into formerly all-white schools and universities.

- **Desegregation versus integration** In the South, segregation by law (*de jure* segregation) was clearly unconstitutional as a result of *Brown*. In the North, segregation was the result of residential segregation (*de facto* segregation). The case of *Swann v. Charlotte-Mecklenburg Board of Education* (1971) upheld the use of busing to integrate schools that had a history of segregation.

Busing was unpopular with many groups, African Americans included. By the early part of the 21st century, the Supreme Court had shifted its support of busing; many school districts have consequently been allowed to discontinue busing plans. Today, schools are once again suffering from *de facto* segregation. In 2007, the Supreme Court struck down desegregation programs in both Seattle and Louisville, ruling that the use of race in assigning students to schools was a violation of the Fourteenth Amendment.

AP Tip

Brown v. Board of Education is one of the most important decisions ever rendered by the Supreme Court and will likely appear on the AP exam.

Getting Congress to pass new civil rights laws required a far more complex and decentralized strategy than campaigning in the federal courts. This part of the movement was aimed at mobilizing public opinion and overcoming the many congressional barriers to action.

The first strategy was to get civil rights issues on the political agenda by mobilizing public opinion through dramatic events. Rosa Parks started a bus boycott, organized by a young minister named Martin Luther King, Jr., in Montgomery, Alabama, when she refused to surrender her seat to a white man. Early demonstrations were based on the philosophy of nonviolent civil disobedience—that is, peaceful violation of a law. Sit-ins at segregated lunch counters and "freedom rides" on segregated bus lines made headlines in the newspapers. Efforts were made to get African Americans registered to vote in counties where whites had used intimidation and harassment to prevent that. Later, racial violence and riots erupted when more militant organizations, such as the Black Panthers, became involved in the civil rights movement.

King, the NAACP, and a new generation of political leaders, including Presidents Kennedy and Johnson, were able to create support for congressional action on civil rights. Five important civil rights bills were passed between 1957 and 1968. Significant voting rights laws were passed in 1957, 1960, and 1965. A housing discrimination law was passed in 1968. The high point of civil rights legislation came in the form of the Civil Rights Act of 1964 and the Voting Rights Act of 1965.

- **The Civil Rights Act of 1964** has six major provisions: it outlawed discrimination in voter registration; it outlawed discrimination in public accommodations; it outlawed discrimination in employment and, further, it created the Equal Employment Opportunity Commission to investigate accusations of discrimination in the workplace; it allowed the federal government to sue to desegregate school districts and other public facilities; and it gave more power to the Civil Rights Commission.

- **The Voting Rights Act** has two major provisions. It outlawed discriminatory voting practices, including literacy tests. In addition, it allowed the federal government to register voters and oversee elections in areas that had a history of voter discrimination.

The civil rights movement boasted many achievements. One is the significant change in political participation—there is an increase in the number of African Americans holding elected office in United States, including President Obama.

WOMEN AND EQUAL RIGHTS

The fight for women's civil rights grew out of their participation in the abolition movement during the 1840s. In 1848, Lucretia Mott and Elizabeth Cady Stanton organized a women's rights convention at Seneca Falls, New York. There, delegates adopted the Declaration of Sentiments, which was based on the Declaration of Independence. After a long fight, in 1920 women earned the right to vote with ratification of the Nineteenth Amendment.

The feminist movement that reappeared in the 1960s challenged the claim that women differ from men in ways that justify differences in legal status. Feminists sought political, social, and economic equality for women. The modern feminist movement had several areas of emphasis:

■ **Equal Rights Amendment** Modern feminist groups, like the National Organization for Women (NOW), sought to eliminate female inequality through a constitutional amendment that would make treatment based on gender illegal. The proposed amendment caused a backlash, especially among conservative religious groups, and failed to receive ratification from the required 38 states.

■ **Title IX** In 1972, Congress created Title IX as part of a larger education bill. Title IX, which outlawed discrimination in educational programs, has had a tremendous impact on athletic opportunities for women at both the high school and the college levels.

■ **Sexual harassment** Sexual harassment occurs when job opportunities, promotions, salary increases, and other opportunities are given in return for sexual favors. One form of sexual harassment is creating a hostile environment—a setting in which harassment impairs a person's ability to work.

■ **Wage discrimination** In 1963, a woman earned, on average, 59 percent of what a man earned. In response, Congress passed the Equal Pay Act, which mandated equal pay for equal work. This law has helped to close the pay gap between men and women, but has not eliminated it altogether. Woman now earn 77.4 percent of what the average man earns.

HISPANICS AND CIVIL RIGHTS

Illegal immigration has become a hot-button topic in recent years—it is estimated that there are approximately 12 million undocumented immigrants in the United States, most of them Hispanics, who are now the largest minority group in the country. Critics of illegal immigration point to the increase in crime along the border, the strain on social services including education, and the need for greater border security.

Civil rights advocates argue that a path to citizenship should be created for illegal immigrants, most of whom are productive members of American society. These advocates also push for the expansion of bilingual education in schools to help the children of immigrants succeed.

Affirmative Action

Despite great strides made by African Americans, women, and other historically disadvantaged groups, they still lag behind white males in most significant quality-of-life indicators, such as educational attainment and average income. This is in part because of past discrimination; they did not have the necessary skills to compete on a level playing field with whites. Affirmative action was created to address this. Affirmative action programs give special preference to disadvantaged groups in education admissions and programs and in employment. Needless to say, affirmative action programs are controversial. Many whites allege that affirmative action programs create reverse discrimination and make it harder for whites to be accepted to college or get job a for which they are qualified.

In *Bakke v. University of California* (1978), the Supreme Court ruled that numerical minority quotas (setting aside a fixed number of minority positions or slots) are not permissible, but that race could be considered in admissions policies. In 2003, the Court again reaffirmed the use of affirmative action. In *Gratz v. Bollinger,* the Court struck down a program that all but ensured minority acceptance to the University of Michigan; however, at the same time, the Court reaffirmed the importance of diversity in education by upholding the use of race as a criterion in *Grutter v. Bollinger,* which dealt with the University of Michigan's law school. In general, the Court supports the concept of affirmative action, but it is reluctant to support the use of quotas.

Other Civil Rights Movements

The African-American civil rights movement paved the way for several other groups in American society to advocate for equal rights:

- **Older Americans** Laws have been passed to protect against discrimination in the workplace. Unless an employer can prove that having an age limit is a necessary part of the job , a person cannot be fired for being too old or be forced to retire.

- **Americans with disabilities** In 1990, Congress passed the Americans with Disabilities Act (ADA). This law extended the protections found under the Civil Rights Act of 1964 to those with physical or mental disabilities. The law set off an avalanche of complaints to the EEOC regarding employers' failures to make accommodations. The courts have limited the application of the ADA since its inception.

- **Gays and Lesbians** The civil rights movement for gays and lesbians had its start with the Stonewall riots in 1969. Since then, gay and lesbian Americans have sought equal protection and treatment under the law. Many state and local governments no longer allow discrimination on the basis of sexual orientation. The most controversial issue regarding homosexual rights at this time is the question of gay marriage. In 1996, Congress passed the Defense of Marriage Act (DOMA), which allows states to refuse to recognize gay marriages performed in other states. DOMA appears to be a direct contradiction to the full faith and credit clause of the Constitution. Currently, gay marriages are legal in a number of states, including Connecticut, Iowa, Massachusetts, New Hampshire, Vermont, New York, Maryland, Maine, Washington state and Washington, D.C. However, most states have constitutional amendments or laws that ban same-sex marriage.

MULTIPLE-CHOICE QUESTIONS

1. In the years following the Civil War, all of the following made it difficult for African Americans to gain equality EXCEPT
   (A) the Constitution did not expressly provide equal rights or voting rights for African Americans
   (B) violence was used to prevent African Americans from exercising their rights
   (C) literacy tests required complex knowledge
   (D) court decisions gave states leeway to maneuver around civil rights laws
   (E) several states imposed fees for voting

2. Which of the following statements best describes the Supreme Court's rationale in *Brown v. Board of Education?*
   (A) The courts must protect groups when the legislature fails to do so.
   (B) Segregated schools are inherently unequal.
   (C) *De* facto segregation is unconstitutional.
   (D) Integrated schools provide educational benefits to all students.
   (E) Schools for African Americans had inferior facilities compared to schools for whites.

3. The federal government took which of the following measures to end southern resistance to desegregation?
   I. sent in the Arkansas National Guard to force schools to desegregate
   II. closed Southern school systems until they agreed to desegregate
   III. provided financial aid for schools that integrated
   IV. ordered federalized troops to escort African-American students to school
   (A) I and II
   (B) I, II, and III
   (C) II and III
   (D) III and IV
   (E) I and IV

4. In the 1960s, Denver, Colorado, had several racially distinct neighborhoods. The Denver public schools developed a neighborhood schools plan in which students would attend the school closest to home. On what grounds was this plan challenged?
   (A) that it was *de jure* segregation
   (B) that it was *de facto* segregation
   (C) that the plan did not allow students the freedom to travel to a school of their choice
   (D) that the plan would not allow African-American students to attend schools with whites
   (E) that there was no valid legal basis for challenging this plan

5. During the past two decades, what has been the trend in federal court decisions regarding school integration?
   (A) The federal courts have been more willing to uphold school busing plans.
   (B) The federal courts have been more willing to impose racial quotas on schools.
   (C) Federal courts have been reluctant to use race-conscious means to achieve integration.
   (D) The federal courts have refused to take cases on grounds of federalism because school district boundaries are set by the states.
   (E) The federal courts have refused to uphold busing because polls show that a majority of the public opposes it.

6. After many delays, all of the following events enabled the passage of the Civil Rights Act of 1964 EXCEPT
   (A) more members in Congress supported civil rights
   (B) the media made the public aware of the discrimination faced by African Americans by showing violence by white segregationists
   (C) President Kennedy, who was a proponent of civil rights, was assassinated
   (D) most Southern whites favored desegregation once public schools became integrated
   (E) President Johnson was committed to passing civil rights legislation

7. Which of the following statements best describes the Supreme Court's position on affirmative action?
   (A) Quotas can be used in college admissions to achieve a racially balanced student body.
   (B) Racial preferences are acceptable as long as a point system is used to rate candidates for college admission.
   (C) "Set-asides" can be used in construction contracts but not in hiring or in college admissions.
   (D) Affirmative action programs are unconstitutional because they are reverse discrimination.
   (E) Affirmative action programs may be acceptable if they are narrowly tailored to meet compelling government interests.

8. All of the following were civil rights laws passed as part of Lyndon Johnson's Great Society EXCEPT
   (A) the Twenty-fourth Amendment
   (B) the Equal Employment Opportunity Act
   (C) *Brown v. Board of Education*
   (D) the Voting Rights Act
   (E) the Fair Housing Act

9. Since the 1990s, all of the following statements about female representation in the federal government are true EXCEPT
   (A) more women are being appointed to the federal bench
   (B) for the first time, a woman was a running mate in a presidential campaign
   (C) more women are serving in Cabinet positions
   (D) more members of Congress are female
   (E) for the first time, a woman was elected to a top leadership position in Congress

10. Which of the following is required by U.S. law?
   (A) States must provide bilingual ballots when more than 5 percent of the population speaks a language other than English.
   (B) States must provide bilingual ballots to any citizen who speaks a language other than English.
   (C) States must create one House district to represent minority interests.
   (D) Television ads must contain bilingual captions in states where 5 percent of the population speaks a language other than English.
   (E) Bilingual translators must be provided at polling places where more than 5 percent of the citizens speak a language other than English.

11. Which of the following statements best describes the Americans with Disabilities Act?
   (A) Public buildings must be made accessible to the disabled as long as it is economically feasible.
   (B) Employers must hire a percentage of disabled employees equal to their percentage in the local population.
   (C) Employers must retain disabled employees even if they are not qualified for their jobs.
   (D) Employers must make reasonable accommodations for disabled employees.
   (E) Employers who hire disabled employees receive subsidies.

12. According to the U.S. Supreme Court, may the Boy Scouts revoke the membership of an openly gay Eagle Scout?
   (A) No, because all individuals have a right of privacy.
   (B) Yes, because the Boy Scouts are a private organization and have a right to freedom of association.
   (C) No, because the law protects people from discrimination on the basis of sexual orientation.
   (D) No, because the Fourteenth Amendment's Equal Protection Clause applies to homosexuals.
   (E) Yes, because the Boy Scouts have a right to protect their system of religious beliefs.

13. Which of the following is true of the Equal Rights Amendment?
   (A) It was ratified in 1977 and became a formal constitutional amendment the following year.
   (B) It was passed by the House of Representative with a two-thirds vote but failed in the Senate by a simple majority.
   (C) Both houses of Congress passed it, but President Nixon vetoed it.
   (D) The vast majority of its opponents were men.
   (E) Both houses of Congress approved it with a two-thirds vote, but it fell short of the three-fourths of the states necessary for ratification.

FREE-RESPONSE QUESTIONS

1. The courts have decided a number of cases involving civil rights.
   a. Identify the clause of the Fourteenth Amendment that is used most frequently in civil rights cases.
   b. For TWO of the following issues, refer to a specific Supreme Court case and summarize the Court's decision.
      • affirmative action
      • gay rights
      • women's rights

2. Both *Brown v. Board of Education* and *Swann v. Charlotte-Mecklenburg Board of Education* deal with school desegregation. For EACH case,
   a. discuss the Court's ruling and its impact
   b. identify and discuss one limitation on school desegregation

Answers

Multiple-Choice Questions

1. **(A)** Although the Fourteenth and Fifteenth Amendments gave African Americans citizenship, equality, and the right to vote, literacy tests, poll taxes, and violence were used to deny voting rights to blacks (*American Government, 2011–2012*, pp. 169–171/ *2013–2014*, pp. 139–140).

2. **(D)** In *Brown v. Board of Education*, the Supreme Court ruled that *de jure* segregation is inherently unequal and violates the equal protection clause of the Fourteenth Amendment (*American Government, 2011–2012*, pp. 172–173/ *2013–2014*, pp. 141–142).

3. **(E)** The federal government sent the National Guard to desegregate schools, including Central High School in Little Rock, Arkansas. Federalized Arkansas National Guard troops escorted African-American students to school (*American Government, 2011–2012*, p. 173/ *2013–2014*, p. 142).

4. **(B)** The neighborhood schools plan was challenged as *de facto* segregation because it resulted in racially separate schools (*American Government, 2011–2012*, p. 174/ *2013–2014*, p. 143, see discussion of similar plan and the Court's ruling in *Swann v. Charlotte-Mecklenburg Board of Education*).

5. **(C)** During the 1990s and early 2000s, the federal courts grew less willing to uphold race-conscious policies to further school integration (*American Government, 2011–2012*, p. 174/ *2013–2014*, p. 143).

6. **(D)** The Civil Rights Act of 1964 was finally passed in response to increasing congressional support, as well as public reaction to the violence against civil rights advocates as shown by the media. President Kennedy's assassination led many—including President Johnson—to support civil rights in his honor (*American Government, 2011–2012*, pp. 177–178/ *2013–2014*, pp. 144–146).

7. **(E)** The Supreme Court has upheld some limited affirmative action programs. These programs must be narrowly tailored to meet a compelling government interest (*American Government, 2011–2012*, p. 198/ *2013–2014*, pp. 166-168).

8. **(C)** The Twenty-fourth Amendment, Equal Employment Opportunity Act, Voting Rights Act, and Fair Housing Act were all passed during the Johnson administration. *Brown v. Board of Education* occurred in 1954, during the Eisenhower presidency (*American Government, 2011–2012*, pp. 178–179/ *2013–2014*, pp. 146–148, 163).

9. **(B)** Since the 1990s, there have been more women in Congress, in the Cabinet, and on the federal bench than ever before. Nancy Pelosi was elected Speaker of the House of Representatives in 2007. In 1984, Geraldine Ferraro was the Democratic candidate for vice president (*American Government, 2011–2012*, pp. 190–191/ *2013–2014*, p. 159).

10. **(A)** Federal law requires states to provide bilingual ballots when 5 percent of the population speaks a language other than English (*American Government, 2011–2012*, p. 179/ *2013–2014*, p. 148).

11. **(D)** The ADA requires employers to make reasonable accommodations for disabled employees (*American Government, 2011–2012*, pp. 200–201/ *2013–2014*, pp. 170–171).

12. **(B)** In *Boy Scouts of America v. Dale*, the Supreme Court ruled that the Boy Scouts were within their rights in revoking Dale's membership because they are a private organization (*American Government, 2011–2012*, p. 202/ *2013–2014*, p. 172).

13. **(E)** Congress approved the Equal Rights Amendment, but it fell three states short of ratification. Some of its most vocal opponents were women (*American Government, 2011– 2012*, pp. 188–189/ *2013–2014*, p. 157).

FREE-RESPONSE QUESTIONS

1. (a) Affirmative action, gay rights, and gender discrimination cases all involve the Equal Protection Clause of the Fourteenth Amendment. The Defense of Marriage Act bans federal recognition of gay marriage, but it may conflict with the Full Faith and Credit Clause. Several laws protect against gender discrimination, including the Equal Pay Act and Title IX of the Civil Rights Act.

   (b) Affirmative action programs use preferential practices in hiring and college admissions. The goals of these programs are to foster more diversity and to make up for past and ongoing discrimination. Affirmative action programs were challenged in *Bakke v. University of California*, when a white medical school applicant with good grades and test scores was not admitted because of a quota system. The Court upheld affirmative action plans in general, but it overturned the quota system. The quota system was found to be race discrimination under the Equal Protection Clause of the Fourteenth Amendment. In a more recent case, the Court overturned a voluntary plan by Seattle schools that was designed to correct a racial imbalance. The Court invalidated the plan under the Equal Protection Clause because it was not "narrowly tailored to meet a compelling government interest." However, some limited affirmative action plans might be acceptable to avoid racial isolation.

   The California Supreme Court ruled that gay couples have a state constitutional right to marry. However, that was superseded in the 2008 elections, when Californians voted for a proposition restricting marriage to a man and a woman. The

   U.S. Supreme Court upheld a rule by the Boy Scouts excluding gays. The Court held that private organizations can choose their own members because they have a right of association. Thus, the status of gay rights is still being determined.

The Supreme Court held that police and firefighting units cannot establish arbitrary rules—such as height and weight requirements—that tend to exclude women from those occupations. The Supreme Court also ruled that life insurance companies cannot charge different rates for women and men. (*American Government, 2011–2012*, pp. 191–193, 197–198, and 201–203 / *2013–2014*, pp. 158, 166–168 and 172–174).

2. (a) In *Brown v. Board of Education,* the issue was whether segregation in public schools was constitutional. The NAACP argued that separate educational facilities were unconstitutional, even if funding and facilities were similar in schools attended by African Americans and by whites. This was the last in a long series of cases designed to chip away at the ruling in *Plessy v. Ferguson.* The Supreme Court held that segregated schools violate the Fourteenth Amendment because they are "inherently unequal." Separate but equal was dead. The immediate impact of the decision was limited because of white resistance. However, over the following decades, public schools were desegregated throughout the South.

   The issue in *Swann v. Charlotte-Mecklenburg* was *de facto* segregation. This means that the law did not segregate the school district, but that it was segregated in fact. Children attended the school nearest home, and because neighborhoods were segregated, so were the schools. The Supreme Court ordered a school busing plan to achieve racial balance within the schools. Because of *Swann,* several large metropolitan school districts implemented busing plans to desegregate. Several years later, the Court ruled that the school district had achieved the goal of integration and that race-based quotas could no longer be imposed.

   (b) The ruling that school districts could not bus students across district lines to achieve integrated schools limited school desegregation. Following the Court's ruling in *Swann,* many cities experienced "white flight" when white families moved to the suburbs. These residential areas were predominantly white, and the cities they left behind had a higher percentage of minorities. The regions remained racially imbalanced because busing could not cross school district boundaries (*American Government, 2011–2012,* pp. 172–174/ *2013–2014,* pp. 139, 141–144).

14

CIVIL LIBERTIES

Civil liberties are the constitutional protections an individual has against government action. In order to understand the nature of civil liberties, it is necessary to understand why the liberties guaranteed in the Bill of Rights are important, how they came to apply to the states, and why they have grown in scope and meaning.

KEY TERMS

actual malice
civil liberties
clear and present danger test
commercial speech
defamation of character
establishment clause
exclusionary rule
free exercise clause
gag order
incorporation theory
libel
prior restraint
public figure
slander
symbolic speech

KEY CONCEPTS

- During the 20th century, the process of selective incorporation was used to apply most of the Bill of Rights to protect citizens from actions by the states.

- The First Amendment is the source of many of the most important civil liberties, including the freedoms of religion, speech, press, assembly, and petition.

185

■ Several rights of the accused are also guaranteed in the Bill of Rights.

■ The USA-PATRIOT Act was created as a result of the 9/11 attacks, and many believe that some of its provisions violate the Constitution.

For a full discussion of order and civil liberties, see the 2011–2012 and 2013–2014 editions of *American Government & Politics Today*, Chapter 4.

Civil Liberties and Selective Incorporation

For most of this nation's history, it was believed that the states were meant to be exempt from the restrictions found in the Bill of Rights. The courts supported this belief until 1925. In *Gitlow v. New York*, the Supreme Court began a process called selective incorporation by using the due process clause of the Fourteenth Amendment—"No State shall make or enforce any law which shall abridge the privileges or immunities of citizens of the United States; nor shall any State deprive any person of life, liberty, or property, without due process of law." Selective incorporation refers to the application of the Bill of Rights to the individual states. As the word *selective* indicates, not all of the rights found in the Bill of Rights have been applied to the states.

AP Tip

Selective incorporation is basic to an understanding of civil liberties and will likely appear on the AP exam.

Freedom of Religion

Freedom of religion has two parts: the establishment clause and the free-exercise clause. Over the years, the Supreme Court has attempted to clarify the meaning of these clauses. The establishment clause states that "Congress shall make no law respecting the establishment of religion." The Court has interpreted this as meaning that the government must maintain a position of neutrality in regard to religion. The free-exercise clause states that "Congress shall make no law prohibiting the free exercise [of religion]." The Court has maintained that the free-exercise clause protects the right to believe in anything one chooses, but there are limits on the practice of one's religion. The following are some important issues regarding the freedom of religion:

■ **Aid to religious schools** The Court ruled in *Lemon v. Kurtzman* (1971) that a law permitting the use of state funds to subsidize teachers to teach secular subjects at religious schools violated the establishment clause. In its decision, the Court laid out the three-part *Lemon* test for state aid: the aid must have a secular purpose; the aid must neither advance nor prohibit religion; the aid must not create excessive government entanglement in religion. In *Agostini v. Felton* (1997), the Court reversed itself on the use of state funds to hire teachers to teach secular subjects in religious schools. In a 5–4 decision, the Court ruled that paying for teachers to teach remedial secular courses did not create *excessive* government entanglement.

In 2002, the Court ruled in *Zelman v. Simmons-Harris* that school vouchers could be used for tuition at religious schools because the money was going to the parents, who then made the decision between religious or secular schools.

- **School prayer** In *Engle v. Vitale* (1962), the Court ruled that school-sponsored prayer violates the establishment clause. This has been extended to include prayer at school activities such as graduations and athletic events. However, the Court has ruled that extracurricular religious activities should have the same support as nonreligious ones. To not provide the same after-school access to such groups would violate the freedom of speech.

- **Public religious displays** In 2005, the Court allowed the Ten Commandments to be displayed at the Texas State Capitol because it was part of a larger secular display. In a separate ruling in 2005, the Court ordered two Ten Commandment displays removed from Kentucky courthouses because they were overtly religious.

- **Evolution** The Court has consistently held that outlawing the teaching of evolution in the classroom or requiring the teaching of creationism (also known as intelligent design) violates the establishment clause because it imposes religious beliefs.

- **Free exercise** In 1990, the Supreme Court ruled in *Oregon v. Smith* that two state employees could be fired for using peyote. The employees argued that their use of peyote—traditionally used in the practice of a Native American religion—was protected under the free exercise clause of the First Amendment. In response, Congress passed the Religious Freedom Restoration Act, which required all local, state, and federal governments to accommodate religious practice. The Supreme Court later struck this law down as too broad.

FREEDOM OF EXPRESSION

The next two clauses of the First Amendment are the freedom of expression clauses, protecting the freedoms of speech and the press. The Founding Fathers believed that a free press was critical to the operation of a democracy; its placement in the First Amendment reflects this importance.

There are several protections accorded to the media by the First Amendment:

- **Prior restraint** A primary safeguard for freedom of the press is the prevention of prior restraint on the publication of any material. This protection was reinforced in *New York Times v. United States*. In this 1971 case, the U.S. government tried to prevent the *New York Times* from publishing a classified Pentagon document pertaining to the Vietnam War. The Court ruled that the government could not prevent publication because it failed to prove that an imminent danger would be produced by the information's publication.

The Court has allowed trial judges to ban news coverage before a trial to begin if news coverage may impede the defendant's ability to receive a fair trial.

- **Slander** Spoken defamation is not protected speech but, like libel, is extremely hard to prove.

- **Libel** Written defamation of a person's character, called libel, is not protected speech. However, the standard to prove libel is extremely high, especially for public figures. To win a libel case, the plaintiff must prove that the publication printed false information knowing it was false and with the intent to cause harm. Because of this high standard, very few libel cases are brought, and even fewer result in any kind of retraction or monetary award.

The Court has consistently held broadcast media to a different standard than print media because broadcasters use publicly owned bandwidth. It has allowed penalties to be imposed for the use of "filthy" words on radio or television broadcasts, and has even allowed films to be banned for their content.

Looking at freedom of speech, the Court has created the following limitations:

- **Symbolic speech** In *Tinker v. Des Moines Independent County School District* (1969), the Court ruled that nonverbal, or symbolic, speech is protected under the First Amendment. Later, in *Texas v. Johnson* (1989), the Supreme Court ruled that burning the flag was a form of protected speech.

- **Commercial speech** In general, the Court has protected advertising as free speech. However, a business can be sued for making false claims in advertising if harm is caused.

- **Clear and present danger rule** In *Schenck v. United States* (1919), the Court created one of the basic limits on a person's freedom of speech: if a person's speech presented a real or imminent danger to him- or herself, to others, or to the general order, the government could limit that speech. A basic test in applying this rule is the difference between advocacy and imminence. Before the government can limit an individual's speech, it must prove that the speech is likely to present an immediate threat. In *Brandenburg v. Ohio* (1969), the Court raised the bar by ruling that threatening speech is protected unless the government can prove it was meant to create an actual and direct danger.

- **Obscenity** One type of speech that is not protected is obscenity. The problem the Supreme Court faces is defining what is considered obscene. In *Miller v. California*, the Court created a four-part test to help determine whether material was obscene:

- The average person finds that the material violates community standards.

- The material, taken as a whole, creates an unnatural or unwholesome interest in sex.
- The material depicts offensive sexual conduct.
- The material lacks any serious artistic, literary, political, or scientific purpose.

Given the criteria above, it should be obvious that definitions of obscenity vary widely from place to place and change with time. More recently, the Supreme Court has struck down several laws that attempted to limit obscenity on the Internet as overly broad in their definitions. However, the Court did uphold a law that required libraries and schools to install Internet filtering software.

PEACEFUL ASSEMBLY AND PETITION

The Court has created a simple test when it comes to restrictions on the right to assemble and petition. These restrictions are called time, place, and manner restrictions; they vary from jurisdiction to jurisdiction. For example, a group of protesters has the right to gather, but not to block traffic or prevent access to an occupied building. The Court even upheld the right of the American Nazi Party to march through a mostly Jewish neighborhood in Skokie, Illinois.

THE RIGHT TO PRIVACY

The most controversial area of civil liberties concerns privacy because the Bill of Rights does not make explicit reference to the right to privacy. In *Griswold v. Connecticut* (1965), the Court ruled that a Connecticut law making it illegal to use contraceptive devices was unconstitutional. In his opinion, Justice William Douglas wrote that the First, Third, Fourth, and Fifth Amendments created "penumbras" that implied a right to privacy, a right protected by the Ninth Amendment.

The *Griswold* decision about the right to privacy has since been used with two controversial areas—abortion rights and the "right to die":

- **Abortion** In the landmark case *Roe v.* Wade (1973), the Supreme Court held that the right to privacy protected a woman's right to an abortion. The Court did allow for government restriction in the second and third trimesters of a pregnancy, but not in the first trimester. Since the *Roe* decision, the Court has grown more conservative and has allowed some limitations on abortion rights. In *Webster v. Reproductive Health Services*, the Court upheld a law that prohibited the use of public funds for abortion services, and in 2007, the Court upheld a federal law that outlawed abortions in the third trimester. In *Planned Parenthood v. Casey*, the Court upheld a Pennsylvania state law that required pre-abortion counseling, a 24-hour waiting period, and parental or judicial permission for girls under the age of 18.
- **"Right to die"** The Court has ruled that the right to privacy includes the right to refuse medical treatment. A family member can make this decision for someone in a coma or a vegetative state

in the absence of a living will. In 2006, the Court upheld a law in Oregon that allowed physician-assisted suicide for terminally ill patients.

PRIVACY AND NATIONAL SECURITY

The war on terrorism created a whole new series of constitutional issues regarding civil liberties. For example, the federal government now uses "roving" wiretaps against a variety of terror suspects. This seems to contradict the earlier Fourth Amendment standard developed by the Court. Previously, in order to receive a warrant for a wiretap, authorities had to describe the place, not the person, being tapped. President George W. Bush ordered wiretaps on conversations between people in the United States and those overseas without a warrant at all, if one of the parties was a terror suspect.

In the aftermath of the 9/11 attacks, Congress passed the USA-PATRIOT Act, which gave the government a host of new powers to track, search, and arrest suspected terrorists.

RIGHTS OF THE ACCUSED

A second area of selective incorporation is the rights of accused criminals. The Court, over time, has incorporated most protections found in the Bill of Rights to the states. The following are some of the ground rules and cases regarding the rights of the accused:

■ **Right to counsel** In *Gideon v. Wainwright* (1963), the Supreme Court ruled that under the Sixth Amendment, states are required to provide counsel in criminal cases. The Court held that the right to a lawyer is fundamental to a fair trial; therefore, each state must provide a lawyer for every defendant if he or she cannot provide one.

■ *Miranda* **rights** The Court has ruled that all accused criminals must be informed of their rights. In *Miranda v. Arizona* (1966), the Court overturned the conviction of Ernesto Miranda because, prior to making a confession, he was not made aware of his Fifth Amendment right to protection from self-incrimination. The Court ruled that accused criminals must be notified of their rights when they are arrested and before questioning can begin. This notification is now called the *Miranda* warnings.

■ **Exclusionary rule** The Supreme Court set out several guidelines regarding the Fourth Amendment, which, along with the First Amendment, has been applied to the states. In *Mapp v. Ohio* (1961), the Court ruled that the exclusionary rule applies to the states. The exclusionary rule prevents evidence obtained through an illegal search and seizure from being used against an accused criminal. The Court later ruled that good faith exceptions could be allowed, which means that evidence obtained when the police believed they had a valid search warrant can be used in a trial.

■ **Death penalty** The Eighth Amendment forbids cruel and unusual punishment. Over the course of U.S. history, critics have challenged the application of the death penalty as a violation of the Eighth

Amendment. In 1972, the Supreme Court ruled in *Furman v. Georgia* that the application of the death penalty was too arbitrary, but capital punishment itself was not cruel and unusual. This decision forced states to adopt more concise laws regarding the death penalty. The Supreme Court upheld these new laws in 1976. More recently, the Court ruled that only juries—not judges— could impose the death penalty. Recent opinion polls have shown declining support for the application of the death penalty.

MULTIPLE-CHOICE QUESTIONS

1. All of the following situations involve civil liberties EXCEPT
   (A) an angry protestor burns an American flag
   (B) a burglary suspect is read her rights before questioning
   (C) a group of parents brings a lawsuit to end *de facto* segregation in a public school district
   (D) a group sacrifices a goat as part of a religious ceremony
   (E) a state law mandates that public school students recite the Pledge of Allegiance each day

2. The Supreme Court has upheld which of the following limits on free speech?
   I. laws against defamation of character
   II. laws against speech that presents a clear and present danger
   III. laws against flag burning
   IV. laws against obscenity
   (A) I and II
   (B) I, II, and III
   (C) II and IV
   (D) I, II, and IV
   (E) I and IV

3. The Ku Klux Klan burns a cross at a rally across the street from a predominantly African-American Baptist church. The members of the church are offended by what they view as a hateful display. How would the courts most likely rule?
   (A) The First Amendment protects hate speech.
   (B) The First Amendment does not protect cross burning because it is intimidating.
   (C) The First Amendment protects hate speech, but burning a cross is not speech and is not protected.
   (D) The First Amendment protects hate speech unless a community decides to ban it.
   (E) The First Amendment does not protect hate speech.

4. May a public school deny funds to a Christian student group if the school provides funding for other groups?
   (A) No, because this policy discriminates against religious speech.
   (B) No, because this policy denies students the right to freely exercise their religious beliefs.
   (C) No, because this policy violates the establishment clause.
   (D) Yes, because giving state funds to a religious group would violate the establishment clause.
   (E) Yes, because giving state funds to a religious group would violate the free exercise clause.

5. Interact Club is a school-sponsored organization that prays around the flagpole of a public school every morning before school. Is the club's activity constitutional?
   (A) No, because the prayer takes place on school grounds and therefore is a violation of the establishment clause.
   (B) No, because the prayer is part of a school-sponsored club and therefore is a violation of the establishment clause.
   (C) No, because it is a violation of both the establishment clause and the free exercise clause to pray on the grounds of a public school.
   (D) Yes, because the prayer takes place before the school day.
   (E) Yes, because the prayer is part of a club, not part of a class, and it could take place at any time during the school day.

6. A house is searched without a valid search warrant, and a corpse is found. What would be the most likely outcome?
   (A) The discovery of the corpse could be used in court because it is the best evidence that a murder occurred.
   (B) The discovery of the corpse could not be used as evidence because it was discovered without a warrant, but hair samples on the corpse could be used in DNA testing.
   (C) The case could not be prosecuted because the exclusionary rule would prevent any evidence of the murder from being presented in court.
   (D) The case could be prosecuted with independent evidence, but the discovery of the corpse could not be used under the exclusionary rule.
   (E) The case would be decided under state law because many states have passed laws eliminating the exclusionary rule.

7. What is the result of the Supreme Court's ruling in *Miranda v. Arizona*?
   (A) Police officers must read a suspect his or her rights upon arrest; otherwise, the case against the defendant must be dismissed.
   (B) If a police officer fails to read a suspect his or her rights upon arrest, the suspect's confession cannot be used in court.
   (C) This case established the exclusionary rule that any illegally obtained evidence cannot be used in court.
   (D) If a defendant is not read his or her rights upon arrest, a confession cannot be used in court unless it is given voluntarily.
   (E) The confession of a defendant who has not been read his or her rights upon arrest may be used in court, but the defendant may bring a civil suit against the arresting officer.

8. The basketball coach at a state university leads her team in a Christian prayer before each game. Participation is voluntary. Is this constitutional?
   (A) Yes, because the prayer is voluntary.
   (B) Yes, because the prayer is recited outside of the school day.
   (C) Yes, because state universities have more academic freedom than secondary schools.
   (D) No, because this violates the free exercise clause.
   (E) No, because this violates the establishment clause.

9. A student walks into a classroom wearing a T-shirt with a drawing of cartoon characters engaged in sexually explicit behavior. The class erupts in laughter, greatly disrupting the lesson. May the school legally require the student to change shirts?
(A) Yes, because the T-shirt substantially interfered with the work and discipline of the school.
(B) No, because wearing a T-shirt is symbolic speech protected by the free exercise clause.
(C) No, because wearing a T-shirt is symbolic speech, protected by the freedom of expression.
(D) Yes, because schools may limit student speech in any way they see fit, including dress codes.
(E) No, because the shirt showed only cartoon characters and was not meant to be taken seriously.

10. What is selective incorporation?
(A) the idea that corporations cannot be held liable for violations of civil liberties because they are nongovernmental entities
(B) the interpretation of the due process clause of the Fourteenth Amendment to apply the fundamental rights in the Bill of Rights to protect people from state action
(C) the interpretation of the due process clause of the Fourteenth Amendment to apply the entire Bill of Rights to protect people from state action
(D) the concept that rights must be balanced with liberties and that the rights of the majority generally prevail
(E) the idea that each state must include the Bill of Rights in its constitution

11. Which of the following statements correctly describe the Supreme Court's position on abortion?
I. States may prohibit abortions in the last trimester of pregnancy.
II. States may not deny public funding for abortions.
III. States may require notification of one parent prior to an abortion for a minor.
IV. States may regulate abortions as long as the regulations do not create an undue burden.
(A) I and II
(B) II and III
(C) III and IV
(D) I, II, and IV
(E) I, III, and IV

12. Which of the following is authorized by the USA PATRIOT Act?
(A) The government may hold a suspect for 90 days without charges.
(B) The government may search a suspect's home without cause.
(C) The government may monitor a suspect's Internet activity.
(D) The government may interrogate a suspect's friends and family.
(E) The government may deport foreign nationals.

13. All of the following statements about the right of privacy are true
EXCEPT
(A) it is expressly protected in the Constitution
(B) it has been used to protect private consensual conduct between
homosexuals
(C) it stems from the First, Third, Fourth, and Fifth Amendments
(D) the Supreme Court recognized the right by reading between the
lines in the Bill of Rights
(E) it has been used to legalize abortion

FREE-RESPONSE QUESTIONS

1. The First Amendment states, "Congress shall make no law . . .
abridging the freedom of speech." However, freedom of speech is
not absolute.
   a. Identify and explain one way freedom of speech may be
restricted.
   b. Give a specific example to support your analysis in part (a).
   c. Identify and explain another way freedom of speech may be
restricted.
   d. Give a specific example to support your analysis in part (c).
2. Civil liberties include the right of criminal defendants to be treated
fairly during investigation, arrest, and trial. Rules against illegal
search and seizure and self-incrimination protect a defendant's
right to due process.
   a. Identify one rule regarding illegal search and seizure, and
explain how that rule operates to protect a defendant's right to
due process.
   b. Identify one rule regarding self-incrimination, and explain how
that rule operates to protect a defendant's right to due process.

Answers

MULTIPLE-CHOICE QUESTIONS

1. **(C)** Civil liberties are protections individuals have from government
action. These include free speech, religious freedom, separation of
church and state, and certain rights of defendants. Civil rights are
rooted in the Fourteenth Amendment's equal protection clause
(*American Government, 2011–2012*, pp. 123, 167/ *2013–2014*, pp. 96–
98, 136).
2. **(D)** Although the First Amendment protects freedom of speech, this
right is not absolute. The Court has upheld laws against defamation
and obscenity and speech that present a clear and present danger
(*American Government, 2011–2012*, pp. 136–139/ *2013–2014*, pp.
107–111).
3. **(A)** The First Amendment protects unpopular and offensive speech,
whether verbal or symbolic, such as burning a cross (*American
Government, 2011–2012*, pp. 134–135/ *2013–2014*, p. 116).
4. **(A)** In *Rosenberger v. University of Virginia*, the Supreme Court
held that the university's policy of denying funds to a religious
group when it provided money to over 100 other groups

unconstitutionally discriminated against religious speech (*American Government, 2011–2012*, p. 131/ *2013–2014*, p. 104).

5. **(D)** The establishment clause does not prohibit all religious activity on school grounds. However, the prayer must take place outside the school building or outside normal school hours (*American Government, 2011–2012*, pp. 129–130/ *2013–2014*, p. 104).

6. **(D)** With some exceptions, the exclusionary rule prohibits evidence from an invalid search from being used in court. It also excludes evidence that is "fruit of the poisonous tree"—evidence that stems from an illegal search. However, the case could still be prosecuted with other evidence (*American Government, 2011–2012*, p. 155/ *2013–2014*, p. 126).

7. **(B)** Under *Miranda,* if a suspect is not read his or her rights upon arrest, a confession cannot be used in court, even if that confession was given voluntarily (*American Government, 2011–2012*, pp. 154–155/ *2013–2014*, p. 124).

8. **(E)** The prayer violates the establishment clause because the school is a state-owned institution and the practice has the effect of coercing those present to participate (*American Government, 2011–2012*, pp. 129–130/ *2013–2014*, p. 101).

9. **(A)** Although students do not leave their First Amendment rights at the schoolhouse door and symbolic speech is protected by the First Amendment, schools may limit speech that is obscene. The T-shirt materially and substantially disrupted the educational process (*American Government, 2011–2012*, pp. 134– 135/ *2013–2014*, p. 106).

10. **(B).** In *Gitlow v. New York* the Supreme Court held that the due process clause of the Fourteenth Amendment protects individuals from state action that violates fundamental rights. Not all of the Bill of Rights has been incorporated (*American Government, 2011–2012*, p. 124/ *2013–2014*, p. 97).

11. **(E)** Abortion remains legal, although states may regulate abortions as long as those regulations are not an undue burden. States are not required to allocate public funding for abortions (*American Government, 2011–2012*, pp. 148–149/ *2013–2014*, p. 118).

12. **(C)** The USA PATRIOT Act allows the government to monitor a suspect's Internet activities, phone conversations, financial records, and book purchases. Opponents argue that these expanded government powers are a threat to civil liberties (*American Government, 2011–2012*, pp. 151–152/ *2013–2014*, p. 121).

13. **(A)** Although privacy is not expressly mentioned in the Constitution, the Supreme Court has held that the right comes from "penumbras" stemming from the First, Third, Fourth, and Fifth Amendments (*American Government, 2011–2012*, p. 146/ *2013–2014*, p. 117).

FREE-RESPONSE QUESTIONS

1. (a) The First Amendment does not protect defamation of character. Libel laws protect people from written statements that are untrue and damaging, and these laws restrict freedom of speech. If freedom of speech were allowed to operate without restriction, anything—no matter how damaging and untrue—could be printed without penalty. To recover damages for libel, an ordinary citizen must prove the falsehood of the statement

and the damage the statement caused. The standard of proof is much higher for public figures. To recover damages for libel, public figures must prove not only that the statement is false, but also that it was made with malice—a reckless disregard for the truth. Although laws against libel infringe on freedom of speech, to balance protection of free speech and protection of a person's reputation, the courts have upheld them.

(b) One specific example of defamation is *New York Times v. Sullivan*. The Supreme Court ruled that a public figure could recover damages for libel only when the statement was made with actual malice—knowledge that it was false or a reckless disregard for the truth.

(c) Another restriction on freedom of speech pertains to statements that present a "clear and present danger." This means that the speech incites imminent, illegal behavior. What constitutes a clear and present danger is open to interpretation.

(d) In *Schenck v. United States,* the Supreme Court upheld Schenck's conviction for making statements that might hinder the military draft. Schenck wrote pamphlets in which he claimed that World War I was being fought to benefit the defense industry, and he urged men to resist the draft. The Court held that the pamphlets created a clear and present danger to the country, because if men had listened to Schenck and avoided the draft, it would have hindered the war effort. Speech that is acceptable in peacetime might be limited during war (*American Government, 2011–2012*, pp. 136–137, 139, 141–142/ *2013–2014*, pp. 108, 111, 113–114).

2. (a) One rule that protects a defendant's right to due process is the exclusionary rule. This rule prevents illegally obtained evidence from being used against a defendant at trial. The Supreme Court established the exclusionary rule in *Mapp v. Ohio*. The defendant was suspected of possessing illegal drugs. When police broke into her home, they did not find drugs, but they did find obscene pictures. The Court ruled that the pornography could not be used as evidence in court because the police had not obtained a search warrant, even though they had had time to do so. The exclusionary rule protects due process because it encourages authorities to obtain search warrants and discourages illegal searches.

(b) *Miranda* warnings also protect defendants' due process rights. In *Miranda v. Arizona,* a rape suspect gave a confession after hours of questioning. He had not been read his rights. The Supreme Court held that the confession was inadmissible because Miranda did not know that he had the right to remain silent or to have an attorney present during questioning. Now when police take suspects into custody, they read from a "*Miranda* card." *Miranda* warnings protect defendants' rights to due process by ensuring that they understand their legal rights. This prevents uninformed self-incrimination (*American Government, 2011–2012*, pp. 154–155/ *2013–2014*, pp. 124–126).

15

DOMESTIC AND ECONOMIC POLICY

Domestic policies such as health care and social welfare programs are a source of political controversy among Americans. When compared with other democracies, the United States' domestic health care and social welfare programs are among the least developed. Another important domestic issue is crime. The United States has the highest rate of incarceration in the world. Finally, the fact that the United States consumes more oil per capita than any other country makes environmental policy a hotly debated issue.

When looking at economic policy making, government officials confront two conflicting pressures: keeping the tax burden under control and maintaining the overall economic health of the country.

KEY TERMS

budget deficit
Environmental Impact Statement
Federal Reserve System
progressive tax
regressive tax
fiscal policy
full employment
inflation
Keynesian economics
loopholes
Medicaid
Medicare
monetary policy
Supplemental Security Income (SSI)
Temporary Assistance to Needy Families (TANF)
unemployment

197

Key Concepts

■ Health care in the United States is costly. After many failed attempts, in 2010 Congress finally passed a health care reform act that is designed to control costs and increase the number of Americans who have health insurance.

■ The United States has created a series of environmental policies since 1969 to reduce pollution and protect endangered species. While these policies have been fairly successful, the government's response to global warming has not been well coordinated, partly because of those who dispute the science of global warming.

■ The cornerstones of social welfare policy in the United States are Social Security and Temporary Assistance to Needy Families.

■ Public assistance in various forms plays a small but controversial role in social welfare policy.

■ Illegal immigration is a growing political issue.

■ Government management of the economy is an effort to balance unemployment and inflation.

■ There are several competing theories about how the government can best manage the economy, including Keynesian economics, supply-side economics, and monetary policy. Recovery plans to deal with the recession of 2007–2009 have caused intense public debate about the effectiveness of these theories.

■ Americans have a comparatively low tax burden. Federal taxes are a mixture of progressive and regressive taxes.

■ The budget indicates how much money the government will collect in taxes, spend in revenues, and allocate among various programs.

For a full discussion of domestic policy and economic policy, see *American Government & Politics Today* 2011–2012 edition, Chapters 16 and 17, and 2013–2014 edition, Chapters 15 and 16. For a full discussion of the budget process, see *American Government & Politics Today*, 2011–2012 edition, Chapter 12, and 2013–2014 edition, Chapter 11.

Health Care Policy

In recent years, the cost of health care in the United States has skyrocketed. Today, Americans spend more on health care than any other country in the world. In 1965, about 6 percent of our income was spent on health care. The percentage of income spent on healthcare is expected to reach 20 by 2020. America's aging population and the availability of more advanced medical technologies account in part—but only in part—for the rise in health care costs.

The government plays a large role in health care policy. Currently, through a variety of government-run health care programs such as Medicaid, Medicare, and the Veterans Administration, government accounts for roughly 45 percent of all health care. Insurance companies and private individuals cover the other 55 percent of health care spending. The most important government health care programs include the following:

- **Medicare** Medicare was created in 1965 and provides health care coverage for Americans over the age of 65. In 2006, a prescription drug component was added to help recipients pay for the cost of expensive drug treatments. Medicare is funded by a payroll tax paid by working Americans. Since its creation, Medicare has become the second-most expensive domestic program, and the growing cost of health care and the increasing number of recipients put its long-term viability in doubt. To keep costs down, the government has capped some reimbursements to doctors and hospitals for Medicare procedures. As a result, a number of HMOs and doctors refuse to accept Medicare patients.

- **Medicaid** This program, which provides health insurance for poor Americans, is jointly administered by the federal government and each state's government. The federal government pays for about 60 percent of Medicaid costs, and the states pay the rest. Eligibility requirements are left up to each individual state. The cost of Medicaid has skyrocketed in recent years, from $150 billion in 1997 to over $300 billion in 2007.

- **The Affordable Care Act** In 2010, Congress passed the Affordable Care Act in an effort to deal with the issue of uninsured American sand increasing health care costs. More than 49 million Americans do not have health insurance. Many of these uninsured are either people in entry-level jobs with companies that did not provide insurance, minorities, or both. The law has several important provisions:

- Americans with preexisting conditions cannot be denied coverage.

- Americans who earn wages will be required to purchase health insurance or pay a penalty.

- Health insurance "exchanges," which allow individuals to purchase health insurance at discounted rates, will be up and running by 2017.

ENVIRONMENTAL POLICY

Over the past several decades, Americans have become more concerned about the environment not only in the United States but worldwide as well. The government has developed environmental policy that tries to balance the costs of environmental programs with the benefits of protecting natural resources, habitats, and wildlife.

Modern U.S. environmental policy began in 1969. In response to an oil spill off the coast of California, Congress passed the National Environmental Policy Act, which created the Environmental Protection Agency (EPA). The EPA was charged with administering all federal law regarding environmental protection. One major provision of the new law was the requirement of environmental impact statements (EIS). Any major federal project was required to file an EIS detailing the possible impact the project might have on the water, air, soil, or wildlife in the area. This requirement has been extended to most—if not all— state and local projects and even to many private projects as well. Environmental interest groups can use the information in an EIS to lobby or sue for project revisions. If they think the environmental damage is too great, they can try and stop a project completely. Other major federal environmental policies include the following:

■ **Air pollution** The Clean Air Act of 1990 created more stringent standards for automobile emissions. It also required old coal plants to reduce emissions by 40 percent and called for the production of CFCs (chemical compounds that deplete the ozone layer) to stop by 2010.

■ **Water pollution** The Clean Water Act, passed in 1972, was designed to make lakes and rivers safe for swimming and fishing, protect fish and wildlife, and eliminate the dumping of pollutants into lakes and rivers.

■ **Endangered species** The Endangered Species Act (1972) made it illegal to harm or kill a plant or animal species on the endangered list. It also authorized the government to purchase the habitats of endangered species in order to protect them. Agricultural and development interest groups have lobbied and sued to remove species (including wolves) from the endangered category when they deem the economic costs of preservation too high.

■ **Global warming** During the early 1990s, evidence began to mount that Earth is getting warmer and that if the trend continues it will have tremendous impacts on the world's environment in the latter half of the 21st century. One of the primary causes of global warming is the emission of so-called greenhouse gases that result from human activity. These gases trap heat in Earth's atmosphere, thus warming it. The science behind global warming has been disputed by a tiny but well-financed group of researchers whose dissent has made it difficult for the government to develop any coherent policy. For example, in 1997, the United States and other industrial countries drew up the Kyoto Protocol, a treaty that called for 38 developed countries to reduce their emission of greenhouse gases by 2010. But in 2001, President George W. Bush refused to submit the treaty to the Senate for ratification.

■ **Energy policy** Energy policy is an important component of environmental policy because much of the air pollution in the United States comes from the creation of energy and the use of automobiles that run on gasoline. Coal and oil power plants and automobiles are primary emitters of greenhouse gases. The United States is the largest user of oil in the world—in 2010, residents used approximately 19 million barrels of oil a day, half of it for gasoline. Fifty percent of this oil was imported. In recent years, critics have called for increased domestic exploration and drilling to lessen our reliance on foreign oil. But as the 2010 Gulf oil spill demonstrated, oil production can have disastrous effects on the environment. Others have called for increased research on and use of alternative energy sources such as wind and solar power. Some experts also contend that the United States should begin to build nuclear power plants again, though this has little public support.

SOCIAL WELFARE PROGRAMS

The United States has two types of social welfare programs. The first are the programs that are available to everyone regardless of income, including Social Security and Medicare. The second type, available only to those whose income falls below a certain level, includes programs such as Medicaid and food stamps. In these programs, threshold income levels are used to determine whether an individual qualifies to receive benefits..

The major social welfare programs in the United States include the following:

- **Social Security** The Social Security Act of 1935 created what is now the nation's largest entitlement program. Social Security is meant to guarantee a minimum pension to all retirees in the United States. However, Social Security is currently under scrutiny because of potential problems looming on the horizon: there will soon be an insufficient number of people paying Social Security taxes to provide benefits for every retired person. Several solutions have been offered, but they are opposed by the public and therefore politically dangerous.

- Raising the retirement age to 70 and raising Social Security taxes would help resolve the problem.

- Privatizing Social Security would allow individuals to invest part of their Social Security taxes in the stock market. President George W. Bush proposed this. It had some support from younger Americans, but very little from older Americans and members of Congress.

- **Welfare** Aid to Families with Dependent Children (AFDC) provided cash support for low- income families. Many viewed the recipients as undeserving; instead of widows with children, recipients increasingly were divorced or unwed mothers who were given assistance year after year. States were constrained by an increasing number of federal regulations. Expensive programs were added, such as food stamps and the earned income tax credit (a cash grant to poor parents who work). AFDC lost more and more political legitimacy until it was abolished.

- The Temporary Assistance for Needy Families (TANF) program was established in place of AFDC. Each state is allocated a federal block grant to help pay the costs of providing TANF. Adults can receive TANF benefits for only five years. Aid is reduced to women who do not help identify the fathers of their children The result has been less spending on welfare payments, but critics contend that this is mostly because those who have exhausted their lifetime benefits now simply fall through the cracks. Since 1996 the number of homeless persons has increased.

AP Tip

Both Social Security and Medicare are controversial policies in the United States. The problems of funding them cut across several aspects of the policy-making process, which makes it likely they will appear in some form on the AP exam.

IMMIGRATION

One issue at the forefront of American politics recently has been immigration. Many Americans believe that illegal immigrants in the United States present an economic drain on our resources. Weak border enforcement may be a national security issue as well. In 2008, all but the most conservative candidates for president supported legislation creating a path to citizenship for illegal immigrants, stronger border security, and tougher penalties for businesses that employ illegal immigrants. In the absence of any meaningful federal reform, many states have taken the issue on themselves. Some states have created requirements for citizens to prove their legal status before receiving nonemergency services. In 2010, Arizona passed a law intended to crack down on illegal immigration. One of the requirements was that, when asked by law enforcement officers, individuals produce documentation of their status as legal residents. In 2011, the Supreme Court overturned several provisions of the Arizona law, although it did uphold the provision allowing law enforcement officials to request proof of citizenship.

ECONOMIC POLICY MAKING

Although the federal government has run deficits most years since 1969, Americans have never liked the idea of the government spending more money than it takes in. The government works hard to manage the economy using a variety of tools, including monetary policy, supply-side theory, and Keynesian theory. No matter which method is used to manage the economy, policy makers try to balance two competing economic issues: inflation and unemployment. "Balance" is the key word here, because inflation and unemployment usually have an inverse relationship—that is, when one increases, the other decreases. The financial crisis of 2008 severely tested the government's traditional tools of economic management.

Unemployment, defined as the percentage of Americans who are looking for a job but cannot find one, is a main concern of U.S. economic policy. One problem with this method of measurement is that it does not count those who have given up trying to find a job, or those who want to work full-time but can only find part-time work. "Full employment" does not mean there is zero percent unemployment; it takes into consideration that a small percentage of the workforce will be out of work during seasonal shifts and while moving between jobs. Not only does the government try to insure full employment through its economic policy making, it also provides temporary unemployment insurance for those workers who have lost jobs and are unable to find new ones.

The other major focus of government economic policy making is an effort to keep inflation under control. Inflation is a general increase in price levels. The government measures inflation through the use of the Consumer Price Index (CPI). The CPI measures the change in prices of a set "basket" of goods and services over time.

BASIC ECONOMIC VOCABULARY

- **Business cycle** refers to the periodic expansion and contraction of an economy. Expansion is marked by inflation; contraction is marked by unemployment.
- **Gross domestic product (GDP)** is the total value of all goods and services produced by a nation, used as a measure of the nation's level of economic activity and health.
- **Economic recession.** Two or more successive quarters in which the economy shrinks instead of grows

ECONOMIC THEORIES

The U.S. government plays an important role in its overall performance. Government's attempts to influence the economy revolve around taxation and spending policies, as well as policies that manipulate interest rates. There are several different theories about how the government should use these tools to manage the economy, and the U.S. government tends to draw on a number of them.

FISCAL POLICY

To help keep the economy healthy and manage both unemployment and inflation, the government can apply fiscal policy, which is the use of taxation and spending to manage the economy. There are two ways the government can implement fiscal policy:

- **Keynesian economics** A British economist working during the Great Depression, John Maynard Keynes argued that in severe economic downturns, a government must take a more active role in stimulating the economy. Keynes argued that the government could stimulate consumer purchasing (demand) through the use of fiscal policy by creating jobs through public works projects or through lowering taxes. Economic management in the United States was dominated by the use of Keynesian theory from the Great Depression until 1980. The stimulus bill passed in the first months of Obama's first term is an example of a Keynesian policy.
- **Supply-side economics** When Ronald Reagan was elected president in 1980, the inflation rate was in the double digits, and both monetary policy (see below) and Keynesian theory had failed to bring it down. Supply-side economic theory, which is heavily influenced by laissez-faire ideas, holds that inflation can be brought under control by increasing the supply of goods. The government can stimulate the supply of goods by cutting taxes on the wealthy and businesses and by deregulating the marketplace. Tax cuts would allow further investment in the economy, which would stimulate production; deregulation would make it easier for the economy to expand. Eventually, the benefit of this increased production would "trickle down" to workers and others. President Reagan and Congress passed huge tax cuts shortly after he took office in 1981. Supply-siders argued that spending cuts would not

be necessary because increased production would offset the loss of tax revenue. The tax cuts were successful in reducing inflation and unemployment, but tax revenues did not increase as predicted.

Monetary Policy

Critics of fiscal policy argued that the impact of government spending took too long to be felt in the economy—jobs finally appeared only after the economic need had passed. An alternative to fiscal policy is monetary policy. Rather than influence the economy through taxing and spending, supporters of monetary policy, believe that the best way to manage the economy is through manipulating the money supply. To manipulate the money supply, the Federal Reserve uses three tools:

- The Fed can sell securities such as U.S. Treasury bonds. When it sells bonds, it takes money out of circulation; when it buys them, it increases the money supply.

- The Fed sets the interest rate that banks charge one another for overnight loans, called the federal funds rate. Sometimes the Fed also changes the reserve rate, which is the interest rate it charges banks for short-term loans.

- The reserve requirement is the percentage of total deposits a bank must keep on hand. By increasing the reserve requirement, the Fed takes money out of circulation and slows inflation and economic growth.

Tax Policy

Americans pay a variety of different taxes. The federal income tax is progressive—as an individual's income increases, so does the percentage of income he or she pays in income tax. The amount of money an individual pays in taxes can be reduced through loopholes. Tax loopholes are provisions in the tax code that reduce potential tax receipts by allowing taxpayers to reduce taxable income. For example, those who invest in oil and gas wells are allowed to deduct some of that investment from their taxable income, thus reducing their tax payments.

However, not all taxes are progressive. Americans pay many taxes that are regressive, especially Social Security taxes. A regressive tax is one that falls in percentage as income increases. Currently, the cap on Social Security–taxable income is $110,100, meaning any money earned in excess of that amount is not taxed to support Social Security.

The Budget Process

The federal budget is important because it validates a set of priorities. There are winners and losers in any budget, and they can be determined by the amount of money they receive from the federal budget.

The budget process starts with the president. Federal law requires that the president prepare and submit a budget to Congress each winter. The Office of Management and Budget (OMB) oversees the president's budget preparation and starts by assessing the overall economic situation and receiving spending priorities from the president. It then gathers budget requests from all of the bureaucratic agencies. The OMB works these requests into a package for the president, who fine-tunes them. The numbers then go back to the bureaucratic agencies, which have to formalize their budgets based on the new guidelines. They submit these formal requests back to the OMB. During this stage of the process, agency heads attempt to influence presidential advisers or the president himself to support their agency with a larger budget. By the winter, the OMB has put the final budget document together, and it is then sent to Congress.

According to the Constitution, Congress is ultimately responsible for the budget. Congress uses the budget submitted by the president as a starting point for its budgetary process. The budgeting process involves two steps:

- **Authorization** This is a formal declaration by a legislative committee that a certain amount of funding may be available to an agency. These authorize a program and attach a dollar amount to the program.

- **Appropriation** This is the passage of a spending bill specifying the amount of funds that will be actually allocated for an agency.

MULTIPLE-CHOICE QUESTIONS

1. Which of the following statements best describes the Social Security program?
   (A) It is funded by a payroll tax on employers and employees.
   (B) It is an insurance program that is available to all Americans on a voluntary basis.
   (C) It is a pension fund.
   (D) It is a needs-based program to help those who cannot afford retirement.
   (E) It is a means of redistributing wealth, because the rich pay for it and the poor receive it.

2. All of the following are problems facing the Social Security system EXCEPT
   (A) people are living longer
   (B) more workers are relying on private pension funds for their retirement benefits
   (C) the average number of workers per Social Security recipient is decreasing
   (D) Medicare expenditures per person are rising
   (E) there is a cap on the amount of wages taxed under Social Security

3. The construction of a dam was halted because it threatened the snail darter fish and its habitat. This is a result of the
   (A) Clean Water Act
   (B) National Environmental Policy Act
   (C) Endangered Species Act
   (D) Environmental Protection Agency
   (E) Wetlands Protection Act

4. What is the result of filing an environmental impact statement (EIS)?
   (A) None. It is merely a statement and does not cause any specific action.
   (B) The statement notifies federal authorities of the potential environmental damage caused by private construction projects.
   (C) Citizens and public interest groups have used the EIS as a way of blocking, changing, or delaying projects.
   (D) The EIS requires private and public builders to take steps to minimize environmental damage.
   (E) The EIS must show that a federal project will be built with the least amount of environmental damage possible.

5. All of the following are available under the Social Security and Medicare programs EXCEPT
   (A) monthly payments to retirees
   (B) health care coverage for retirees
   (C) a prescription drug benefit
   (D) payments to the totally and permanently disabled
   (E) payments to needy families with dependent children

6. Which of the following statements best describes the poverty level?
   (A) a minimum fair market value of a family's total assets, adjusted for inflation and depreciation
   (B) the amount of income needed to meet a family's basic needs, plus a savings account for emergencies
   (C) the minimum cash income that will provide for a family's basic needs
   (D) the total amount of income for a family with two adults, both working 40 hours per week at minimum wage
   (E) a family income in the bottom 20 percent of all wage earners

7. How did the Welfare Reform Act of 1993 affect the relationship between the states and the federal government?
   (A) States have been given less flexibility in deciding how to structure welfare benefits.
   (B) Funding was implemented through a formula grant, based on the number of welfare recipients living in each state.
   (C) The law was an unfunded mandate.
   (D) The law was implemented through a block grant, and states bear the burden of increased welfare spending.
   (E) The federal government directly administers welfare and food stamp programs.

8. What is the major difference between Medicare and Medicaid?
   (A) Medicare is needs based, and Medicaid is available to all Americans over age 65.
   (B) Medicaid acts as a supplement to private insurance.
   (C) Medicare is available only to retired Americans.
   (D) Medicaid provides coverage to all children in the United States, while Medicare provides coverage for the elderly.
   (E) Medicare is available to all Americans over age 65, while Medicaid is needs-based.

9. An economist believes that inflation can be reduced by limiting the amount of money in circulation. This can best be described as
   (A) Keynesianism
   (B) supply-side economics
   (C) a loose monetary policy

(D) a tight monetary policy

(E) fiscal conservatism

10. All of the following are responsibilities of the Federal Reserve Board EXCEPT

(A) buying and selling federal government securities

(B) regulating the amount of money a member bank must keep on hand as reserve

(C) reviewing the federal budget and making recommendations to prevent deficits

(D) changing the interest rates charged to banks that borrow from the Fed

(E) setting monetary policy and making predictions about the economy

11. Which of the following best describes the federal budget?

(A) It is a document that announces how much the government expects to collect in taxes and how expenditures will be allocated to various programs.

(B) It is a document that just predicts a bottom line, including the dollar amount of a projected surplus or deficit.

(C) It is a document that describes the federal debt and proposes a payment plan.

(D) It is a document that changes over the course of a year as revenues and expenditures change.

(E) It is a general policy statement outlining the economic goals of the federal government for the upcoming year.

12. Which of the following statements best describes Keynesian economic theory?

(A) controlling the money supply to control the economy

(B) using deficit spending to combat an economic slump

(C) using tax cuts to stimulate economic growth

(D) reducing the number of government regulations on businesses to stimulate economic growth

(E) the belief that free economic competition eliminates the weak and preserves the strong

13. Which of the following terms best describes an increase in the price of goods resulting in a decrease in the value of currency?

(A) economic depression

(B) economic recession

(C) inflation

(D) deflation

(E) deficit spending

14. Which of the following is the best example of a fiscal policy?

(A) reducing the money supply in order to reduce the inflation rate

(B) the Federal Reserve Board selling securities on the open market

(C) raising the reserve requirement, meaning that banks must keep more money on hand

(D) lowering the income tax rate on the middle class in order to stimulate the demand for goods

(E) lowering the interest rate banks pay for money borrowed from the Federal Reserve

Free-Response Questions

1. Social Security and Medicare are badly in need of reform if they are to continue for future generations.
   a. Describe the Social Security program.
   b. Identify one problem faced by Social Security and explain one possible solution to that problem.
   c. Describe Medicare.
   d. Identify one problem faced by Medicare and explain one possible solution to that problem.
2. The American government uses fiscal policy to influence the economy.
   a. Define fiscal policy.
   b. Identify and explain one reason that government spending is difficult to control.
   c. Identify and explain one way the government can reduce budget deficits.

Answers

Multiple-Choice Questions

1. **(A)** Social Security is funded by a payroll tax on employers and employees. It is a pay-as-you-go transfer system where those who are working fund the benefits of those who are retired (*American Government, 2011–2012*, p. 612/ *2013–2014*, pp. 523–525).
2. **(B)** The Social Security program is running out of money because people are living longer, and there are fewer workers to support each retiree. Medicare spending is rising, due to the increased cost of health care. There is a cap on wages taxed by Social Security; this reduces the amount of money that could be available for the program (*American Government, 2011– 2012*, pp. 612–613/ *2013– 2014*, pp. 523–526).
3. **(C)** Environmental groups sued under the Endangered Species Act to stop the Tennessee Valley Authority from completing a dam because it threatened the habitat of the snail darter, a tiny fish (*American Government, 2011–2012*, p. 563/ *2013–2014*, p. 488).
4. **(C)** An Environment Impact Statement is a report showing the costs and benefits of major federal actions that could significantly affect the quality of the environment. This provides notice to citizens and interest groups who may take action against the project (*American Government, 2011– 2012*, p. 560/ *2013–2014*, p. 486).
5. **(E)** Social Security and Medicare are entitlements that provide retirees and the disabled with monthly payments, health care, and a prescription drug benefit. Payments to poor families are given under Temporary Assistance to Needy Families, a means-tested program (*American Government, 2011– 2012*, pp. 555, 572/ *2013– 2014*, pp. 481-482, 498, 523–525).
6. **(C)** The poverty level estimates the minimum cash income that will provide for a family's basic expenses (*American Government, 2011– 2012*, p. 572/ *2013–2014*, p. 497).

7. **(D)** The Welfare Reform Act was funded through a block grant, placing the burden of increased welfare spending on the states (*American Government, 2011–2012*, pp. 572– 573/ *2013–2014*, p. 498).

8. **(E)** All Americans over the age of 65 qualify for Medicare. Medicaid is need-based (*American Government, 2011–2012*, pp. 554–555/ *2013–2014*, pp. 481–483).

9. **(D)** A tight monetary policy slows the rate of inflation (*American Government, 2011–2012*, p. 601/ *2013–2014*, p. 527–528).

10. **(C)** The Federal Reserve Board makes economic forecasts and sets monetary policy. This includes establishing the amount of money a bank must keep on reserve and setting the interest rates charged to banks that borrow from the Fed. In addition, the Federal Reserve Board buys and sells government securities (*American Government, 2011–2012*, pp. 600–603/ *2013–2014*, pp. 526–527).

11. **(A)** The budget is the government's annual financial plan announcing proposed revenue collections and explaining how the money will be spent (*American Government, 2011–2012*, pp. 436–438, 595/ *2013–2014*, pp. 370–372).

12. **(B)** Keynesianism is an economic theory that includes the technique of using deficit spending to combat an economic slump. Under this theory, the deficits will be paid off with budget surpluses after the economy recovers (*American Government, 2011–2012*, pp. 595–596/ *2013–2014*, pp. 513–514).

13. **(C)** Inflation occurs when increasing prices make the dollar worth less (*American Government, 2011–2012*, pp. 592– 594/ *2013–2014*, p. 512).

14. **(D)** Fiscal policies are economic policies that involve government spending and taxing (*American Government, 2011–2012*, pp. 595–596/ *2013–2014*, pp. 514–515).

FREE-RESPONSE QUESTIONS

1. (a) Social Security is a federal program that provides economic assistance to the elderly and disabled.

    (b) Social Security is facing a crisis. Rather than being an insurance fund, as was originally envisioned, it is now an intergenerational contract. The problem is that soon there will not be enough working people to support the people who have retired. This is because new groups, such as the disabled, have been added to the program. In addition, baby boomers are starting to retire, and their numbers exceed those of later generations. Furthermore, the amounts already contributed to the system are not enough to make ends meet with inflation. One proposal to alleviate this problem is to allow people to invest their Social Security funds in the stock market. The market usually performs better than mutual funds or savings accounts in the long run. The market also usually performs better in the long run than government bonds, which are now the required form of securities for Social Security surpluses.

    However, there is the risk that people will lose their retirement funds in unsafe investments or stock market downturns—a possibility that was made vivid by the financial crisis in the fall of 2008. Another proposal is that the upper income limit on Social Security taxes be removed.

(c) Medicare is a federal program that pays for some of the hospitalization costs of those who qualify for Social Security benefits and allows those people to purchase insurance for doctors' fees and prescription drugs.

(d) The major problem facing Medicare is the skyrocketing costs of medical care. One solution has been to offer subsidized insurance for prescription drugs. Other solutions are to encourage or even require Medicare recipients to be served by nonprofit organizations, change the way hospitals are reimbursed for care of Medicare patients in order to discourage overtreatment and fraud, and put nonnegotiable limits on reimbursements for particularly expensive treatments like cardiac bypass surgery (*American Government, 2011–2012*, pp. 554–555, 612–613/ *2013–2014*, pp. 481–482, 523–525).

2. (a) Fiscal policies are economic policies that involve government spending and taxation. These policies are reflected in the federal budget.

(b) One reason government expenditures are hard to control is that the government must provide certain programs by law, including Social Security and Medicare. It is politically difficult to reduce or eliminate these payments because voters have come to expect them.

(c) One way the government could reduce budget deficits would be to raise taxes. This would result in more federal revenue. However, this is an unpopular solution (*American Government, 2011–2012*, pp. 436–438, 595–596/ *2013–2014*, pp. 481–482, 514, 519–521, 523–525).

16

FOREIGN POLICY AND NATIONAL SECURITY

The importance of foreign policy and national security was brought into sharp focus by the terrorist attacks of September 11, 2001. In addition to several pre-existing issues, the attacks created a new focus and a new set of problems for American foreign–policy makers. Creating foreign policy involves many questions: How great are the powers of the president? What role should Congress play? How important is public opinion?

KEY TERMS

attentive public
Cold War
containment
defense policy
détente
diplomacy
economic aid
foreign policy
foreign policy process
intelligence community
isolationist foreign policy/isolationism
military-industrial complex
Monroe Doctrine
moralist foreign policy
national security policy
negative constituents
realist foreign policy
Soviet bloc
Strategic Arms Limitation Treaty (SALT I)
technical assistance
Truman Doctrine

KEY CONCEPTS

- American foreign policy is carried out through a mixture of diplomacy, economic aid, technical assistance, and military intervention.

- Ensuring national security is a primary goal of U.S. foreign policy.

- The Constitution sets the stage for a power struggle between the president and Congress over foreign policy.

- World War II and the Cold War created a need to coordinate foreign policy in new ways.

- Foreign policy decision making involves a complex cast of officials, agencies, and interest groups.

- Global policy issues include human rights, trade, and the environment.

For a full discussion of global policy, see *American Government & Politics Today*, 2011-2012 edition, Chapter 18 and 2013-1024 edition, Chapter 17.

FOREIGN POLICY BASICS

The United States' global importance cannot be denied. The American approach to foreign policy blends moral idealism and political realism. Moral idealism is American foreign policy should be based on our beliefs and values . On the other hand, some argue that the world is full of dangerous actors; political realism demands that every nation do whatever it must to ensure its own survival and prosperity.

The United States executes its foreign policy using a variety of tools:

- **Diplomacy** Diplomacy includes all of the external relationships that a country maintains. Often, diplomacy involves negotiations over issues that exist between two or more nations. The United States frequently acts as a diplomatic mediator in disputes between other nations. For example, in 1978, President Carter used diplomacy to encourage a negotiated peace agreement among Israel and Egypt. Currently, the United States is working with some European and Asian nations to find a diplomatic solution to the problem of Iranian nuclear development.

- **Economic aid** The United States spends billions of dollars every year in economic assistance in the form of grants or loans to foreign governments.

- **Technical assistance** The United States sends experts in areas such as engineering, agriculture, and business to foreign countries to help underdeveloped nations educate their populations, build infrastructures, or reform their economies.

- **Military intervention** As a last resort, the United States uses military intervention to achieve its foreign policy goals. Often, military intervention has been used when there was a perceived threat to vital U.S. interests.

A HISTORY OF RECENT U.S. FOREIGN POLICY

During the 20th century, the U.S. approach to foreign policy changed in response to world affairs:

- **Isolationism** During the 1920s and 1930s, the goal of U.S. foreign policy was to avoid getting involved in wars. This view was adopted after World War I.

- **Cold War** After World War II, the United States and the Soviet Union were locked in a competition for global dominance known as the Cold War. The primary U.S. foreign policy goal was containment, or the effort to stop the spread of communism. The following are important ideas and events from the Cold War:

- **The Truman Doctrine** This was a policy adopted in 1947 by President Truman that was aimed at stopping the expansion of communism in southeastern Europe.

- **Korean War and Vietnam War** The United States joined the Korean War (1950–53) and the Vietnam War (1965–73) as efforts to prevent the spread of communism. In Korea, the United States succeeded in protecting South Korea from communism, but the communists were victorious in Vietnam.

- *Détente* **and the fall of the Soviet Union** In the late 1960s and early 1970s, tensions between the United States and the Soviet Union decreased, and the two countries signed the first major treaty reducing nuclear weapons, SALT I. In the 1980s, President Reagan continued arms reduction talks with the Soviet Union. Finally, in 1991, communism in the Soviet Union came to an end, and with it, the Cold War.

- **Unipolar world** After the fall of the Soviet Union, some experts argued that the United States was the world's sole superpower. With the perceived reduction of threats to U.S. power and security in the world, President Clinton reduced the size of the military and shifted the focus of CIA information gathering from military threats to economic issues. At the same time, the United States aggressively expanded NATO to include former communist countries in Eastern Europe, among them, Poland.

FOREIGN POLICY CHALLENGES TODAY

- **War on terror** In the aftermath of the 9/11 attacks, President Bush recast U.S. foreign policy. This new approach includes policies that advocate unilateral and preemptive actions to protect the United States and its allies from terrorism. The Bush Doctrine, which held that the United States would use "preemptive war" to prevent possible terrorist actions, was used to justify the invasion of Iraq in 2003.

- **Nuclear proliferation** Today, there are several nations that are known to possess nuclear weapons. Several other nations, most notably Iran, are working to develop them. The United States has worked hard to prevent the spread of nuclear weapons technology and to ensure that those nations that already possess such weapons maintain tight control over them to ensure the technology does not fall into the hands of terrorists. The most pressing example of this difficulty is the current Iranian attempt to acquire nuclear weapons.

■ **Israeli-Palestinian peace process** The United States has long sought to mediate an end to the conflict between Israel and the Palestinians. Israel occupies the Palestinian territories in the Gaza Strip and the West Bank.. Tension and even outright warfare have regularly flared between Israel and the Palestinians in the occupied territories, as Israel contends that terrorist attacks against Israel from Gaza and the West Bank justify the Israeli occupation.

■ **Economic challenges** U.S. economic dominance is currently being challenged and changed by the dramatic economic growth of countries such as Brazil and, especially, China.

WHO MAKES FOREIGN POLICY?

The Constitution's ambiguous definition of the foreign policy powers of the president and Congress invites conflict between the two branches. But experts agree that the president usually has the leading voice in crafting American foreign policy. The president's formal foreign policy powers include:

■ **War powers** The Constitution makes the president the commander in chief of U.S. armed forces. Since the establishment of the United States, there have been at least 125 instances in which combat troops have been deployed without a declaration of war, including the Korean War, the Vietnam War, and the current wars in Iraq and Afghanistan.

■ **Treaties and executive agreements** The Constitution also allows the president to negotiate treaties with foreign countries, though treaties must be ratified by a two-thirds vote in the Senate before they can be implemented. The president can also enter into executive agreements with foreign countries; those agreements do not need to be ratified by the Senate.

■ **Other powers** The president has the power to grant diplomatic recognition to foreign governments and to appoint ambassadors and other important diplomats. These appointments are subject to Senate confirmation.

In addition to these formal powers, the president has several informal advantages over Congress in creating foreign policy, including greater access to information and the ability to influence public opinion.

However, Congress is not without influence in the area of foreign policy. Perhaps the most important power that Congress has in that area is its control over the budget. Any funds used for foreign policy programs must be approved by Congress. This gives Congress an important tool in regulating the president's role in creating and implementing foreign policy. Congress also tried to limit the president's use of military force in 1973 by passing the War Powers Resolution, which contained these important provisions:

■ The president must report all commitments of troops in hostile situations to Congress within 48 hours.

■ The president may make only a 60-day commitment of troops, unless there is a declaration of congressional approval.

The War Powers Resolution has had very little influence on American military actions. Every president since its passage has said the act is unconstitutional and sent troops abroad without congressional approval. Furthermore, Congress has been reluctant to cut off appropriations for popular military actions.

One other check that Congress has on the president's foreign policy powers is oversight by intelligence committees. House and Senate intelligence committees must be fully informed of all intelligence activities, including any covert operations.

AP Tip

The struggle between the president and Congress for control of foreign policy, including the War Powers Resolution, is often covered on the AP exam.

THE FOREIGN POLICY–MAKING APPARATUS

Several bureaucratic agencies and other bodies are responsible for making foreign policy in the United States:

■ **Department of State** This Cabinet agency is responsible for formulating and monitoring U.S. foreign policy. The secretary of state is usually the president's most important adviser on foreign policy. However, the secretary's actual power depends on the president. The Department of State has over 32,000 employees.

■ **Department of Defense** This Cabinet agency is responsible for the creation, coordination, and implementation of U.S. military policy. Like the Department of State, the Department of Defense is headed by a secretary and deputy secretaries. In addition to these civilian appointees, the Department of Defense employs soldiers, pilots, sailors, and civilian contractors.

■ **National Security Council (NSC)** Created to coordinate all departments and agencies that play a role in foreign policy, the NSC is chaired by the president and includes the vice president and the secretaries of state and defense. The national intelligence director, the chairman of the Joint Chiefs of Staff, and the attorney general are usually included, as well. The national security adviser heads the staff of the NSC. The goal of the staff is to integrate domestic, foreign, and military policies and facilitate presidential foreign policy decisions.

■ **Intelligence community** The Central Intelligence Agency (CIA), the National Security Agency (NSA), and military intelligence commands gather information on foreign countries for other agencies in the United States to act on. In response to the 9/11 attacks, Congress created an intelligence czar, called the director of national intelligence, to coordinate information brought in from the various parts of the intelligence community.

Multiple-Choice Questions

1. All of the following are struggles over foreign policy between the president and Congress EXCEPT
   (A) the president is commander in chief, but Congress must authorize funding for the armed forces
   (B) the president appoints ambassadors, but the Senate must confirm them
   (C) the president negotiates treaties, but the Senate must ratify them with a two-thirds vote
   (D) the president declares war, but Congress must authorize troop deployments
   (E) the president appoints ambassadors, but the Senate must confirm them

2. What has been the presidential response to the War Powers Act?
   (A) The War Powers Act has had a limited impact on presidents' decisions regarding military actions.
   (B) Because of the War Powers Act, Congress has consistently refused to appropriate funds for troops once they have been deployed.
   (C) The War Powers Act has been successfully used by Congress to prevent troop commitments.
   (D) The War Powers Act has encouraged every president since Nixon to consult with Congress before taking military action.
   (E) The War Powers Act was challenged in court by President Nixon and found to be unconstitutional.

3. Which of the following coordinates domestic, foreign, and military policies?
   (A) Department of State
   (B) Department of Defense
   (C) National Security Council
   (D) Central Intelligence Agency
   (E) Department of Homeland Security

4. What is the major difference between an executive agreement and a treaty?
   (A) Treaties apply to foreign relations, and executive agreements apply to domestic policy making.
   (B) The Senate must approve treaties; executive agreements do not require Senate approval.
   (C) The Supreme Court has ruled that treaties are constitutional, but executive agreements are unconstitutional.
   (D) Treaties are reserved for important issues, and executive agreements are used for routine matters.
   (E) Treaties have the force of law; executive agreements do not.

5. Which of the following is in charge of formulating and executing foreign policy?
   (A) Department of Defense
   (B) National Security Agency

(C) Defense Intelligence Agency
(D) Central Intelligence Agency
(E) Department of State

6. All of the following have been used to expand the president's authority over foreign affairs EXCEPT
    (A) the War Powers Resolution
    (B) executive agreements
    (C) the president's authority to transfer funds from one program to another
    (D) the president's control over surplus or infrequently used equipment
    (E) the power as commander in chief to commit troops in emergency situations

7. All of the following were a part of U.S. foreign policy during the Cold War EXCEPT
    (A) the containment doctrine
    (B) the Vietnam War
    (C) *détente*
    (D) a focus on global economic competition
    (E) the Korean War

8. Which of the following is often considered to be President Nixon's most influential contribution to foreign policy?
    (A) keeping the Soviet Empire constricted within its boundaries
    (B) setting the stage for diplomatic recognition of China
    (C) limiting the growth of nuclear weapons
    (D) escalating the Vietnam War
    (E) developing aggressive new weapons systems

9. The Strategic Defense Initiative best illustrates which foreign policy theory?
    (A) *détente*
    (B) containment
    (C) isolationism
    (D) nation building
    (E) deterrence

10. Which of the following statements best describes the Strategic Arms Limitation Treaty (SALT I) negotiated by President Carter in 1972?
    (A) It required countries to reduce their stockpiles of nuclear weapons.
    (B) It set a goal of the year 2020 for eliminating nuclear weapons worldwide.
    (C) It limited the growth of nuclear weapons.
    (D) It limited the growth of both conventional and nuclear weapons.
    (E) The Republican Senate failed to ratify the treaty.

11. Which of the following policies reduces restrictions on trade?
    (A) eliminating tariff barriers
    (B) imposing import quotas
    (C) outlawing pirated intellectual property, such as CDs and DVDs
    (D) preventing the dumping of goods below cost
    (E) outlawing unfair business practices

12. The United States does business with 10 big emerging markets even though some of those countries have dubious human rights records. Which best describes the conflict posed by these contacts?
    (A) the conflict between democratic and authoritarian states
    (B) the conflict between moralism and realism
    (C) the conflict between developed and developing countries
    (D) the conflict between consolidated and emerging nations the conflict between commercial and government interests

13. Which of the following best describes the military-industrial complex?
    (A) the complicated relationship between the president and Pentagon officials
    (B) the difficult set of issues the government must face in defending against foreign threats
    (C) the cozy relationship between members of Congress and the president in appropriating funds for foreign conflicts
    (D) a group of buildings that house the Pentagon and Department of State
    (E) the mutually beneficial relationship between defense contractors and the armed forces

14. All of the following are tools of U.S. foreign policy EXCEPT
    (A) military intervention
    (B) technical assistance
    (C) monetary policy
    (D) diplomacy
    (E) economic aid

FREE–RESPONSE QUESTIONS

1. The president's powers in making military and foreign policy are extensive and have expanded over time.
   (a) Identify and explain two reasons that the president is powerful in military and foreign affairs.
   (b) Identify and explain one constraint on the president's policy making in military and foreign affairs.

2. Global policy making includes diverse issues such as trade, human rights, and the environment.
   (a) Pick TWO policy areas from the list below and explain one specific policy that has been proposed to address each policy-making area.
     i. Investment and trade
     ii. human rights
     iii. environmental policy
     iv. Identify one international organization of which the United States is a member, and explain the impact of that organization on the U.S. ability to make policy.

Answers

1. **(D)** Congress has the power to declare war, although the War Powers Act allows the president to commit troops for 60 days (*American Government, 2011–2012,* pp. 409, 453, 642–643/ *2013–2014,* pp. 345, 386, 547–548).

2. **(A)** Many presidents believe that the War Powers Act is an unconstitutional infringement on their powers as commander in chief. As a result, it has had a limited impact (*American Government, 2011–2012,* pp. 453, 648– 649/ *2013–2014,* pp. 386, 547–548).

3. **(C)** The National Security Council advises the president on the integration of domestic, foreign, and military policies (*American Government, 2011–2012,* p. 646/ *2013–2014,* p. 544).

4. **(B)** The Senate must ratify treaties. Presidents enter into executive agreements without the approval of the Senate (*American Government, 2011–2012,* p. 455/ *2013–2014,* pp. 542–543).

5. **(E)** The State Department formulates American foreign policy throughout the world. One of its most important missions is diplomacy (*American Government, 2011– 2012,* pp. 644–646/ *2013–2014,* p. 544).

6. **(A)** The War Powers Resolution was meant to limit the president's power to commit troops to 60 days unless Congress authorizes additional troop commitments (*American Government, 2011–2012,* pp. 453, 642–643/ *2013–2014,* pp. 386, 547–548).

7. **(D)** Cold War policies included containment, conflicts in Vietnam and Korea, and periods of *détente*. Since the Cold War, U.S. foreign policy has shifted toward global economic competition and combating terrorism (*American Government, 2011–2012,* pp. 627–629/ *2013–2014,* pp. 551–553).

8. **(B)** President Nixon was the first U.S. president to visit China. This set the stage for formal diplomatic recognition of that country (*American Government, 2011–2012,* p. 629/ *2013–2014,* p. 553).

9. **(E)** President Reagan urged the development of aggressive new weapons systems, like the proposed Strategic Defense Initiative, commonly called Star Wars, as part of his policy of combating communism by building up the military to deter nuclear war (*American Government, 2011–2012,* p. 629/ *2013–2014,* p. 553).

10. **(C)** SALT I was a result of a brief period of *détente*. The pact limited the growth of strategic nuclear weapons (*American Government, 2011–2012,* p. 629/ *2013–2014,* p. 553).

11. **(A)** Reducing tariffs is a free trade policy that seeks to eliminate commercial restrictions among nations (*American Government, 2011–2012,* general discussion pp. 604–606/ *2013–2014,* p. 530).

12. **(B)** The United States balances its desire for commercial ties with its objective of supporting human rights. This is an example of the blending of political realism and moral idealism (*American Government, 2011–2012,* pp. 624–625/ *2013–2014,* p. 549).

13. **(E)** The military-industrial complex is the mutually beneficial relationship between the armed forces and defense contractors (*American Government, 2011–2012,* pp. 649– 650/ *2013–2014,* pp. 548–549).

14. **(C)** Foreign policy tools include military intervention, diplomacy, economic aid, and technical assistance *(American Government, 2011–2012,* pp. 621–622/ *2013–2014,* p. 539).

FREE-RESPONSE QUESTIONS

1. (a) Although Congress has the power to declare war, the president is the commander in chief. Presidents have asserted the ability to commit troops on numerous occasions. This gives the president great power in foreign affairs. For example, both Presidents Kennedy and Johnson sent troops to Vietnam even though there was no official declaration of war. This eventually put half a million troops overseas. The fact that a president can initiate and maintain such a large military action in the absence of a formal declaration of war demonstrates the power of the presidency.

    Another reason the president has so much power in foreign affairs is the number of defense and national security agencies under his authority. The Central Intelligence Agency engages in covert activities designed to provide the government with information about threats from abroad. The National Security Council is made up of a group of advisers who help the president develop a coherent approach to foreign policy. In an attempt to coordinate military and foreign policy, it includes the secretaries of state and defense. Because of the wide range of executive agencies that are involved in making foreign and defense policy, the president has considerable power.

    (b) One constraint on a president's ability to make foreign policy is that the Senate must ratify treaties. Although the president negotiates treaties, they are no more than a promise until the Senate ratifies them. This means that the Senate has the ultimate authority over formal agreements made with foreign nations, and the president's power is constrained. Other constraints include congressional oversight in intelligence committees, the appropriations power of Congress, and public opinion *(American Government, 2011–2012,* pp. 405, 642–643, 646–647/ *2013–2014,* pp. 541–548, 552–553).

2. (a) The North American Free Trade Agreement resulted in the elimination of trade barriers among the United States, Mexico, and Canada. Although many labor unions were opposed to the treaty, President Clinton supported the agreement (originally negotiated by President George H. W. Bush) because he supported free trade policies.

    The United States opposes human rights abuses. In 1989, the Chinese government crushed demonstrations in Tiananmen Square, killing students and imprisoning protestors. After criticizing the George H. W. Bush administration for not being hard enough on China, President Clinton supported most favored nation status for China. An important reason for this change was the growing trade ties between China and the United States.

    One proposed environmental policy was an accord on global warming worked out by most nations in Kyoto, Japan. This set target goals for reductions in carbon emissions. The administration of President George W. Bush deemphasized global warming and did not support the Kyoto Agreement.

(b) The United States is a member of NATO. This means that the United States has agreed to defend its allies in case of attack and would be expected to follow this policy. The United States is also a member of the United Nations. This means it has agreed to abide by the ruling of the World Court in certain cases. The United States is also a member of the World Trade Organization, World Bank, and International Monetary Fund, which set the terms of trade between countries. Membership in these organizations limits the policies the United States may pursue because it has agreed to abide by the rules of the organizations (*American Government, 2011–2012,* pp. 564–565, 605–607, 624– 625, 638–639/ *2013–2014,* pp. 231, 490, 497, 530, 552, 555, 559, 565–566).

Part III

Practice Tests

Practice Test 1

UNITED STATES GOVERNMENT AND POLITICS EXAMINATION
Section I: Multiple-Choice Questions
Time: 45 minutes

Directions The questions or incomplete statements below are each followed by five suggested answers. Select the best answer.

1. What kind of federal grants are awarded based on competitive applications for specific undertakings?
   (A) formula grants
   (B) block grants
   (C) revenue sharing
   (D) program grants
   (E) broad-based aid

2. Why was the Voting Rights Act successful in meeting its goal of increasing African-American voter registration in the South?
   I. because the goal was clear—to increase African-American voter registration
   II. because federal officials oversaw the law
   III. because local officials agreed with the law
   IV. because black voters were protected when going to the polls
   (A) I and II
   (B) I, II, and IV
   (C) II, III, and IV
   (D) I, III, and IV
   (E) II and IV

3. When does a president have the best chance of getting his program enacted?
   (A) during a period at the beginning of his term, when he can claim a mandate
   (B) halfway through his first term, after he has established himself
   (C) during his second term, after he has had time to develop relationships with members of Congress
   (D) after he holds a press conference and asks the public to support a program during wartime
   (E) when his approval ratings have increased because of a prolonged war or economic recession

4. What was the result of the Court's ruling in *Miranda v. Arizona*?
   (A) It established the exclusionary rule.
   (B) It established the good-faith exception to the exclusionary rule.
   (C) If a suspect has not been informed of his rights, his confession cannot be used as evidence.
   (D) If a suspect has not been informed of his rights, the charges against him must be dropped.
   (E) The state must provide an attorney if a defendant cannot afford one.

5. The president has all of the following expressed powers under the Constitution EXCEPT
   (A) to grant reprieves and pardons for federal offenses
   (B) to convene Congress in special sessions
   (C) to declare war
   (D) to appoint ambassadors, subject to Senate confirmation
   (E) to veto bills passed by Congress

6. All of the following are cited as reasons for low voter turnout EXCEPT
   (A) registration procedures make voting more difficult
   (B) American elections are dominated by the two major parties
   (C) felons are not allowed to vote, and this significantly decreases turnout
   (D) elections are held frequently
   (E) negative campaigning discourages voters

7. What encourages a two-party system in the United States?
   (A) the inclusion of ballot initiatives and referendums
   (B) the selection of candidates through primaries
   (C) the selection of candidates through caucuses
   (D) ticket-splitting by voters between the Republican and Democratic parties
   (E) the fact that elections are for single-member districts, with plurality representation

8. Which of the following serves as a check by Congress over the executive?
   (A) Congress can change the number and jurisdiction of the lower courts.
   (B) The Senate can refuse to confirm a person nominated to be a judge.
   (C) All revenue bills must originate in the House of Representatives.
   (D) Congress can override a presidential veto by a majority vote of both houses.
   (E) Congress can remove Cabinet secretaries.

9. What role does political party affiliation play in the selection of federal judges?
   (A) Presidents usually appoint members of their political party, and these people are generally qualified.
   (B) None. Federal judges are appointed based upon their qualifications rather than their party affiliation.
   (C) Some. Federal judges are appointed based upon their qualifications, but equally qualified candidates are judged based upon party affiliation.
   (D) Party affiliation is much more important than qualifications. Many unqualified judges are appointed because they are faithful to the party.
   (E) Under the merit rules for civil service, presidents are barred from considering party affiliation in appointing federal judges.

10. Why has the custom of senatorial courtesy been criticized?
    (A) because senators block the nomination of judges on the basis of party politics
    (B) because presidents find it difficult to find judicial candidates who would be accepted by their state senators
    (C) because senators from the opposing party use it to block the president's nominations for partisan purposes
    (D) because it results in unqualified candidates being confirmed
    (E) because it forces presidents to share the nomination power with the members of the Senate

11. Beginning in 2006, it was difficult for President George W. Bush to get his domestic program passed. What is the best explanation for this?
    (A) His approval ratings suffered a steady decline.
    (B) The government was unified.
    (C) The poor economy made it difficult for Congress to fund new programs.
    (D) He refused to work with Congress on bipartisan legislation.
    (E) He concentrated on foreign affairs and did not put forth a domestic agenda.

12. Why is the threat of a veto a powerful presidential tool?
    (A) because Congress does not want the negative media attention associated with a presidential veto
    (B) because a presidential veto kills a bill until the next session of Congress
    (C) because it is difficult for Congress to obtain the two-thirds vote necessary to override a presidential veto
    (D) because the president can use the line-item veto to cut out pet projects favored by certain members of Congress
    (E) because the public usually supports the president more than it supports Congress

13. What is the basis of James Madison's argument in Federalist No. 10?
    (A) Factions are dangerous and must be destroyed.
    (B) The government can eliminate the causes of faction.
    (C) Political parties should be encouraged to form so that all viewpoints are represented.
    (D) A balanced government can control factions and prevent one faction from gaining too much power.
    (E) State government will prevent factions from forming.

14. Colorado is not required to recognize a gay marriage from Massachusetts. This is a result of the
    (A) Defense of Marriage Act
    (B) Full Faith and Credit Clause
    (C) Privileges and Immunities Clause
    (D) Tenth Amendment
    (E) Civil Unions Act

15. What was the biggest change to campaign financing made by the Campaign Finance Reform Act of 2002 (McCain-Feingold)?
(A) the elimination of PAC contributions to candidates
(B) the elimination of "soft money"
(C) new requirements for full disclosure of campaign contributions
(D) the creation of a new, nonpartisan, board of directors of the Federal Election Commission
(E) the banning of all advertising by any political party in the sixty days before an election

16. Which of the following statements best describes the public debt?
(A) It represents the annual shortfall when expenditures exceed revenues.
(B) It is the amount of interest the United States government owes on the money it borrows.
(C) It does not occur in years when there is a budget surplus.
(D) It is a figure used for accounting purposes and does not represent real money owed.
(E) It is the total amount owed by the federal government to individuals, businesses, and foreigners.

17. Under which of the following principles has the due process clause of the Fourteenth Amendment been applied to protect individuals from violations of fundamental rights by the states?
(A) equal protection
(B) constitutional federalism
(C) the incorporation doctrine
(D) the inclusionary doctrine
(E) the wall of separation

18. What is the primary source of political socialization?
(A) family
(B) opinion leaders
(C) television
(D) the Internet
(E) public schools

19. What was the Supreme Court's ruling in *Webster v. Reproductive Health Services*?
(A) States may prohibit abortions during the third trimester of pregnancy.
(B) States may require parental notification prior to an abortion.
(C) States may require counseling prior to an abortion.
(D) States may ban tax-supporting facilities from performing abortions.
(E) States may impose a waiting period prior to an abortion.

20. What was the biggest problem with the Articles of Confederation?
(A) The national government imposed heavy taxes on the wealthy.
(B) The states did not have enough power.
(C) Individual states could not control their economies.
(D) The national government did not have the power to regulate intrastate commerce.
(E) The national government could not lay and collect taxes.

21. A judge believes that cases should be decided by closely adhering to statutes and precedents. Which of the following terms best describes this judicial philosophy?
(A) judicial activism
(B) judicial restraint
(C) limited jurisdiction
(D) dual federalism
(E) states' rights

22. Which of the following is a difference between the House of Representatives and the Senate?
    (A) The Senate has stricter rules for floor debate.
    (B) There is no leader in the Senate, except for the vice president in case of a tie vote.
    (C) Revenue bills must originate in the Senate.
    (D) There are fewer rules governing debate in the Senate than in the House.
    (E) The Senate has standing committees, but the House uses only select committees.

23. All of the following statements about filibusters are true EXCEPT
    (A) either political party may use the filibuster
    (B) senators who filibuster may speak about any topic
    (C) filibusters have been used to block judicial appointments
    (D) cloture votes are rare, because they require seventy-five votes
    (E) the Senate gives its members the right of unlimited debate

24. What are political action committees (PACs)?
    (A) registered organizations that pool contributions and donate money to campaigns
    (B) committees that work as part of an iron triangle to change bureaucratic regulations
    (C) interest groups that have raised more than $200,000 in a single fiscal year
    (D) groups of people who are interested in a cause and lobby on its behalf
    (E) organizations whose primary purpose is to lobby Congress

25. How does an executive order differ from legislation?
    (A) Executive orders are submitted by the president to Congress for approval; bills are submitted by the Congress to the president for approval.
    (B) Executive orders have the force of law but do not have to be approved by Congress.
    (C) Executive orders expire after five years.
    (D) Executive orders require ratification by the Senate but not the House.
    (E) The Supreme Court cannot rule on the constitutionality of an executive order.

26. Which of the following caused the sharpest decline in the level of political trust among Americans?
    (A) the terrorist attacks of September 11, 2001
    (B) the war in Iraq
    (C) the Vietnam War and Watergate scandal
    (D) the campaign finance scandals of the late 1980s and early 1990s
    (E) President Clinton's relationship with Monica Lewinsky

27. What is judicial review?
    (A) the review of judicial appointments by members of the Senate, who have the power to confirm nominees
    (B) the ability of the Supreme Court to overturn rulings by federal district court judges
    (C) the power of the Supreme Court to overturn rulings by federal appeals court judges
    (D) the power of the chief justice of the Supreme Court to preside over impeachment hearings
    (E) the power of the Supreme Court to declare acts of Congress null and void if they violate the Constitution

28. Which of the following programs are entitlements?
    (I)   Medicaid
    (II) Medicare
    (III) food stamps
    (IV) Social Security
    (A) I and II
    (B) I, II, and III
    (C) II and IV
    (D) I and IV
    (E) II, III, and IV

29. Elections serve all of the following important functions EXCEPT
    (A) they allow citizens to choose among candidates
    (B) they socialize political activity
    (C) they provide a way to remove the president from office prior to the end of his term
    (D) they institutionalize access to political power
    (E) they increase the state's legitimacy

30. Which of the following is a check on the president's powers over foreign affairs?
    (A) Congress must approve of troop commitments before the military can be deployed.
    (B) The Senate may refuse to ratify a treaty.
    (C) Congress may impeach the president for an unjust war.
    (D) Congress may cut funding for a Cabinet-level department.
    (E) Two-thirds of both houses of Congress may overturn a presidential veto.

31. All of the following are necessary for an accurate public opinion poll EXCEPT
    (A) the question must be asked in an unbiased manner
    (B) the persons interviewed must be selected based on a random sample
    (C) the questions must be understandable
    (D) the answer categories must offer people a choice between different responses
    (E) the number of people sampled must be at least 10 percent of the population

32. Which constitutional provision gives states most of their powers?
    (A) the Ninth Amendment
    (B) the Tenth Amendment
    (C) the commerce clause
    (D) the necessary and proper clause
    (E) the full faith and credit clause

33. What is the main reason for the shift from dual to cooperative federalism?
    (A) court decisions that required the states and federal government to coordinate policies
    (B) inconsistent welfare policies at the state level, which required national coordination
    (C) the increase in federal grants-in aid to the states
    (D) the global economy and the importance of improving the trained workforce
    (E) revenue sharing, which occurred during budgetary surpluses

34. What is the role of the federal courts of appeals?
    (A) to send cases to the Supreme Court when there is a constitutional issue involved
    (B) to hear appeals from the federal district courts
    (C) to hear new testimony in cases being retried
    (D) to hear appeals from state supreme courts when there is a constitutional issue involved
    (E) to review acts of Congress before they are sent to the Supreme Court for final judicial review

35. Several interest groups filed briefs in the affirmative action cases brought by college applicants against the University of Michigan. What is the best description of these briefs?
    (A) amicus curiae
    (B) stare decisis
    (C) per curiam
    (D) reply briefs
    (E) appellate briefs

36. Which of the following is the best example of the shift in power toward states' rights?
    (A) the use of the commerce clause to regulate public places and accommodations
    (B) the Court's decision in United States v. Lopez
    (C) grants-in-aid provided by the national government to the states
    (D) the Court's decision in McCulloch v. Maryland
    (E) state budget cuts as a result of rising inflation

37. A state, which is not Maine or Nebraska, has eight members in the House of Representatives. In a presidential election, that state's population votes 40 percent for the Democratic candidate and 60 percent for the Republican candidate. How are that state's electoral votes allocated?
    (A) Eight electoral votes are pledged to the Republican candidate.
    (B) Ten electoral votes are pledged to the Republican candidate.
    (C) Four votes are pledged to the Democrat, and six votes are pledged to the Republican.
    (D) Six votes are pledged to the Democrat, and four votes are pledged to the Republican.
    (E) It is impossible to determine the allocation of electoral college votes from the facts given.

38. When the House and Senate pass different versions of a bill, where is the language of the bill resolved?
    (A) joint committee
    (B) standing committee
    (C) conference committee
    (D) select committee
    (E) in a meeting with the leadership of both houses

39. Which constitutional provision has expanded the power of the federal government in regulating privately owned businesses?
    (A) commerce clause
    (B) Tenth Amendment
    (C) full faith and credit clause
    (D) power to lay and collect taxes
    (E) power to borrow money

40. What is the term for an event that produces a sharp change in the existing pattern of party loyalties among groups of voters?
    (A) readjustment
    (B) deviating election
    (C) electoral shift
    (D) realignment
    (E) party reorganization

41. Under which doctrine are judges obligated to follow precedents set by their own courts or by courts of higher authority?
    (A) common law
    (B) judicial restraint
    (C) original intent
    (D) stare decisis
    (E) judicial review

42. When the Supreme Court ruled that laws against flag burning are unconstitutional, many citizens disagreed with the Court's ruling and wanted Congress to take action. What could Congress do to make flag burning illegal?
    (A) pass a federal law that bans flag burning
    (B) pass a constitutional amendment banning flag burning
    (C) with a two-thirds vote, approve a constitutional amendment, to be ratified by three-fourths of the states
    (D) pressure the president for an executive order banning flag burning
    (E) there is nothing Congress can do once the Supreme Court rules a law unconstitutional; the Supreme Court is a court of last resort

43. Congressional committees and their members do all of the following tasks EXCEPT
    (A) revise bills
    (B) hold hearings
    (C) refer bills to subcommittees
    (D) give advice on bills to other members of Congress
    (E) enact legislation

44. All of the following involve civil rights EXCEPT
    (A) school desegregation
    (B) affirmative action
    (C) sex discrimination
    (D) flag burning
    (E) the treatment of disabled Americans

45. Which of the following requires equal treatment of men and women in university athletic programs?
    (A) the Equal Rights Amendment
    (B) the Fourteenth Amendment
    (C) Title IX of the Educational Amendments
    (D) the Civil Rights Act of 1964
    (E) the Equal Opportunity in Education Act

46. What is the typical method for becoming a member of the White House staff?
    (A) be a longtime associate of the president
    (B) be a longtime member of Congress with substantial experience in policymaking
    (C) serve on the staff of the president's predecessor if the former president was a member of the president's political party
    (D) have experience in business and industry and apply for the job based upon qualifications
    (E) have experience in academia, preferably as a professor at an Ivy League college

47. What is the difference between a primary and a caucus?
    (A) Party membership is required to vote in a primary, but anyone may attend a caucus.
    (B) Caucuses are more influential in selecting candidates than primaries.
    (C) Voters are more likely to attend a caucus than a primary.
    (D) A caucus is a meeting of party members, and a primary is a vote.
    (E) There is no significant difference between a primary and a caucus.

48. The census is important for which of the following purposes?
    (I) to determine the number of representatives a state will have in the House of Representatives
    (II) to determine the number of senators each state will have
    (III) for the purpose of receiving categorical grant money
    (IV) to determine the number of electoral college votes a state will have
    (A) I and III
    (B) I, II, and III
    (C) II, III, and IV
    (D) I and IV
    (E) I, III, and IV

49. All of the following are advantages of incumbency for members of Congress EXCEPT
    (A) the recognition they receive by sitting on oversight committees
    (B) the use of franking privileges to let members of their districts know what they have been doing
    (C) the ability to provide casework
    (D) the ability to bring pork-barrel projects to their states
    (E) name recognition

50. All of the following arguments have been made about the electoral college EXCEPT
   (A) it benefits small states because they receive a disproportionate share of votes
   (B) it benefits large states because they receive a disproportionate share of attention from the candidates
   (C) it benefits third parties because they can control entire regions of the country
   (D) it is undemocratic because the winner of the popular vote may not win in the electoral college
   (E) states with large urban populations get more attention from the candidates

51. What is the term for drawing electoral district boundaries in odd shapes in order to benefit a particular political party?
   (A) political redistricting
   (B) gerrymandering
   (C) patronage
   (D) divided government
   (E) political reapportionment

52. A state law that requires posting of the Ten Commandments in all public school classrooms would most likely be challenged as a violation of the
   (A) establishment clause
   (B) free exercise clause
   (C) First Amendment protection of symbolic speech
   (D) Tenth Amendment
   (E) First Amendment protection of the right to petition

53. States separate death penalty cases into a trial phase and a sentencing phase. This is a result of
   (A) Furman v. Georgia
   (B) Gideon v. Wainright
   (C) Gregg v. Georgia
   (D) United States v. McVeigh
   (E) Ring v. Arizona

54. John F. Kennedy believed that government should use spending and tax policies to fine-tune the economy. Which economic theory does this represent?
   (A) supply-side economics
   (B) Keynesianism
   (C) laissez-faire
   (D) deficit financing
   (E) monetarism

55. In the following scenario, the Senate has fifty Republicans and fifty Democrats and the president is Republican. What would be the result if one Republican senator changed his affiliation to become an independent?
   (A) No major changes would occur in the conduct of the Senate.
   (B) The Senate would have a Democratic majority, and it would become impossible for the president to enact his program.
   (C) The Republican whip would be used to make sure the independent senator voted with the Republicans.
   (D) The Republican committee heads would be replaced with Democrats.
   (E) The vice president would no longer be the president of the Senate.

STOP
END OF SECTION I

IF YOU FINISH BEFORE TIME IS CALLED, YOU MAY CHECK YOUR WORK ON THIS SECTION. DO NOT GO ON TO SECTION II UNTIL YOU ARE TOLD TO DO SO.

UNITED STATES GOVERNMENT AND POLITICS EXAMINATION
Section II: 4 Free-Response Questions
Time: 100 minutes

Directions You have 100 minutes to answer all four of the following questions. Unless the directions indicate otherwise, respond to all parts of each question. It is recommended that you take a few minutes to plan and outline each answer. Spend approximately 25 minutes on each question. In your response, use specific examples where appropriate. Be sure to number each of your answers.

1. Civil rights have expanded over time, and new groups continue to ask the federal government for protection from discrimination.
   a. Identify and explain one decision made by the Supreme Court that expanded civil rights.
   b. Identify and explain one law passed by Congress that expanded civil rights.
   c. Identify a group that has encountered roadblocks in obtaining civil rights protection, and explain two reasons for these roadblocks.

2. The federal government cannot control the economy, but it can take measures to improve the health of the American economy.
   a. Identify and explain one way that the government uses monetary policy to influence the economy.
   b. Identify and explain one way that the government uses the budget to influence the economy.
   c. Identify and explain one way Congress can influence the economy.
   d. Identify and explain one way the president can influence the economy.

3. The power of incumbency in the outcome of an election is pivotal and, after surviving their second reelection, can garner tremendous loyalty amongst the constituents.
   a. Define the term "incumbency advantage," and explain why the incumbency advantage is greater for members of the House of Representatives.
   b. Identify and explain two reasons why members of Congress have an incumbency advantage.
   c. Explain one way in which the redistricting process might benefit incumbents.

4. The power of the president is the power to persuade rather than the power to command.
   a. Identify and explain one formal power and one informal power used by the president to influence domestic policy.
   b. Identify and explain one formal power and one informal power used by the president to influence foreign policy.

END OF EXAMINATION

ANSWERS TO THE MULTIPLE-CHOICE QUESTIONS

Using the table below, score your test.

Determine how many questions you answered correctly and how many you answered incorrectly. You will find explanations of the answers on the following pages.

1. D	11. A	21. B	31. E	41. D	51. B
2. B	12. C	22. D	32. B	42. C	52. A
3. A	13. D	23. D	33. C	43. E	53. C
4. C	14. A	24. A	34. B	44. D	54. B
5. C	15. B	25. B	35. A	45. C	55. D
6. C	16. E	26. C	36. B	46. A	
7. E	17. C	27. E	37. B	47. D	
8. B	18. A	28. C	38. C	48. E	
9. A	19. D	29. C	39. A	49. A	
10. E	20. E	30. B	40. D	50. C	

1. (D) Program grants are based on competitive application and are used for specific programs, like substance abuse and AIDS prevention (American Government, 2011–2012, p. 108/ 2013–2014, 170–171).

2. (B) The Voting Rights Act of 1965 had a clear goal of increasing registration and voting by blacks. Federal officials oversaw its implementation, and blacks were protected when going to the polls (American Government, 2011– 2012, p. 178/ 2013–2014, p. 147).

3. (A) A president's popularity tends to be highest right after he is elected, when he can claim a mandate from the voters in support of his program (American Government, 2011–2012, p. 463/ 2013–2014, pp. 395–396).

4. (C) In *Miranda v. Arizona*, the court held that suspects must be read their rights. Otherwise, their confessions are not admissible in court (American Government, 2011–2012, pp. 154–155/ 2013–2014, p. 124).

5. (C) Although the president is the commander in chief, Congress has the power to declare war (American Government, 2011–2012, p. 409/ 2013–2014, pp. 385–386).

6. (C) Registration procedures, the frequency of elections, negative campaigning, and the two-party system all negatively impact voter turnout (American Government, 2011–2012, pp. 319–321/ 2013–2014, pp. 285–286).

7. (E) Single-member districts with majority representation favor two parties and make it difficult for third parties to compete (American Government, 2011–2012, p. 299/ 2013–2014, pp. 264–267).

8. (B) The Senate can refuse to confirm a judge nominated by the president. This is a check on both the executive and judicial branches (American Government, 2011–2012, pp. 533–534/ 2013–2014, pp. 462–463).

9. (A) Presidents usually appoint judges from the ranks of their political party. These candidates are also chosen based upon their qualifications (American Government, 2011–2012, pp. 531–532/ 2013–2014, pp. 461–462).

10. (E) Senatorial courtesy allows a senior senator from the president's party to block the nomination of a federal district judge from his or her home state (American Government, 2011–2012, p. 531/ 2013–2014, p. 460).

11. (A) Beginning in 2006, President George W. Bush faced divided government, in which the party opposing the president holds one or both houses of Congress. Although this does not cause gridlock, it does make it more difficult for a president to get programs passed (American Government, 2011–2012, p. 456/ 2013–2014, p. 396).

12. (C) It is difficult for Congress to obtain the two-thirds vote necessary to override a presidential veto (American Government, 2011–2012, p. 460/ 2013–2014, p. 393).

13. (D) Madison believed that a balanced government (including separation of powers, checks and balances, and federalism) could "break and control the violence of faction" (American Government, 2011–2012, pp. 52–53/ 2013–2014, pp. 45-46, 48).

14. (A) In 1996, Congress passed the Defense of Marriage Act, which bans federal recognition of gay marriages and allows state governments to ignore same-sex marriages performed in other states (American Government, 2011–2012, pp. 203–204/ 2013–2014, pp. 63, 173, 214).

15. (B) The McCain-Feingold law bans soft-money contributions— these were unlimited contributions to political parties, which were considered the largest loophole in previous campaign finance reform laws (American Government, 2011–2012, pp. 353–354/ 2013–2014, p. 323).

16. (E) The debt is the amount owed by the federal government. It is the accumulation of all past federal government deficits. (American Government, 2011–2012, p. 597-598/ 2013–2014, p. 515-16).

17. (C) In 1925, the Supreme Court held that the due-process clause of the Fourteenth Amendment protects individuals from state action that violates fundamental rights. Other rights have been added over time. This is known as the incorporation doctrine (American Government, 2011–2012, p. 124/ 2013–2014, pp. 97–98).

18. (A) Families have the most influence in political socialization (American Government, 2011–2012, p. 215/ 2013–2014, p. 184).

19. (D) In *Webster v. Reproductive Health Services,* the Supreme Court ruled that states may prohibit tax-supported facilities from performing abortions (American Government, 2011–2012, p. 148/ 2013–2014, p. 118).

20. (E) Under the Articles of Confederation, the national government did not have the power to tax. This was a big problem because it could not pay its debts and did not have enough money to carry on the functions of government (American Government, 2011–2012, pp. 41–43/ 2013–2014, pp. 37–38).

21. (B) Judicial restraint is a philosophy whereby judges adhere closely to statutes and precedents in reaching their decisions (American Government, 2011–2012, p. 535/ 2013–2014, p. 464).

22. (D) The House is more formal and has more rules in the conduct of its business (American Government, 2011–2012, p. 411/ 2013–2014, p. 348).

23. (D) Sixty votes are required to end a filibuster by cloture (American Government, 2011–2012, pp. 411–412/ 2013–2014, p. 349).

24. (A) PACs are committees set up to raise and spend money on campaigns (American Government, 2011–2012, pp. 349–351/ 2013–2014, pp. 320–321).

25. (B) Executive orders are presidential directives that have the force of law but do not need to be approved by Congress (American Government, 2011–2012, p. 465/ 2013–2014, p. 398).

26. (C) The Vietnam War and Watergate scandal caused a steep decline in Americans' level of political trust (American Government, 2011–2012, pp. 232–233/ 2013–2014, pp. 202–203).

27. (E) Judicial review was established in Marbury v. Madison. It is the power of the Supreme Court to declare state or federal laws unconstitutional (American Government, 2011–2012, p. 517/ 2013–2014, pp. 446, 449).

28. (C) Medicare and Social Security are entitlement programs. Entitlements are guaranteed benefits to which every eligible person has a legal right. They are not based on financial need (American Government, 2011–2012, pp. 555 and 572/ 2013–2014, pp. 522–525).

29. (C) Elections allow voters to choose among candidates. They also socialize political activity, provide a means of accessing power, and bolster the state's power and authority (legitimacy). There is no recall election to remove the president from office prior to the end of his term. This may be done through impeachment (American Government, 2011–2012, pp. 314–315/ 2013–2014, pp. 281, 293).

30. (B) The Senate may refuse to ratify a treaty approved by the president (American Government, 2011–2012, pp. 409–410/ 2013–2014, p. 387).

31. (E) For a national poll, 95 percent of the time most polling organizations sample 1,500 people to achieve a sampling error of plus or minus 3 percent (American Government, 2011–2012, p. 228/ 2013–2014, pp. 195–199).

32. (B) The Tenth Amendment reserves powers neither delegated to the national government nor prohibited to the states, to the states and the people. It is the main basis for state power (American Government, 2011–2012, p. 94/ 2013–2014, p. 71).

33. (C) Federal grants-in-aid often come with strings attached. This was a major reason for the move from dual to cooperative federalism (American Government, 2011–2012, pp. 107–108/ 2013–2014, pp. 81–84).

34. (B) The federal courts of appeals hear appeals from the federal district courts. If a litigant is unhappy with an appeals court decision, the final level of appeal is the Supreme Court, which may or may not grant a writ of certiorari to decide the case (American Government, 2011–2012, pp. 523–525/ 2013–2014, pp. 452–454).

35. (A) An individual or group that is not a party to a legal action but has an interest in it files an amicus curiae brief (American Government, 2011–2012, p. 527/ 2013–2014, p. 455).

PRACTICE TEST 1 ❖ **237**

36. (B) The Supreme Court's decision in *United States v. Lopez* shifted power to the states by limiting the national government's power to pass legislation using the commerce clause (American Government, 2011–2012, pp. 113–114/ 2013–2014, p. 87).

37. (B) In all states except Maine and Nebraska, a winner-take-all system is used. The state has ten electoral college votes, eight for its members in the House of Representatives and two for its senators, all of which will be pledged to the Republican candidate. Maryland, Minnesota, and Wisconsin each has 10 votes in the electoral college (American Government, 2011–2012, pp. 298–299 and 331/ 2013–2014, pp. 298–300).

38. (C) Conference committees with members of both houses work on the language of bills that were passed in different versions (American Government, 2011–2012, pp. 426– 427/ 2013–2014, p. 363).

39. (A) The commerce clause, in conjunction with the necessary and proper clause, allows the federal government to regulate private businesses (American Government, 2011–2012, pp. 93–94 and 101–102/ 2013–2014, pp. 69, 76-77).

40. (D) A realigning period occurs when there is a major and permanent shift in the groups supporting the political parties (American Government, 2011– 2012, pp. 281–283/ 2013–2014, pp. 271–272).

41. (D) Under the principle of *stare decisis*, courts must follow precedent set by their own courts or by higher courts that have authority over them (American Government, 2011–2012, p. 517/ 2013–2014, pp. 446–447).

42. (C) An amendment to the Constitution can, in effect, overturn a Supreme Court decision. An amendment requires the approval of two-thirds of both houses of Congress and ratification by three-fourths of the states (American Government, 2011–2012, pp. 58–59/ 2013–2014, pp. 53–54).

43. (E) Congressional committees revise bills, hold hearings, and give advice to other members of Congress. They can also refer bills to subcommittees for further review (American Government, 2011–2012, pp. 424–425/ 2013–2014, pp. 360–361).

44. (D) Civil rights are powers or privileges guaranteed by the Equal Protection Clause of the Fourteenth Amendment. Discrimination on the basis of race, gender, or disability invokes civil rights. Civil liberties are personal freedoms guaranteed to individuals, such as freedom of speech (American Government, 2011– 2012, pp. 123 and 167/ 2013–2014, pp. 96, 136).

45. (C) The goal of Title IX of the Educational Amendments was to equalize the numbers of men and women playing varsity sports (American Government, 2011–2012, p. 189/ 2013–2014, p. 158).

46. (A) The president must rely heavily on his staff, which is typically drawn from his longtime associates (American Government, 2011–2012, pp. 470–471/ 2013–2014, pp. 403-404).

47. (D) A primary is a special election; a caucus is a meeting of party members. Both are methods of choosing delegates to the national convention (American Government, 2011–2012, pp. 359–360/ 2013–2014, pp. 291–292, 307–308).

© 2014 Cengage Learning. All Rights Reserved. May not be scanned, copied or duplicated, or posted to a publicly accessible website, in whole or in part.

48. (E) The census determines the number of representatives a state will have in the House of Representatives. This also impacts the number of electoral college votes. Census data are also important for receiving formula grant money (American Government, 2011–2012, pp. 108–109 and 413–414/ 2013–2014, p. 82, 354–357).

49. (A) Incumbent members of Congress benefit from name recognition, the use of franking privileges, casework, and by bringing pork-barrel projects to their states. Sitting on oversight committees usually does not bring much attention (American Government, 2011–2012, pp. 415– 416/ 2013–2014, p. 353).

50. (C) The electoral college hurts third parties because it is difficult for them to get a majority in any state. Thus it is difficult for third parties to get any electoral college votes (American Government, 2011–2012, pp. 298–299/ 2013–2014, p. 265).

51. (B) Gerrymandering is the redrawing of districts to benefit a political party (American Government, 2011–2012, p. 418/ 2013–2014, p. 355).

52. (A) A law requiring the posting of the Ten Commandments in public schools could be challenged under the establishment clause as violating the separation between church and state (American Government, 2011–2012, p. 130/ 2013–2014, p. 102).

53. (C) In Gregg v. Georgia, the Supreme Court upheld the constitutionality of the death penalty as long as states adopted precise rules in applying it. The Patriot Act balanced privacy rights with national security (American Government, 2011–2012, p. 157/ 2013–2014, pp. 120-121, 127–128).

54. (B) Keynesian economics is the theory that the government should actively use taxing and spending policies to stimulate economic growth (American Government, 2011–2012, p. 595/ 2013–2014, pp. 513–514).

55. (D) The majority party in the Senate appoints committee heads (American Government, 2011–2012, pp. 427 and 438–439/ 2013–2014, pp. 366–367).

ANSWERS TO THE FREE-RESPONSE QUESTIONS

QUESTION 1

Part (a): The Supreme Court decision in Brown v. Board of Education expanded civil rights. The plaintiffs claimed that separate schools for blacks and whites violated the Fourteenth Amendment. The Court agreed, ruling that segregated schools were inherently unequal. This overturned the separate but equal doctrine established in Plessy v. Ferguson. The Brown case paved the way for more equal educational opportunities for black children.

Part (b): The Voting Rights Act of 1965 also expanded civil rights. Although blacks were given the right to vote in the Fifteenth Amendment, Southern states used several tactics to block this right, including grandfather clauses, literacy tests, and terrorism. Under the Voting Rights Act, federal marshals were sent to the offending states to register blacks and protect them at the polls. The result was increased registration and turnout by blacks.

Part (c): One group that has encountered roadblocks in obtaining civil rights protection is homosexuals. For example, domestic partner benefits are not recognized uniformly throughout the nation, and same-sex partners are not able to take advantage of inheritance laws. Several states have passed laws limiting marriage to between a man and a woman. The Defense of Marriage Act prohibits federal recognition of gay marriages and allows states to ignore same-sex marriages performed in other states. One reason for the roadblocks facing homosexuals is that gay and lesbian relationships go against some people's deeply help religious beliefs. As a result, it is difficult for gay people to get widespread support for civil rights protections. For example, California voters passed an initiative banning gay marriage (American Government, 2011–2012, pp. 172–173, 178, and 201–204/ 2013–2014, pp. 141–142, 146–147, 171–174).

SCORING This essay is worth 7 points.

Part (a) is worth 2 points—1 point for identifying a case (Brown v. Board of Education), and 1 point for explaining how the case expanded civil rights (it ended segregation and provided educational opportunities). There are a number of civil rights cases that could be identified and explained in this section, including a companion case to the Brown decision and Swann v. Charlotte-Mecklenburg County Schools.

Part (b) is worth 2 points—1 point for identifying a law (the Voting Rights Act of 1965), and 1 point for explaining how the law expanded civil rights (it sent federal marshals to enable blacks to register and vote). Other laws could be identified, such as the Civil Rights Act of 1964, Title IV, and the Americans with Disabilities Act.

Part (c) is worth 3 points—1 for identifying a group that has faced roadblocks (homosexuals), and 1 point for each of two obstacles identified (homosexuals may not benefit from inheritance laws, and several states limit marriage to one man and one woman). Other groups could be identified as well, including women, the disabled, and immigrants.

QUESTION 2

Part (a): One way that monetary policy is used to influence the economy is by changing interest rates. The Federal Reserve Board sets the interest rates it charges banks to borrow from the federal government. This is called the discount rate. If the Fed raises the discount rate, banks pay more to borrow money, and they pass these higher interest rates on to their customers. This makes money more expensive to borrow and slows the rate of inflation.

Part (b): One way the budget is used to influence the economy is through taxation policy. For example, President Bill Clinton obtained a tax increase in 1993. This increased federal revenues. The tax increase, along with a boom in high-tech industries, resulted in budget surpluses from 1998–2002.

Part (c): One way Congress can influence the economy comes from its role in approving all taxes and almost all expenditures. Appropriations committees in both houses must approve all spending.

Budget committees, assisted by the Congressional Budget Office, make recommendations about the budget submitted by the president.

Part (d): The president has some influence over the economy because he appoints the members of the Federal Reserve Board (subject to Senate confirmation). This board sets monetary policy, and the president appoints candidates who share his philosophy about regulating the money supply. Members serve for staggered terms of fourteen years, and this gives them significant influence over the economy (American Government, 2011–2012, pp. 409, 595–596, and 600–603/ 2013–2014, pp. 371, 512–513, 526–527

SCORING This essay is worth 8 points.

Part (a) is worth 2 points—1 point for identifying a monetary tool (interest rates), and 1 point for explaining how this tool influences the economy (higher interest rates control inflation). Points would be awarded for other identifications and explanations, such as changing the amount of reserves a bank must keep on hand.

Part (b) is worth 2 points—1 point for identifying a budgetary tool (taxation), and 1 point for explaining how this tool influences the economy (lower taxes may stimulate growth). Points would be awarded for identifying and explaining other budgetary tools, such as using government spending to stimulate the economy.

Part (c) is worth 2 points—1 point for identifying a way Congress influences the economy (by approving taxing and spending) and 1 point for the explanation (Congress can influence the budget by proposing its own plan with the assistance of the CBO). Points would be awarded for identifying other ways Congress influences the economy, such as Senate confirmation of members of the Federal Reserve Board.

Part (d) is worth 2 points—1 point for identifying a way the president influences the economy (by appointing members of the Federal Reserve Board), and 1 point for the explanation (members are appointed for long terms and share the president's monetary philosophy). Points would be awarded for identifying other ways the president can influence the economy, such as by proposing an annual budget.

QUESTION 3

Part (a): The incumbency advantage is the trend that members of Congress who run for reelection are elected at much higher rates than challengers. Members of the House of Representatives are reelected at higher rates than senators are. This is because House members are elected every two years and are therefore constantly campaigning. Also, House members represent smaller constituencies than most senators do, and it is easier for them to stay in touch with their constituents through casework

Part (b): One reason for the incumbency advantage is that incumbents can do casework for constituents in their districts, and satisfied constituents will vote for their reelection. Another reason for the incumbency advantage is that incumbents can bring special benefits to their states in the form of pork barrel spending. They can take credit with constituents for bringing these projects to their states, thus garnering constituent support for reelection.   In addition, incumbents have higher name recognition than challenger, and this fact can help incumbents get reelected.

Part (c): Redistricting benefits incumbents when the incumbent is from the same party as the one dominating the state legislature. The state legislature draws district boundaries. This creates safe districts where incumbents will most likely be reelected, thus maintaining party control (American Government, 2011–2012, pp. 415–418/ 2013–2014, pp. 354–357).

SCORING This essay is worth 7 points.

Part (a) is worth 2 points—1 point for defining the incumbency advantage (incumbents are elected at higher rates than challengers), and 1 point for the explaining why House members have a greater incumbency advantage (they are elected every two years and come from smaller districts than senators). Points would be awarded for identifying other trends, such as the fact that many members of the House of Representatives live in "safe" districts.

Part (b) is worth 4 points—1 point each for identifying a reason for the incumbency advantage (casework and pork barrel spending) and one point each for an explanation of the advantage (casework helps constituents personally and gives them a reason to reelect the incumbent and pork barrel spending brings money to a district which encourages voters to support the incumbent. Points would be awarded for identifying other trends, such as name recognition and the creation of "safe" districts.

Part (c) is worth 1 point for explaining that redistricting benefits incumbents because the party in power in the state legislature will draw district lines to create safe districts benefiting their party.

QUESTION 4

Part (a): One formal power of the president in influencing domestic policy is the power to appoint Cabinet secretaries. There are fifteen Cabinet-level departments. When the Department of Homeland Security was created, President George W. Bush appointed someone to lead it. These appointments are subject to Senate confirmation. Presidents try to select candidates who agree with their domestic agendas and will carry out their wishes.

One informal power the president has to influence domestic policy is the power to call a televised address to ask for the public's support for a program. Presidents use media coverage, remarks to the reporters, and public appearances to speak directly to the American people. This is called "going public," and is designed to raise public support and pressure for the president's program.

Part (b): One formal power of the president in foreign affairs is the power as commander in chief to commit troops. Although the War Powers Resolution allows presidents to do so for only sixty days, most presidents have ignored this. President Bush obtained congressional approval for a troop commitment in Iraq. One informal power of the president in foreign affairs is signing an executive agreement with a leader of another nation. Executive agreements do not require Senate approval. For example, President Franklin Roosevelt signed an executive agreement with Great Britain, trading destroyers for bases during World War II (American Government, 2011–2012, pp. 452–460/ 2013–2014, pp. 383–384, 385–386, 396–397).

SCORING This essay is worth 8 points.

Part (a) is worth 4 points—1 point for the formal power identified (presidents appoint Cabinet secretaries) and 1 point for the explanation (they set policy in accordance with his wishes), 1 point for an informal power (the power to "go public") and 1 point for the explanation (raise public support for the president's program). Points would also be awarded for identifying and explaining other formal powers, such as the power to approve laws, and other informal powers, such as the power to offer a member of Congress support with his or her campaign in exchange for favorable legislation.

Part (b) is worth 4 points—1 point for the formal power identified (commander in chief) and 1 point for the explanation (commit troops), 1 point for identifying an informal power (executive agreements) and 1 point for the explanation (executive agreements are signed with leaders of other countries and do not require Senate approval). Points would also be awarded for identifying and explaining other formal powers, such as the power to appoint the secretary of defense, and other informal powers, such as the ability to work with international organizations, such as NATO.

CALCULATING YOUR SCORE

SECTION I: MULTIPLE-CHOICE QUESTIONS

(Because this practice test contains 55 questions and the AP exam contains 60 questions, you will need to multiply the number you answered correctly by 1.09. This is the number of questions you might have answered correctly on a 60-question test).

Number answered correctly (multiplied by 1.09) equals ___

SECTION II: FREE-RESPONSE QUESTIONS

Question 1   ___   × 2.143 equals _____
out of 7   do not round
Question 2   ___   × 1.875 equals _____
out of 8   do not round
Question 3   ___   × 2.143 equals _____
out of 7   do not round
Question 4   ___   × 1.875 equals _____
out of 8   do not round
Total for Section II _____

COMPOSITE SCORE
_____ + _____ = _____
Section I   Section II   Composite Score

Student scores are weighted differently each year to determine the final AP grade. The chart below is an estimate.

COMPOSITE SCORE RANGE	AP GRADE
93–120	5
82–92	4
66–81	3
48–65	2
0–47	1

PRACTICE TEST 2

UNITED STATES GOVERNMENT AND POLITICS EXAMINATION
Section I: Multiple-Choice Questions
Time: 45 minutes

Directions The questions or incomplete statements below are each followed by five suggested answers. Select the best answer.

1. How can the executive branch check the judicial branch?
   (A) by approving the nomination of federal judges
   (B) by nominating federal judges, subject to senate approval
   (C) by issuing an executive order overturning a court's decision
   (D) by firing a federal judge for cause
   (E) by reducing the number of federal courts

2. All of the following are part of conservative ideology EXCEPT
   (A) opposition to interference with the free market
   (B) belief that sexually explicit material should be banned
   (C) opposition to affirmative action
   (D) support for increased spending on public housing
   (E) a cautious approach to change

3. An election is held in which a voter must be registered to a political party before he or she is allowed to participate. Which of the following terms best describe this election?
   (A) general election
   (B) election for party leaders
   (C) open primary
   (D) closed primary
   (E) caucus

4. Which statement best describes the importance of the vice president?
   (A) The vice president checks on the health of the president daily and attends the funerals of Third World dictators.
   (B) The vice president has an important role as the president of the Senate.
   (C) The importance of the vice president depends on his or her relationship with the president and the duties the president asks him or her to assume.
   (D) The vice president is a lightning rod for criticism that would be otherwise directed at the president.
   (E) The vice president does not have an important role; his or her function is largely ceremonial.

5. Which of the following is most likely to result in a budget deficit?
   (A) increasing military spending and raising taxes
   (B) reducing means-tested social programs
   (C) cutting taxes for the wealthiest Americans
   (D) increasing taxes for the middle class
   (E) increasing military spending without raising taxes

6. Why was the election of 2000 significant?
   (A) because there was no winner in the electoral college, and the election was decided by a majority vote in the House of Representatives
   (B) because there was no winner in the electoral college, and the election was decided by one vote per state in the House of Representatives
   (C) because for the first time in more than a century, the winner in the electoral college lost the popular vote
   (D) because a third party, the Green party, won electoral college votes in three states
   (E) because the Supreme Court overturned the electoral college's decision

7. The House Judiciary Committee is best described as
   (A) standing
   (B) conference
   (C) select
   (D) joint
   (E) appropriations

8. What is the best rationale for allowing Supreme Court justices to serve for life terms?
   (A) It takes time for a justice to gain experience in decision making.
   (B) The Court should be able to make decisions without reprisal, even when their rulings go against public opinion.
   (C) Congress should not be able to remove them, because the average member of Congress does not have a legal background.
   (D) Their salaries are so low that it is difficult to attract good candidates; job security makes their positions more attractive.
   (E) They serve for life terms so that presidents who appoint them may leave a legacy after they leave office.

9. In what respects is the Senate more powerful than the House of Representatives?
   I. It has the power to ratify treaties.
   II. It has the power to confirm judicial appointments.
   III. All revenue bills must originate there.
   IV. Each senator represents an entire state rather than a congressional district.
   (A) I and II
   (B) I, II, and III
   (C) II and III
   (D) I, II, and IV
   (E) III and IV

10. Which of the following cases fall under the original jurisdiction of the Supreme Court?
    (A) cases involving a state law that is alleged to violate the United States Constitution
    (B) cases involving a federal law that is alleged to violate the United States Constitution
    (C) controversies between two or more states
    (D) cases where the amount in controversy exceeds $50,000
    (E) conflicts between the president and Congress

11. The president can influence legislation in all of the following ways EXCEPT
    (A) by having his staff write a legislative program that is then introduced by a member of his party in Congress
    (B) by asking the public to call Congress and express support for his legislative agenda
    (C) by threatening to veto a bill when there is not enough likely support in Congress to override the veto
    (D) by personally contacting members of Congress and asking for their support
    (E) by issuing an executive order overturning an act of Congress

12. What do the decisions of the Court led by Chief Justice Earl Warren illustrate about the relationship between the Court and the presidency?
    (A) Supreme Court justices closely follow the views of the presidents who appointed them, and try to use those views in making decisions.
    (B) Supreme Court justices stay in close contact with the presidents who nominate them, and they often become close friends.
    (C) Supreme Court justices are independent. You can never predict with certainty what they will do once in office.
    (D) Supreme Court justices are more likely to consider the opinions of the public if the president supports those beliefs.
    (E) Supreme Court justices are hesitant to lose the political support of the party that nominated them.

13. Which of the following have been used to expand civil rights?
    I.   commerce clause
    II. due process clause
    III. full faith and credit clause
    IV. equal protection clause
    (A) I, II, and IV
    (B) I and IV
    (C) II and IV
    (D) I and II
    (E) II, III, and IV

14. Two students who attended a public high school were suspended because they wore black armbands to protest the war in Vietnam. Their clothing might have caused a disruption, but no disruption occurred. They challenged the suspension, arguing that their First Amendment rights were violated. What is the most likely outcome of their case?
    (A) It will be dismissed, because wearing an armband is not speech protected by the First Amendment.
    (B) It will be dismissed, because students do not have free speech rights while they are in school.
    (C) It will be dismissed, because students do not have a right to be disruptive in school.
    (D) The students will win, because wearing an armband is protected symbolic speech.
    (E) The students will win, because teenagers have the same free speech rights as adults.

15. The House Rules Committee has all of the following powers EXCEPT
    (A) the power to make revisions to bills
    (B) the power to set strict time limits for debate
    (C) the power to specify the kinds of amendments that can be added to bills
    (D) the power to govern the procedures under which the house will consider bills
    (E) the power to forbid amendments to bills

16. What has been the impact of the War Powers Resolution on American military actions?
    (A) Presidents have carefully followed the law and have asked Congress for permission before committing troops.
    (B) Presidents have committed troops and then asked for Congress to continue the troop commitments beyond sixty days.
    (C) Its impact has been minimal, and several presidents have committed troops worldwide since its enactment.
    (D) Congress has used the law to call troops home once they have been committed for more than sixty days.
    (E) None. The Supreme Court ruled the War Powers Resolution unconstitutional under the political questions doctrine.

17. When Newt Gingrich became Speaker of the House of Representatives in the 1990s, what changes were made to House rules?
    I.   Some senior members were passed over in selection of committee chairs.
    II. Term limits were placed on committee chairs.
    III. Members of the opposing party were not placed on committees.
    IV. The House Rules Committee was abolished.
    (A) I and II
    (B) II and III
    (C) I, II, and III
    (D) I, II, and IV
    (E) II, III, and IV

18. The Civil Rights Act of 1964 did all of the following EXCEPT
    (A) bar race discrimination in public accommodations
    (B) ban discrimination in housing
    (C) outlaw race discrimination in hiring and firing
    (D) bar race discrimination in movie theaters, stadiums, and arenas
    (E) strengthen voting rights legislation

19. Which of the following statements best describes incorporation theory?
    (A) The Bill of Rights protects individuals from the federal government but not from state government.
    (B) The Fourteenth Amendment protects individuals from state violations of all of the rights in the Bill of Rights.
    (C) The Fourteenth Amendment protects individuals from state violations of all of the rights in the Bill of Rights plus other fundamental rights.
    (D) The First Amendment protects individuals from state violations of free speech rights.
    (E) The Fourteenth Amendment protects individuals from state violations of fundamental personal rights.

20. What case established that the necessary and proper clause could be used to extend the national government's power beyond its expressed authority?
    (A) McCulloch v. Maryland
    (B) Marbury v. Madison
    (C) Gitlow v. New York
    (D) Gibbons v. Ogden
    (E) Barron v. Baltimore

21. Which of the following most accurately describes the origins of political attitudes (political socialization)?
    (A) The media has the biggest influence on the political attitudes of people ages eighteen to twenty-one.
    (B) Young people ages eighteen to twenty-one tend to vote opposite of their parents because they want to rebel against their parents.
    (C) The family usually plays the largest role in political socialization, and people tend to vote the same way as their parents vote.
    (D) Schools play a large role in socialization, and high school students tend to follow the ideology of their social studies teachers.
    (E) There are so many influences on political socialization that no single factor determines ideology.

22. Which of the following candidates is most likely to get elected to Congress?
    (A) an incumbent senator
    (B) an incumbent member of the House of Representatives
    (C) a challenger for a seat in the Senate
    (D) a challenger for a seat in the House of Representatives
    (E) It is impossible to tell from this scenario who is more likely to be reelected because reelection depends mostly on party affiliation.

23. Why is the filibuster criticized as being undemocratic?
    (A) because it allows a member of the House of Representatives to block legislation that has substantial popular support
    (B) because it can be used in the Senate but not in the House of Representatives
    (C) because it can be used by a member of either house to block legislation that has substantial popular support
    (D) because it allows a senator to block legislation that has substantial popular support
    (E) because there is no procedure for ending a filibuster once it has started

24. Which of the following accurately describes the outcome of impeachment in United States history?
    (A) President Nixon was impeached, but he resigned before he was removed from office.
    (B) Nixon and Clinton are the only presidents who have faced impeachment.
    (C) Articles of impeachment were approved against President Clinton, but he was not impeached.
    (D) Bill Clinton and Andrew Johnson were impeached but not convicted or removed from office.
    (E) Andrew Johnson is the only president to have been impeached and removed from office.

25. Interested individuals and organizations may join together to support a specific policy position or cause. What is the best term for these groups?
    (A) interest groups
    (B) policy allies
    (C) issue networks
    (D) PACs
    (E) social networks

26. The Supreme Court is most likely to issue a writ of certiorari in which of the following cases?
    (A) a conflict between two lower courts concerning an issue of national importance
    (B) a conflict between the president and Congress over the War Powers Resolution
    (C) a criminal case from a state court in which the defendant proclaims his innocence
    (D) a conflict between a federal agency and a state government
    (E) a conflict over the meaning of an unclear regulation issued by an administrative agency

27. How are congressional district boundaries determined?
    I. They are redrawn every ten years according to census data.
    II. They are drawn so that they are roughly equal in square miles.
    III. They are drawn so that, as much as possible, one person's vote will be worth the same as another person's vote.
    IV. They are drawn to favor minority racial groups.
    (A) I and II
    (B) III and IV
    (C) I and III
    (D) II, III, and IV
    (E) II and IV

28. There are 538 total votes in the electoral college. The Democrat receives 265, the Republican receives 255, and an Independent candidate receives 18. How will the election be decided?
    (A) The Democrat will win because he received the most electoral college votes.
    (B) The Democrat will win because no candidate received the majority of the electoral votes and the Democrat won the popular vote.
    (C) There will be a runoff election between the Democrat and the Republican.
    (D) The House of Representatives will decide, with each representative casting one vote.
    (E) The House of Representatives will decide, with each state casting one vote.

29. Which statement best describes why the Tea Party did not splinter the vote for the Republican Party in the 2010 midterm elections?
    (A) Third parties rarely have an impact on elections.
    (B) The Tea Party had so few supporters that the Republican Party was not weakened significantly.
    (C) The Tea Party is an ideological group within the Republican Party.
    (D) The Tea Party drew more support from Democrats than from Republicans.
    (E) Tea Party candidates received no public funding, because the Tea Party was classified as a third party.

30. How did voter turnout in the 2008 presidential elections differ from previous years?
    (A) There was a significant realignment among voters.
    (B) The voter turnout rate remained the same as it was in 2004.
    (C) It was lower than in the three previous elections.
    (D) There was a larger turnout among younger voters.
    (E) It is difficult to determine, because most people weren't willing to answer questions about whether they had voted.

31. Which of the following was a realigning election?
    (A) the 1996 presidential election, because the vote fell below 50 percent
    (B) the 2000 presidential election, because the electoral college vote did not mirror the popular vote
    (C) the 1932 presidential election, because African Americans made a permanent shift to the Democratic party
    (D) the 1972 reelection of Richard Nixon, because he won in a landslide
    (E) none of these elections meet the criteria for being a critical election

32. Which of the following constitutional provisions has been used to strengthen state powers?
    (A) Tenth Amendment
    (B) full faith and credit clause
    (C) necessary and proper clause
    (D) privilege and immunities clause
    (E) commerce clause

33. All of the following were problems under the Articles of Confederation EXCEPT
    (A) Shays' Rebellion
    (B) state constitutions did not contain bills of rights
    (C) the national government was in debt
    (D) inflation
    (E) states fought over western lands

34. Which of the following is an advantage of a federal system?
    (A) Local governments are more likely to be dominated by factions.
    (B) It is easy to determine which level of government is responsible for a particular problem.
    (C) States can experiment with programs, and the successful ones can be adopted on the national level.
    (D) A federal system is less expensive than a unitary system because there are fewer national government entities.
    (E) States have traditionally protected the rights of minority groups more than the national government has.

35. How do political parties choose their presidential nominee?
    (A) by a majority vote in the primaries
    (B) by a majority vote in the caucuses
    (C) through a majority vote of delegates at the national convention
    (D) through a vote of party leaders at the national convention
    (E) through a primary runoff election between the top two candidates

36. In studying government and politics, what does the term "political agenda" mean?
    (A) the scope of government regulation in a particular policy area
    (B) a set of issues that is important to the public and the government
    (C) the platform set forth by the president's political party
    (D) the issues that are subject to legislation currently pending in Congress
    (E) the list of issues determined by the media as meriting public attention

37. Which statement best describes how presidential power has changed over time since ratification of the Constitution?
    (A) Presidential power over foreign affairs has increased, but power over the bureaucracy has decreased over time.
    (B) Presidential power over foreign affairs has decreased because the War Powers Resolution requires presidents to consult with Congress.
    (C) Presidential power over legislation has decreased because of negative press coverage of presidential proposals.
    (D) Presidential power over foreign affairs has increased.
    (E) Presidential power has not changed significantly since the Constitution was ratified.

38. All of the following are ways that Congress oversees the bureaucracy EXCEPT
    (A) it can fire agency heads
    (B) the Senate confirms the appointment of Cabinet heads
    (C) Congress can submit legislation to the president that cuts an agency's budget
    (D) congressional committees can hold oversight hearings
    (E) Congress can write legislation to clarify agency regulations and procedures

39. Which statement best describes the Warren Court?
    (A) It made decisions to increase personal liberties, including abortion.
    (B) It made decisions that ended school segregation and restricted defendants' rights.
    (C) It frequently used judicial restraint.
    (D) It made decisions that expanded civil rights and civil liberties.
    (E) It supported affirmative action.

40. Which of the following has been used to weaken the exclusionary rule?
    (A) Several states have passed laws ending the use of the exclusionary rule.
    (B) Some courts provide a good faith exception to the exclusionary rule.
    (C) Several states allow the use of confessions as evidence, even when the defendant was not read his rights, as long as the confession was not coerced.
    (D) Some states now allow civil suits against the police, rather than excluding evidence, as a deterrent to illegal searches.
    (E) States cannot weaken the exclusionary rule because the Supreme Court settled the matter.

41. All of the following features of elections in the United States favor a two-party system EXCEPT
    (A) winner-take-all in the electoral college
    (B) single-member, plurality representation districts
    (C) a plurality vote determines the winner
    (D) one member of Congress is elected from each district
    (E) proportional representation

42. What checks does Congress have over the judiciary?
    I. The Senate confirms federal judges.
    II. Senatorial courtesy can be used to block a nomination.
    III. Congress can overcome an unpopular court decision by proposing a constitutional amendment, subject to ratification.
    IV. Congress can rewrite legislation to overcome a negative court ruling.
    (A) I and II
    (B) I, II, and III
    (C) II and III
    (D) II, III, and IV
    (E) I, II, III, and IV

43. The House of Representatives and Senate pass different versions of a bill. What happens next?
    (A) The bill is sent to a conference committee, then back to both houses for final approval, and then to the president.
    (B) The bill is sent to a conference committee, then back to its original committees for approval, and then to the president.
    (C) The bill is sent to a conference committee, and if the changes are not significant, it is sent directly to the president.
    (D) Both versions of the bill are sent to the president, who signs the version that he prefers.
    (E) The bill is sent to the Speaker of the House and the president pro tempore of the Senate, who agree on common language and then send the bill to the president for signature.

44. Congress passes bills that provide funding for each agency. This is called
    (A) an authorization
    (B) an appropriation
    (C) an earmark
    (D) a budget resolution
    (E) a continuing resolution

45. How can Congress check the executive branch?
    I. by overriding a presidential veto
    II. by rejecting the president's proposed budget
    III. by refusing to allow the Vice President to cast a tie-breaking vote in the Senate
    IV. the Senate can refuse to approve the president's nomination for a position as Cabinet secretary
    (A) I and II
    (B) II and III
    (C) I, II, and III
    (D) III and IV
    (E) I, II, and IV

46. What is the most important factor in predicting the winner in congressional elections?
    (A) the amount of casework done for a district
    (B) the number of pork barrel projects brought to a district
    (C) incumbency
    (D) the number of times franking privileges have been used to contact constituents
    (E) whether the economy is doing well or poorly

47. When presented with a bill passed by Congress, the president may take all of the following actions EXCEPT
    (A) sign the bill
    (B) hold onto the bill for 10 days without signing it
    (C) sign part of the bill, and send a veto message about part of the bill
    (D) veto the bill and send a veto message to Congress
    (E) pocket veto the bill

48. What kind of bill is most likely to include a pork barrel project with money earmarked for a particular state?
    (A) authorization bill
    (B) continuing resolution
    (C) reapportionment bill
    (D) appropriations bill
    (E) joint resolution

49. Which of the following have an impact on policymaking?
    I. congressional committees and subcommittees
    II. issue networks
    III. bureaucratic agencies
    IV. interest groups
    (A) I, II, and III
    (B) II, III, and IV
    (C) I, III, and IV
    (D) I, II, and IV
    (E) I, II, III, and IV

50. A voting district was created to benefit a "minority-majority." It was drawn in the shape of earmuffs. Did the courts uphold this redistricting plan?
    (A) No, because the district was drawn in a strange shape.
    (B) No, because race-based redistricting is unconstitutional.
    (C) No, because the district was drawn to benefit the Democratic Party.
    (D) Yes, because the district was drawn to comply with the Voting Rights Act of 1965.
    (E) Yes, because states have wide latitude in drawing district boundaries.

51. If voting patterns among African Americans and Hispanics continue, what is the likely implication of having a minority-majority?
    (A) More Republicans will be elected.
    (B) More Independents will be elected.
    (C) Voter turnout will decrease.
    (D) More Democrats will be elected.
    (E) There are so many minorities that having a minority-majority is unlikely to affect elections.

52. All of the following provisions govern how states deal with one another EXCEPT
    (A) extradition clause
    (B) full faith and credit clause
    (C) supremacy clause
    (D) privileges and immunities clause
    (E) Article I, Section 10 (states may not place tariffs on one another)

53. *Griswold v.* Connecticut, in which the Supreme Court held that the Fourth Amendment includes a right to privacy, is an example of what judicial philosophy?
    (A) original intent
    (B) judicial activism
    (C) judicial restraint
    (D) statutory construction
    (E) political questions doctrine

STOP
END OF SECTION

IF YOU FINISH BEFORE TIME IS CALLED, YOU MAY CHECK YOUR WORK ON THIS SECTION. DO NOT GO ON TO SECTION II UNTIL YOU ARE TOLD TO DO SO.

UNITED STATES GOVERNMENT AND POLITICS EXAMINATION
Section II: 4 Free-Response Questions
Time: 100 minutes

Directions You have 100 minutes to answer all four of the following questions. Unless the directions indicate otherwise, respond to all parts of each question. It is recommended that you take a few minutes to plan and outline each answer. Spend approximately 25 minutes on each question. In your response, use specific examples where appropriate. Be sure to number each of your answers.

1. Congress exercises control over both the judiciary and the bureaucracy.
   a. Identify and explain two checks that Congress has over the judiciary.
   b. Identify and explain two checks that Congress has over the bureaucracy.

2. Political parties nominate presidential candidates in a process that varies from state to state. Candidates from one of the two major parties win elections, because third parties are weak in America.
   a. Explain the caucus process. Describe one criticism of presidential caucuses.
   b. Explain the primary process. Describe one criticism of presidential primaries.
   c. Identify and explain two reasons why third parties rarely win elections.

3. Interest groups and PACs have several ways to influence the political process. However, several factors limit their ability to influence the political process.
   a. Identify and explain two ways interest groups or PACs attempt to influence the political process.
   b. Identify and explain one factor that limits interest groups or PACs.

4. The president is the chief legislator, and he shares lawmaking powers with Congress. Presidents have varying degrees of success in getting the legislation they propose passed by Congress.
   a. Define split-ticket voting.
   b. Define divided government.
   c. Identify and explain one reason why divided government impacts presidential success in Congress.
   d. Identify and explain one factor, other than divided government, that impacts presidential leadership in Congress.

END OF EXAMINATION

ANSWERS TO THE MULTIPLE-CHOICE QUESTIONS

Using the table below, score your test.
Determine how many questions you answered correctly and how many you answered incorrectly. You will find explanations of the answers on the following pages.

1. B	11. E	21. C	31. C	41. E	51. D
2. D	12. C	22. B	32. A	42. E	52. C
3. D	13. A	23. D	33. B	42. A	53. B
4. C	14. D	24. D	34. C	44. B	
5. E	15. A	25. C	35. C	45. E	
6. C	16. C	26. A	36. B	46. C	
7. A	17. A	27. C	37. D	47. C	
8. B	18. B	28. E	38. A	48. D	
9. D	19. E	29. C	39. D	49. E	
10. C	20. A	30. D	40. B	50. B	

1. (B) The executive has a check on the judiciary by nominating federal judges, subject to Senate confirmation (*American Government, 2011–2012*, pp. 532–553/ 2013–2014, pp. 459–462).

2. (D) Conservatives want to limit government-sponsored social programs. They oppose regulations on the free market (*American Government, 2011–2012*, p. 19/ 2013–2014, p. 19).

3. (D) Voters in closed primaries must be registered with a party (*American Government, 2011–2012*, p. 358/ 2013–2014, p. 292).

4. (C) The duties and importance of vice presidents have varied, depending on the relationship between the president and the vice president and the duties the president wants the vice president to assume (*American Government, 2011– 2012*, pp. 472–474/ 2013–2014, pp. 405–406).

5. (E) A deficit results when federal expenditures exceed revenues. For example, under President George W. Bush, military spending increased. This, coupled with the president's reluctance to raise taxes, resulted in a deficit (*American Government, 2011–2012*, p. 595/ 2013–2014, p. 515).

6. (C) In the 2000 presidential election, for the first time since 1888, the winner of the popular vote lost the election because of the electoral college vote (*American Government, 2011–2012*, pp. 329–332/ 2013–2014, pp. 301).

7. (A) The House Judiciary Committee is a standing committee because it is permanent (*American Government, 2011–2012*, p. 426/ 2013-2014, pp. 361-362).

8. (B) Supreme Court justices serve for life to protect them from political retribution if they make a decision the public dislikes (*American Government, 2011–2012*, pp. 530–531/ 2013–2014, general discussion, p. 446).

9. (D) The Senate is the upper house, and it ratifies treaties and confirms judicial nominations. Each senator represents an entire state, which means senators usually represent a bigger constituency than members of the House. Revenue bills must originate in the House (*American Government, 2011–2012,* pp. 407–410/ *2013–2014,* p. 347).

10. (C) The Supreme Court has original jurisdiction over controversies between states. There are a few other kinds of cases in which the Court has original jurisdiction; most of the Court's jurisdiction is appellate (*American Government, 2011–2012,* p. 525/ *2013–2014,* pp. 450–451).

11. (E) An executive order does not require the agreement of Congress. However, Congress has the power to write a bill overturning an executive order (*American Government, 2011–2012,* p. 465/ *2013–2014,* pp. 398).

12. (C) Chief Justice Earl Warren presided over the Court that issued the Brown v. Board of Education decision. President Eisenhower, who nominated him, was not very concerned about civil rights. This shows that justices can be very independent once in office (*2011–2012,* p. 535/ *2013–2014,* pp. 141–142, 464).

13. (A) The courts have used the due process and equal protection clauses of the Fourteenth Amendment to protect groups from discrimination by the states. Congress used the commerce clause to pass the Civil Rights Act of 1964, which prohibits racial discrimination (*American Government, 2011–2012,* p. 178/ *2013–2014,* general discussion, pp.141–142, 146–147).

14. (D) Wearing an armband is symbolic speech that is protected by the First Amendment, as long as it does not cause a substantial disruption in the learning environment (*American Government, 2011–2012,* pp. 134–135/ *2013–2014,* p. 106).

15. (A) The House Rules Committee adopts a rule that governs procedures for considering a bill in the House. It sets time limits on debates, and it can specify the kinds of amendments allowed or prohibit amendments entirely (*American Government, 2011–2012,* p. 427/ *2013–2014,* p. 348).

16. (C) The impact of the War Powers Resolution has been minimal. Several presidents have committed troops for more than sixty days without congressional approval (American Government, *2011–2012,* p. 453/ *2013–2014,* pp. 386, 547–548).

17. (A) The role of seniority lessened, and Republicans passed over some senior members as committee heads and placed term limits on committee chairs (*American Government, 2011–2012,* p. 424/ *2013–2014,* p. 363).

18. (B) The Civil Rights Act of 1964 banned discrimination in public places and employment and strengthened voting rights legislation. A similar law passed in 1968 banned racial discrimination in housing (*American Government, 2011– 2012,* pp. 178–179/ *2013–2014,* pp. 146–148).

19. (E) Under incorporation theory, the Fourteenth Amendment protects individuals from state violations of fundamental freedoms (*American Government, 2011–2012,* p. 124/ *2013–2014,* pp. 97–98).

20. (A) In McCulloch v. Maryland, the Supreme Court held that the necessary and proper clause enabled the federal government to establish a bank because such a power was implied in the power to regulate the currency (*American Government, 2011–2012,* pp. 94, 100–101/ 2013–2014, pp. 75–76).

21. (C) The family plays the largest role in political socialization (*American Government, 2011–2012,* p. 215/ 2013–2014, p. 184).

22. (B) Incumbent members in the House of Representatives have the highest reelection rates (*American Government, 2011–2012,* pp. 415–417/ 2013–2014, p. 353).

23. (D) A filibuster, which takes place only in the Senate, has been criticized as being undemocratic because one senator can talk a popular bill to death (*American Government, 2011–2012,* pp. 411–412, 418–419/ 2013–2014, pp. 348–349).

24. (D) Presidents Andrew Johnson and Bill Clinton were impeached. Impeachment is a process in which a president is charged by the House and tried by the Senate. Neither president was convicted or removed (*American Government, 2011– 2012,* pp. 468–469/ 2013–2014, pp. 400–401).

25. (C) Issue networks are groups of people from interest groups, congressional staffs, scholars, and public relations specialists that support a particular policy position on a certain issue (*American Government, 2011–2012,* p. 508/ 2013–2014, p. 438).

26. (A) The Supreme Court is most likely to take a case when an important conflict between lower court decisions needs to be resolved (*American Government, 2011– 2012,* p. 529/ 2013–2014, p. 457).

27. (C) Congressional district boundaries are drawn every ten years, following the census. As much as possible, they are drawn so that every person's vote counts equally (*American Government, 2011–2012,* pp. 417/ 2013–2014, p. 354).

28. (E) If no candidate receives a majority vote (270 votes) in the electoral college, the House of Representatives decides, with each state casting one vote (*American Government, 2011–2012,* pp. 329–332/ 2013–2014, p. 300).

29. (C) The Tea Party is not a third party; it is a group within the Republican Party. As a result, it did not splinter the Republican Party (*American Government, 2011–2012,* general discussion p. 304/ 2013–2014, pp. 352–353).

30. (D) There was a larger turnout among younger voters in the 2008 presidential election (*American Government, 2011–2012,* p. 318/ 2013–2014, p. 284).

31. (C) A realigning election occurs when there is a major and permanent electoral shift. In 1932 African Americans began voting for the Democratic Party (*American Government, 2011–2012,* p. 284/ 2013–2014, pp. 269–271).

32. (A) The Tenth Amendment reserves for the states and the people those powers that are not expressly given to the national government or prohibited to the states (*American Government, 2011–2012,* p. 94/ 2013–2014, p. 71).

33. (B) Under the Articles of Confederation, there was inflation, the nation was in debt, and states fought over western lands. Shays's Rebellion illustrated the weaknesses of the national government. Most state constitutions contained bills of rights (American Government, 2011–2012, pp. 41–43/ 2013–2014, pp. 37–39).

34. (C) Under federalism, states can become laboratories for experimental programs and policies (American Government, 2011–2012, pp. 89–90,112/ 2013–2014, pp. 67–68).

35. (C) Delegates are pledged to candidates during state primaries and caucuses. The candidate is formally selected by a vote of the delegates at the national convention (American Government, 2011–2012, p. 359/ 2013–2014, pp. 332–333).

36. (B) The political agenda is a set of issues thought by the public or those in government to merit action by the government (American Government, 2011–2012, pp. 549–550/ 2013–2014, pp. 476–477).

37. (D) Presidential power over foreign affairs has increased. Several modern presidents have used their power as commander in chief to enter into foreign conflicts without a formal declaration of war (American Government, 2011–2012, pp. 452–456/ 2013–2014, pp. 385–386).

38. (A) Congress can rewrite agency regulations, propose cuts in their budgets, and hold oversight hearings. The Senate confirms the appointments of Cabinet secretaries (American Government, 2011–2012, pp. 487, 508/ 2013–2014, pp. 347, 438–440).

39. (D) The Warren Court used judicial activism to expand civil rights and civil liberties (American Government, 2011–2012, general discussion pp. 535, 538–539/ 2013–2014, pp. 141–142, 464–465).

40. (B) Some courts allow a good faith exception to the exclusionary rule; evidence obtained under the good faith belief that the search was legal can be used in court (American Government, 2011–2012, p. 115/ 2013–2014, p. 126).

41. (E) The winner-take-all, simple plurality, majority representation system favors a two-party system. In proportional systems used in some European countries and elsewhere, smaller parties benefit by being allocated a proportional number of seats in the legislature (American Government, 2011–2012, pp. 298–299/ 2013–2014, pp. 265–266).

42. (E) Congress can check the judiciary by rejecting nominations, rewriting legislation, and proposing a constitutional amendment. Senatorial courtesy allows a senator from the president's party to block the nomination of a district judge from his or her home state (American Government, 2011– 2012, pp. 58–59, 61–62, 531/ 2013–2014, pp. 45–46, 460, 467–468).

43. (A) When the House and Senate pass different versions of a bill, it is sent to a conference committee to work out the language. Both houses must approve it before the bill is sent to the president (American Government, 2011–2012, pp. 426– 427/ 2013–2014, p. 363).

44. (B) Congress passes appropriation bills that authorize funds to be used by an agency (American Government, 2011–2012, p. 508/ 2013–2014, p. 371).

45. (E) Congress can check the executive by rejecting legislation and rejecting the president's budget. The Senate can refuse to confirm the appointment of a Cabinet secretary (American Government, 2011–2012, pp. 460, 487/ 2013–2014, pp. 347, 370-371).

46. (C) Incumbency is the most important factor in congressional elections (*American Government, 2011–2012*, pp. 415–416/ 2013–2014, pp. 353–354).

47. (C) The president does not have line-item veto power (*American Government, 2011–2012*, p. 460/ 2013–2014, p. 393).

48. (D) Pork barrel legislation, with earmarks for particular projects, is attached to appropriations bills, which allocate funds for certain programs (*American Government, 2011–2012*, p. 434/ 2013–2014, p. 368).

49. (E) Congressional committees, bureaucratic agencies, interest groups, and issue networks, all have an impact on policy making (*American Government, 2011–2012*, pp. 549–551/ 2013–2014, pp. 437–438).

50. (B) The Supreme Court ruled that the intentional creation of a "minority-majority" district was unconstitutional (*American Government, 2011–2012*, p. 421/ 2013–2014, p. 357).

51. (D) African Americans and Hispanics are the largest ethnic groups. They tend to vote for the Democratic Party. The most likely outcome of having a minority-majority district is that more Democrats will be elected (*American Government, 2011–2012*, p. 222/ 2013–2014, p. 192).

52. (C) The extradition clause, the full faith and credit clause, and the privileges and immunities clause are provisions of the Constitution governing states' relationships with one another. In addition, Article I, Section 10 prohibits interstate tariffs (*American Government, 2011–2012*, pp. 98–99/ 2013–2014, pp. 73–74).

53. (B) The Supreme Court found a right to privacy implied in the language of the Fourth Amendment. This is a case of judicial activism (*American Government, 2011–2012*, p.146/ 2013–2014, pp. 117, 464–465).

ANSWERS TO THE FREE-RESPONSE QUESTIONS

QUESTION 1

Part (a): One check that Congress has over the judiciary is that the Senate must confirm the president's judicial nominees. Of course, presidents nominate candidates for the federal bench who support the president's judicial philosophies. However, these candidates must face the scrutiny of the Senate. In addition, they might face a filibuster by a senator from the opposing party to block their nomination. This means that the Senate has the final say over who is appointed to the federal bench.

Another check that Congress has over the judiciary is the power to propose a constitutional amendment, approved by a two-thirds vote in each house, if it does not agree with a decision reached by the Supreme Court. For example, the Supreme Court once ruled that the income tax was unconstitutional. This ruling was overcome with a constitutional amendment. Of course, amendments must be approved by three-fourths of the states in order be ratified.

Part (b): One check that Congress has over the bureaucracy is the power of the purse. Appropriations bills originate in the House, and passage is required for funding all government programs.

Authorization bills set limits on what agencies can spend. Federal agencies must be able to justify their budgets, since they are under congressional scrutiny, and subject to congressional cuts or increases in their budgets.

Another check that Congress has over the bureaucracy is oversight hearings. Congressional committees can hold hearings in which agency heads and personnel are required to testify. Congress investigates whether agencies are operating efficiently and effectively. If necessary, committees can recommend legislation that changes the agency's procedures (*American Government, 2011–2012*, pp. 58–59, 437–438, 508–510/ 2013–2014, pp. 45–46, 53–54, 438–440, 462–463, 467–468).

SCORING This essay is worth 8 points.

Part (a) is worth 4 points—1 point is awarded for each identification of a check Congress has over the judiciary (the Senate confirms appointments, and Congress can propose an amendment), and 1 point is awarded for each explanation (the Senate has the final say over who sits on the federal bench, and amendments can overturn a court decision). Points would be awarded for identifying and explaining other powers Congress has over the judiciary, such as enlarging or reducing the number of courts.

Part (b) is worth 4 points—1 point is awarded for each identification of a check Congress has over the bureaucracy (power of the purse and oversight hearings), and 1 point is awarded for each explanation (Congress can cut or increase an agency's budget and Congress can determine how well an agency is operating). Points would be awarded for other checks Congress has over the bureaucracy, such as confirming the appointment of Cabinet heads.

QUESTION 2

Part (a): A caucus is a method to select delegates to attend a party's national convention. Party members meet and select delegates to attend the next level of meetings within the state. Eventually, a state caucus is held to select delegates to attend the national convention. One criticism of the caucus process is that it takes more time and energy than simply voting and only party regulars will attend.

Part (b): A primary is a special election to select delegates to attend the party's national convention. One criticism of the primary process is that many states hold closed primaries, which require voters to register in advance with the party. This discourages participation from nonaffiliated voters who are interested in a particular candidate.

Part (c): There are several reasons why third parties do not do well in elections. One reason is the electoral college. Because almost all states use a winner-take-all system, a third party candidate who does relatively well nationwide still may not win a single electoral college vote. Another reason third parties do not do well is the incumbency advantage. Incumbents usually win, and they are overwhelmingly Republicans and Democrats (*American Government, 2011–2012*, pp. 298–299, 339–340, 359–360/ 2013–2014, pp. 264–267, 291–293).

SCORING This essay is worth 6 points.

Part (a) is worth 2 points—1 point is awarded for defining a caucus (a meeting of party members to choose delegates), and 1 point is awarded for explaining a criticism of the caucus process (it is time-consuming). Other criticisms are that the first caucus is in Iowa, which gives that state too much attention, and those who attend caucuses are more liberal or conservative in their ideology than most party members, making them unrepresentative.

Part (b) is worth 2 points—1 point is awarded for defining a primary (a special election to select delegates), and 1 point is awarded for explaining a criticism of primaries (voters must register with a party).Other criticisms are that the New Hampshire primary is held first, giving that state too much influence, and primaries are expensive for states to conduct.

Part (c) is worth 2 points—1 point is awarded for each explanation of why third parties do not do well in elections (the electoral college and incumbency advantage). Other explanations are that we use a majority vote, single seat system for the House of Representatives (rather than proportional representation) and third parties do not appeal to mainstream voters, who tend to be in the ideological middle.

QUESTION 3

Part (a): One way that PACs attempt to influence the political process is by spending money to help candidates they favor get elected. This spending can take two forms—campaign contributions and independent expenditures. Donations usually go to candidates who are already sympathetic to the PAC's positions. Congressional candidates do not get any federal money to run their campaigns. By giving money to campaigns, PACs hope that a candidate will be elected and will pursue policies favored by the PAC. In addition, through independent expenditures, PACs may spend money on their own advertising campaigns.

One way that interest groups can influence the political process is by providing credible information to members of Congress. Members of Congress are policy generalists who must make decisions in very specific and often technical policy areas. Interest groups can provide congressmen with the kind of detailed, specific, and up-to-date information politicians need. By presenting organized and persuasive information to Congress, lobbyists can develop and maintain the confidence of a legislator and further their group's policy interests.

Part (b): One constraint on PACs is campaign finance reform. Although there is no limit on independent expenditures, PACs cannot contribute more than $5,000 to a particular candidate (*American Government, 2011–2012,* pp. 264–265, 350–353/ 2013–2014, pp. 229, 320–326, 352).

SCORING This essay is worth 6 points.

Part (a) is worth 4 points—1 point is awarded for each identification of a way that PACs or interest groups influence the political process (giving money), and 1 point is awarded for the explanation (money helps sympathetic candidates get elected). You would receive 1 point for identifying a second way that PACs or interest groups influence the political process (giving needed information) and 1 point for an explanation (persuasive information helps congressmen further the group's interests). Points would be awarded for identifying and explaining other ways interest groups or PACs influence the political process, such as hiring the former heads of agencies to help them lobby current members of the agency.

Part (b) is worth 2 points—1 point is awarded for identifying a constraint on interest group influence (campaign finance reform laws), and 1 point is awarded for an explanation (PACs are limited in how much money they can donate to a campaign). Points would be awarded for identifying and explaining other constraints on PACs and interest groups, such as the rule that ads by 527 independent organizations must state the name of the organization. Another limit on interest group and PAC behavior is the harm that is caused to the group's reputation if a high profile member is indicted for criminal behavior.

QUESTION 4

Part (a): Split-ticket voting occurs when a person votes for a president from one political party and for a member of either house of Congress from the opposing political party. The result of split-ticket voting is divided government.

Part (b): Divided government occurs when the president is from one political party and the other political party controls one or both houses of Congress.

Part (c): One reason divided government impacts presidential leadership in Congress is that the president will probably have less success in getting the legislation he favors passed. Presidents must cross party lines and persuade Congressmen and women of a different political viewpoint to support his program. This is much more difficult than getting the support of those who already support his ideological view.

Part (d): Approval ratings impact a president's ability to pursue his legislative program. When a president's approval ratings are high, he can be much more persuasive in Congress, because the American people are behind him and support his goals (*American Government, 2011–2012,* pp. 306, 463/ 2013–2014, pp. 263, 394–395).

SCORING This essay is worth 6 points.

Part (a) is worth 1 point for defining ticket splitting (voting for a president of one party and a member of Congress from a different party).

Part (b) is worth 1 point for defining divided government (the president is from one party and the other party controls one or both houses of Congress).

Part (c) is worth 1 point for identifying the impact of divided government (the president has less success in Congress), and 1 point is awarded for explaining the impact of divided government on the president's success in Congress (presidents have more difficulty persuading Congress to support their programs). Other explanations are that the president will have to compromise more on legislation, and the president may have to rely more on key members of his party to persuade others in Congress to support the president's plans.

Part (d) is worth 1 point for identifying another factor that impacts presidential success in Congress (approval ratings) and 1 point is awarded for explaining how that factor impacts presidential success in Congress (high approval ratings show public support and make it easier for the president to persuade Congress). Other factors would include a mandate following an election or the president's lame duck status.

CALCULATING YOUR SCORE

SECTION I: MULTIPLE-CHOICE QUESTIONS

(Because this practice test contains 53 questions and the AP exam contains 60 questions, you will need to multiply the number you answered correctly by 1.13. This is the number of questions you might have answered correctly on a 60-question test).

Number answered correctly (multiplied by 1.13) equals ___

SECTION II: FREE-RESPONSE QUESTIONS

Question 1 _____ × 1.875 equals _____
out of 8   do not round
Question 2 _____ × 2.5 equals _____
out of 6   do not round
Question 3 _____ × 2.5 equals _____
out of 6   do not round
Question 4 _____ × 2.5 equals _____
out of 6   do not round
Total for Section II _____

COMPOSITE SCORE

_____ + _____ = _____
Section I   Section II   Composite Score

Student scores are weighted differently each year to determine the final AP grade. The chart below is an estimate.

COMPOSITE SCORE RANGE	AP GRADE
93–120	5
82–92	4
66–81	3
48–65	2
0–47	1

GLOSSARY

ACQUISITIVE MODEL A model of bureaucracy that views top-level bureaucrats as seeking to expand the sizes of their budgets and staffs to gain greater power.

ACTUAL MALICE Either knowledge of a defamatory statement's falsity or a reckless disregard for the truth.

ADMINISTRATIVE AGENCY A federal, state, or local government unit established to perform a specific function. Administrative agencies are created and authorized by legislative bodies to administer and enforce specific laws.

ADVICE AND CONSENT Terms in the Constitution describing the U.S. Senate's power to review and approve treaties and presidential appointments.

AFFIRM To declare that a court ruling is valid and must stand.

AFFIRMATIVE ACTION A policy in educational admissions or job hiring that gives special attention or compensatory treatment to traditionally disadvantaged groups in an effort to overcome effects of past discrimination.

AGENDA SETTING Determining which public-policy questions will be debated or considered.

ANARCHY The absence of any form of government or political authority.

ANTI-FEDERALIST An individual who opposed the ratification of the new Constitution in 1787. The Anti-Federalists were opposed to a strong central government.

APPELLATE COURT A court with jurisdiction to review cases and issues that were originally tried in lower courts.

APPOINTMENT POWER The authority vested in the president to fill a government office or position. Positions filled by presidential appointment include those in the executive branch and the federal judiciary, commissioned officers in the armed forces, and members of the independent regulatory commissions.

APPROPRIATION The passage by Congress of a spending bill specifying the amount of authorized funds that actually will be allocated for an agency's use.

ARISTOCRACY Rule by the "best"; in reality, rule by the upper class.

265

ATTENTIVE PUBLIC That portion of the general public that pays attention to policy issues.

AUSTRALIAN BALLOT A secret ballot prepared, distributed, and tabulated by government officials at public expense. Since 1888, all U.S. states have used the Australian ballot rather than an open, public ballot.

AUTHORITARIANISM A type of regime in which only the government is fully controlled by the ruler. Social and economic institutions are not under the government's control.

AUTHORIZATION A formal declaration by a legislative committee that a certain amount of funding may be available to an agency. Some authorizations terminate in a year; others are renewable automatically, without further congressional action.

BALANCE OF TRADE The difference between the value of a nation's exports of goods and the value of its imports of goods.

BATTLEGROUND STATE A state that is likely to be so closely fought that the national campaigns devote exceptional effort to winning the popular and electoral votes there.

"BEAUTY CONTEST" A presidential primary in which contending candidates compete for popular votes but whose results do not control the selection of delegates to the national convention. .

BICAMERAL LEGISLATURE A legislature made up of two parts, called chambers. The U.S. Congress, composed of the House of Representatives and the Senate, is a bicameral legislature.

BICAMERALISM The division of a legislature into two separate assemblies.

BLACK CODES Laws passed by Southern states immediately after the Civil War that denied most legal rights to freed slaves.

BLOCK GRANTS Federal programs that provide funds to state and local governments for general functional areas, such as criminal justice or mental health programs.

BLUE DOG DEMOCRATS Members of Congress from more moderate states or districts who sometimes "crossover" to vote with Republicans on legislation.

BOYCOTT A form of pressure or protest—an organized refusal to purchase a particular product or deal with a particular business.

BROAD CONSTRUCTION A judicial philosophy that looks to the context and purpose of a law when making an interpretation.

BUDGET DEFICIT Government expenditures that exceed receipts.

BUREAUCRACY A large organization that is structured hierarchically to carry out specific functions.

BUSING In the context of civil rights, the transportation of public school students from areas where they live to schools in other areas to eliminate school segregation based on residential racial patterns.

CABINET An advisory group selected by the president to aid in making decisions. The Cabinet includes the heads of 15 executive departments and others named by the president.

CABINET DEPARTMENT One of the 15 departments of the executive branch(State, Treasury, Defense, Justice, Interior, Agriculture, Commerce, Labor, Health and Human Services, Homeland Security, Housing and Urban Development, Education, Energy, Transportation, and Veterans Affairs).

CAPITALISM An economic issue characterized by the private ownership of wealth-creating assets, free markets, and freedom of contract.

CAPTURE The act by which an industry being regulated by a government agency gains direct or indirect control over agency personnel and decision makers.

CASE LAW Judicial interpretations of common-law principles and doctrines, as well as interpretations of constitutional law, statutory law, and administrative law.

CASEWORK Personal work for constituents by members of Congress.

CATEGORICAL GRANTS Federal grants to states or local governments that are for specific programs or projects.

CAUCUS A meeting of party members designed to select candidates and propose policies.

CHARTER A document issued by a government that grants to a person, a group of persons, or a corporation the right to carry on one or more specific activities. A state government can grant a charter to a municipality.

CHECKS AND BALANCES A major principle of the American system of government whereby each branch of the government can check the actions of the others.

CHIEF DIPLOMAT The role of the president in recognizing foreign governments, making treaties, and effecting executive agreements.

CHIEF EXECUTIVE The role of the president as head of the executive branch of the government.

CHIEF LEGISLATOR The role of the president in influencing the making of laws.

CHIEF OF STAFF The person who is named to direct the White House Office and advise the president.

CIVIL DISOBEDIENCE A nonviolent public refusal to obey allegedly unjust laws.

CIVIL LIBERTIES Those personal freedoms that are protected for all individuals. Civil liberties typically involve restraining the government's actions against individuals.

CIVIL RIGHTS All rights rooted in the Fourteenth Amendment's guarantee of equal protection under the law.

CIVIL SERVICE A collective term for the body of employees working for the government. Generally, civil service is understood to apply to all those who gain government employment through a merit system.

CIVIL SERVICE COMMISSION The initial central personnel agency of the national government, created in 1883.

CLASS-ACTION SUIT A lawsuit filed by an individual seeking damages for "all persons similarly situated."

CLEAR AND PRESENT DANGER TEST The test proposed by Justice Oliver Wendell Holmes for determining when government may restrict free speech. Restrictions are permissible, he argued, only when speech creates a *clear and present danger* to the public order.

CLIMATE CONTROL The use of public relations techniques to create favorable public opinion toward an interest group, industry, or corporation.

CLOSED PRIMARY A type of primary in which the voter is limited to choosing candidates of the party of which he or she is a member.

COATTAIL EFFECT The influence of a popular candidate on the electoral success of other candidates on the same party ticket. The effect is increased by the party-column ballot, which encourages straight-ticket voting.

COLD WAR The ideological, political, and economic confrontation between the United States and the Soviet Union following World War II.

COMMANDER IN CHIEF The role of the president as supreme commander of the military forces of the United States and of the state National Guard units when they are called into federal service.

COMMERCE CLAUSE The section of the Constitution in which Congress is given the power to regulate trade among the states and with foreign countries.

COMMERCIAL SPEECH Advertising statements, which increasingly have been given First Amendment protection.

COMMON LAW Judicially made law that originated in England from decisions shaped according to prevailing custom. Decisions were applied to similar situations and gradually became common to the nation.

COMMUNICATIONS DIRECTOR A professional specialist who plans the communications strategy and advertising campaign for a candidate.

CONCURRENT POWERS Powers held jointly by national and state governments.

CONCURRING OPINION A separate opinion prepared by a judge who supports the decision of the majority of the court but who wants to make or clarify a particular point or voice disapproval of the grounds on which the decision was made.

CONFEDERAL SYSTEM A system consisting of a league of independent states, each having essentially sovereign powers. The central government created by such a league has only limited powers over the states.

CONFEDERATION A political system in which states or regional governments retain ultimate authority except for those powers they expressly delegate to a central government. A voluntary association of independent states, in which the member states agree to limited restraints on their freedom of action.

CONFERENCE COMMITTEE A special joint committee appointed to reconcile differences when bills pass the two chambers of Congress in different forms.

CONSENSUS General agreement among the citizenry on an issue.

CONSERVATISM A set of beliefs that includes the advocacy of a limited role for the national government in helping individuals, support for traditional values and lifestyles, and a cautious response to change._

CONSERVATIVE COALITION An alliance of Republicans and Southern Democrats that can form in the House or the Senate to oppose liberal legislation and support conservative legislation.

CONSOLIDATION The union of two or more government units to form a single unit.

CONSTITUENT One of the persons represented by a legislator or other elected or appointed official.

CONSTITUTIONAL INITIATIVE An electoral device whereby citizens can propose a constitutional amendment through petitions signed by a required number of registered voters.

CONSTITUTIONAL POWER A power vested in the president by Article II of the Constitution.

CONSUMER PRICE INDEX (CPI) A measure of the change in price over time of a specific group of goods and services used by the average household.

CONTAINMENT A U.S. diplomatic policy adopted by the Truman administration to contain communist power within its existing boundaries.

CONTINUING RESOLUTION A temporary funding law that Congress passes when an appropriations bill has not been decided by the beginning of the new fiscal year, October 1.

COOLEY'S RULE The view that cities should be able to govern themselves, presented in an 1871 Michigan decision by Judge Thomas Cooley.

COOPERATIVE FEDERALISM The theory that the states and the national government should cooperate in solving problems.

CORRUPT PRACTICES ACTS A series of acts passed by Congress in an attempt to limit and regulate the sizes and sources of contributions and expenditures in political campaigns.

COUNCIL OF GOVERNMENTS (COG) A voluntary organization of counties and municipalities concerned with area-wide problems.

COUNTY The chief governmental unit set up by the state to administer state law and business at the local level. Counties are drawn up by area, rather than by rural or urban criteria.

CREDENTIALS COMMITTEE A committee used by political parties at their national conventions to determine which delegates may participate. The committee inspects the claim of each prospective delegate to be seated as a legitimate representative of his or her state.

DE FACTO SEGREGATION Racial segregation that occurs because of past social and economic conditions and residential racial patterns.

DE JURE SEGREGATION Racial segregation that occurs because of laws or administrative decisions by public agencies.

DEALIGNMENT A decline in party loyalties that reduces long-term party commitment.

DEFAMATION OF CHARACTER Wrongfully hurting a person's good reputation. The law imposes a general duty on all persons to refrain from making false, defamatory statements about others.

DEFENSE POLICY A subset of national security policies having to do with the U.S. armed forces.

DEMOCRACY A system of government in which political authority is vested in the people. Derived from the Greek words *demos* ("the people") and *kratos* ("authority").

DEMOCRATIC PARTY One of the two major American political parties, it evolved out of the Republican Party of Thomas Jefferson.

DEMOCRATIC REPUBLIC A republic in which representatives elected by the people make and enforce laws and policies.

DÉTENTE A French word meaning a relaxation of tensions. The term characterized U.S.–Soviet relations as they developed under President Richard Nixon and Secretary of State Henry Kissinger.

DEVOLUTION The transfer of powers from a national or central government to a state or local government.

DILLON'S RULE The narrowest possible interpretation of the legal status of local governments, outlined by Judge John E. Dillon, who in 1872 stated that a municipal corporation can exercise only those powers expressly granted by state law.

DIPLOMACY The process by which states carry on political relations with each other; settling conflicts among nations by peaceful means.

DIPLOMATIC RECOGNITION The formal acknowledgment of a foreign government as legitimate.

DIRECT DEMOCRACY A system of government in which political decisions are made by the people directly, rather than by their elected representatives; probably attained most easily in small political communities.

DIRECT PRIMARY An intraparty election in which the voters select the candidates who will run on a party's ticket in the subsequent general election.

DIRECT TECHNIQUE An interest group activity that involves interaction with government officials to further the group's goals.

DISCHARGE PETITION A procedure by which a bill in the House of Representatives may be forced (discharged) out of a committee that has refused to report it for consideration by the entire House. The petition must be signed by an absolute majority (218) of representatives and is used only on rare occasions.

DISSENTING OPINION A separate opinion in which a judge dissents from (disagrees with) the conclusion reached by the majority on the court and expounds his or her own views about a case.

DIVERSITY OF CITIZENSHIP The condition that exists when the parties to a lawsuit are citizens of different states, or when the parties are citizens of a U.S. state and citizens or the government of a foreign country. Diversity of citizenship can provide a basis for federal jurisdiction.

DIVIDED GOVERNMENT A situation in which one major political party controls the presidency and the other controls the chambers of Congress, or in which one party controls a state governorship and the other controls the state legislature.

DIVISIVE OPINION Public opinion that is polarized between two vastly different positions.

DOMESTIC POLICY Public plans or courses of action that concern internal issues of national importance, such as poverty, crime, and the environment.

DUAL FEDERALISM A system in which the states and the national government each remain supreme within their own spheres. The doctrine looks on nation and state as coequal sovereign powers. Neither the state government nor the national government should interfere in the other's arena.

EARMARKS Funding appropriations that are specifically designated for a named project in a member's state or district.

EARNED-INCOME TAX CREDIT (EITC) PROGRAM A government program that helps low-income workers by giving back part or all of their Social Security taxes.

ECONOMIC AID Assistance to other nations in the form of grants, loans, or credits to buy the assisting nation's products.

ELASTIC CLAUSE, OR NECESSARY AND PROPER CLAUSE The clause in Article I, Section 8, that grants Congress the power to do whatever is necessary to execute its specifically delegated powers.

ELECTOR A member of the electoral college, which selects the U.S. president and vice president. Every state's electors are chosen in each presidential election year according to state laws.

ELECTORAL COLLEGE A group of persons called *electors* selected by the voters in each state and the District of Columbia; this group officially elects the president and vice president of the United States. The number of electors in each state is equal to the number of each state's representatives in both chambers of Congress.

ELITE THEORY A perspective holding that society is ruled by a small number of people who exercise power to further their own self-interest.

EMERGENCY POWER An inherent power exercised by the president during a period of national crisis.

EMINENT DOMAIN A power set forth in the Fifth Amendment to the U.S. Constitution that allows government to take private property for public use under the condition that just compensation is offered to the landowner._

ENABLING LEGISLATION A statute enacted by Congress that authorizes the creation of an administrative agency and specifies the name, purpose, composition, functions, and powers of the agency being created.

ENERGY POLICY Laws concerned with how much energy is needed and used by the nation as a whole.

ENUMERATED POWER A power specifically granted to the national government by the Constitution. The first 17 clauses of Article I, Section 8, specify most of the enumerated powers of Congress.

ENVIRONMENTAL IMPACT STATEMENT (EIS) A report that must show the costs and benefits of major federal actions that could significantly affect the quality of the environment.

EQUALITY As a political value, the idea that all people are of equal worth.

ESTABLISHMENT CLAUSE The part of the First Amendment prohibiting the establishment of a church officially supported by the national government. It is applied to questions of state and local government aid to religious organizations and schools, the legality of allowing or requiring school prayers, and the teaching of evolution versus intelligent design.

EXCLUSIONARY RULE A policy forbidding the admission at trial of illegally seized evidence.

EXECUTIVE AGREEMENT An international agreement made by the president, without senatorial ratification, with the head of a foreign state.

EXECUTIVE BUDGET The budget prepared and submitted by the president to Congress.

EXECUTIVE OFFICE OF THE PRESIDENT (EOP) An organization established by President Franklin D. Roosevelt to assist the president in carrying out major duties.

EXECUTIVE ORDER A rule or regulation issued by the president that has the effect of law. Executive orders can implement and give administrative effect to provisions in the Constitution, to treaties, and to statutes.

EXECUTIVE PRIVILEGE The right of executive officials to withhold information from or to refuse to appear before a legislative committee.

EXPORTS Goods and services produced domestically for sale abroad.

EXPRESSED POWER A power of the president that is expressly written into the Constitution or statutory law.

EXTRADITE To surrender an accused or convicted criminal to the authorities of the state from which he or she has fled; to return a fugitive criminal to the jurisdiction of the accusing state.

FACTION A group or bloc in a legislature or political party acting in pursuit of some special interest or position.

FALL REVIEW The annual process in which the Office of Management and Budget, after receiving formal federal agency requests for funding for the next fiscal year, reviews the requests, makes changes, and submits its recommendations to the president.

FEDERAL MANDATE A requirement in federal legislation that forces states and municipalities to comply with certain rules.

FEDERAL OPEN MARKET COMMITTEE The most important body within the Federal Reserve System. The Federal Open Market Committee decides how monetary policy should be carried out.

FEDERAL QUESTION A question that has to do with the U.S. Constitution, acts of Congress, or treaties. A federal question provides a basis for federal jurisdiction.

FEDERAL REGISTER A publication of the U.S. government that prints executive orders, rules, and regulations.

FEDERAL RESERVE SYSTEM (THE FED) The agency created by Congress in 1913 to serve as the nation's central banking organization.

FEDERAL SYSTEM A system of government in which power is divided between a central government and regional, or sub-divisional, governments. Each level must have some domain in which its policies are dominant and some genuine political or constitutional guarantee of its authority.

FEDERALISM A system of government in which power is divided by a written constitution between a central government and regional or subdivisional governments. Each level must have some domain in which its policies are dominant and some genuine constitutional guarantee of its authority.

FEDERALIST The name given to one who was in favor of the adoption of the U.S. Constitution and the creation of a federal union with a strong central government.

FEMINISM The philosophy of political, economic, and social equality for women and the gender consciousness sufficient to mobilize women for change.

FILIBUSTER The use of the Senate's tradition of unlimited debate as a delaying tactic to block a bill.

FINANCE CHAIRPERSON The campaign professional who directs fundraising, campaign spending, and compliance with campaign finance laws and reporting requirements.

FIRST BUDGET RESOLUTION A resolution passed by Congress in May that sets overall revenue and spending goals for the following fiscal year.

FISCAL POLICY The federal government's use of taxation and spending policies to affect overall business activity.

FISCAL YEAR (FY) A 12-month period that is used for bookkeeping or accounting purposes, the fiscal year does not usually coincide with the calendar year. For example, the federal government's fiscal year runs from October 1 through September 30.

FOCUS GROUP A small group of individuals who are led in discussion by a professional consultant as part of an effort to gather opinions on and responses to candidates and issues.

FOOD STAMPS Benefits issued by the federal government to low-income individuals to be used for the purchase of food; originally provided as coupons, but now typically provided electronically through a card similar to a debit card.

FOREIGN POLICY A nation's external goals and the techniques and strategies used to achieve them.

FOREIGN POLICY PROCESS The steps by which foreign policy goals are decided and acted upon.

FRANKING A policy that enables members of Congress to send material through the mail by substituting a facsimile signature (frank) for postage.

FREE EXERCISE CLAUSE The provision of the First Amendment guaranteeing the free exercise of religion.

FREE RIDER PROBLEM The difficulty interest groups face in recruiting members when the benefits they achieve can be gained without joining the group.

FRONT-LOADING The practice of moving presidential primary elections to the early part of the campaign to maximize the impact of these primaries on the nomination.

FRONT-RUNNER The presidential candidate who appears to be ahead at a given time in the primary season.

FULL EMPLOYMENT An arbitrary level of unemployment that corresponds to "normal" friction in the labor market. In 1986, a 6.5 percent rate of unemployment was considered full employment. Today, it is assumed to be around 5 percent.

FULL FAITH AND CREDIT CLAUSE This section of the Constitution requires states to recognize one another's laws and court decisions. It ensures that rights established under deeds, wills, contracts, and other civil matters in one state will be honored in other states.

FUNCTIONAL CONSOLIDATION Cooperation by two or more units of local government in providing services to their inhabitants. This is generally done by unifying a set of departments (e.g., police departments) into a single agency.

GAG ORDER An order issued by a judge restricting the publication of news about a trial or a pretrial hearing to protect the accused's right to a fair trial.

GENDER DISCRIMINATION Any practice, policy, or procedure that denies equality of treatment to an individual or a group because of gender.

GENDER GAP The difference between the percentage of women who vote for a particular candidate and the percentage of men who vote for the same candidate.

GENERAL JURISDICTION Exists when a court's authority to hear cases is not significantly restricted. A court of general jurisdiction normally can hear a broad range of cases.

GENERAL LAW CITY A city operating under general state laws that apply to all local governmental units of a similar type.

GENERAL SALES TAX A tax levied as a proportion of the retail price of a commodity at the point of sale.

GENERATIONAL EFFECT A long-lasting effect of the events of a particular time on the political opinions of those who came of political age at that time.

GERRYMANDERING The drawing of legislative district boundary lines to obtain partisan or factional advantage. A district is said to be gerrymandered when its shape is manipulated by the dominant party in the state legislature to maximize electoral strength at the expense of the minority party.

GET OUT THE VOTE (GOTV) This phrase describes the multiple efforts expended by campaigns to get voters out to the polls on election day.

GOVERNMENT The preeminent institution in which decisions are made that resolve conflicts or allocate benefits and priveleges. It is unique because it has the ultimate authority within society.

GOVERNMENT CORPORATION An agency of government that administers a quasi-business enterprise. These corporations are used when activities are primarily commercial.

GOVERNMENT IN THE SUNSHINE ACT A law that requires all committee-directed federal agencies to conduct their business regularly in public sessions.

GRANDFATHER CLAUSE A device used by Southern states to disenfranchise African Americans. It restricted voting to those whose grandfathers had voted before 1867.

GREAT COMPROMISE The compromise between the New Jersey and the Virginia plans that created one chamber of the Congress based on population and one chamber representing each state equally; also called the Connecticut Compromise.

GROSS DOMESTIC PRODUCT (GDP) The dollar value of all final goods and services produced in a one-year period.

GROSS PUBLIC DEBT The net public debt plus interagency borrowings within the government.

HARD MONEY Political contributions and campaign spending that are recorded under the regulations set forth in law and by the Federal Election Commission.

HATCH ACT An act, passed in 1939, that restricted the political activities of government employees. It also prohibited any political group from spending more than $3 million in a campaign and limited individual contributions to a campaign committee to $5,000.

HATE CRIME A criminal offense committed against a person or property that is motivated—in whole or in part—by the offender's bias against a race, color, ethnicity, national origin, sex, gender identity or expression, sexual orientation, disability, age, or religion.

HEAD OF STATE The role of the president as ceremonial head of the government.

HILLSTYLE The actions and behaviors of a member of Congress in Washington, D.C., intended to promote policies and the member's own career aspirations.

HOME RULE CITY A city permitted by the state to let local voters frame, adopt, and amend their own charters.

HOMESTYLE The actions and behaviors of a member of Congress aimed at his or her constituents and intended to win their support and trust.

IDEOLOGY A comprehensive set of beliefs about the nature of people and the role of an institution or government.

IMPEACHMENT An action by the House of Representatives to accuse the president, vice president, or other civil officer of the United States of committing "Treason, Bribery, or other high Crimes and Misdemeanors."

IMPORT QUOTA A restriction imposed on the value or number of units of a particular good that can be brought into a country. Foreign suppliers are unable to sell more than the amount specified in the import quota.

IMPORTS Goods and services produced outside a country but sold within its borders.

INCOME TRANSFER A redistribution of income from some individuals in the economy to others, generally by government action.

INCORPORATION THEORY The view that most of the protections of the Bill of Rights apply to state governments through the Fourteenth Amendment's due process clause.

INDEPENDENT A voter or candidate who does not identify with a political party.

INDEPENDENT EXECUTIVE AGENCY A federal agency that is not part of a Cabinet department but reports directly to the president.

INDEPENDENT EXPENDITURES Nonregulated contributions from PACs, organizations, and individuals. The funds may be spent on advertising or other campaign activities, so long as the expenditures are not coordinated with those of a candidate.

INDEPENDENT REGULATORY AGENCY An agency outside the major executive departments charged with making and implementing rules and regulations.

INDIRECT TECHNIQUE A strategy employed by interest groups that uses third parties to influence government officials.

INFLATION A sustained rise in the general price level of goods and services.

INHERENT POWER A power of the president derived from statements in the Constitution that "the executive Power shall be vested in a President" and that the president should "take Care that the Laws be faithfully executed"; defined through practice rather than through law.

INITIATIVE A procedure by which voters can propose a law or a constitutional amendment.

IN-KIND SUBSIDY A good or service—such as food stamps, housing, or medical care— provided by the government to low-income groups.

INSTITUTION   An ongoing organization that performs certain functions for society.

INSTRUCTED DELEGATE A legislator who is an agent of the voters who elected him or her and who votes according to the views of constituents, regardless of personal beliefs.

INTELLIGENCE COMMUNITY The government agencies that gather information about the capabilities and intentions of foreign governments or that engage in covert actions.

INTEREST GROUP An organized group of individuals sharing common objectives who actively attempt to influence policy makers.

INTERSTATE COMPACT An agreement between two or more states. Agreements on minor matters are made without congressional consent, but any compact that tends to increase the power of the contracting states relative to other states or relative to the national government generally requires the consent of Congress. Such compacts serve as a means by which states can solve regional problems.

IRON CURTAIN The term used to describe the division of Europe between the Soviet bloc and the West; coined by Winston Churchill.

IRON TRIANGLE The three-way alliance among legislators, bureaucrats, and interest groups to make or preserve policies that benefit their respective interests.

ISOLATIONIST FOREIGN POLICY A policy of abstaining from an active role in international affairs or alliances; it characterized U.S. foreign policy toward Europe during most of the 1800s.

ISSUE ADVOCACY ADVERTISING Advertising paid for by interest groups that support or oppose a candidate or a candidate's position on an issue without mentioning voting or elections.

ISSUE NETWORK A group of individuals or organizations—which may consist of legislators and legislative staff members, interest group leaders, bureaucrats, the media, scholars, and other experts—that supports a particular policy position on a given issue.

ITEM VETO The power exercised by the governors of most states to veto particular sections or items of an appropriations bill while signing the remainder of the bill into law.

JIM CROW LAWS Laws enacted by Southern states that enforced segregation in schools, on transportation, and in public accommodations.

JOINT COMMITTEE A legislative committee composed of members of both chambers of Congress.

JUDICIAL ACTIVISM A doctrine holding that the Supreme Court should take an active role by using its powers to check the activities of governmental bodies when those bodies exceed their authority.

JUDICIAL IMPLEMENTATION The way in which court decisions are translated into action.

JUDICIAL RESTRAINT A doctrine holding that the Supreme Court should defer to the decisions made by the elected representatives of the people in the legislative and executive branches.

JUDICIAL REVIEW The power of the Supreme Court or any court to hold a law or other legal action as unconstitutional.

JURISDICTION The authority of a court to decide certain cases. Not all courts have the authority to decide all cases. Two jurisdictional issues are where a case has arisen, and its subject matter.

JUSTICIABLE QUESTION A question that may be raised and reviewed in court.

KEYNESIAN ECONOMICS A school of economic thought that tends to favor active federal government policy making to stabilize economy-wide fluctuations, usually by implementing discretionary fiscal policy.

KITCHEN CABINET The group of informal advisers to the president.

LABOR MOVEMENT Generally, the economic and political expression of working-class interests; politically, the organization of working-class interests.

LATENT INTERESTS Public-policy interests that are not recognized or addressed by a group at a particular time.

LAWMAKING The process of establishing the legal rules that govern society.

LEGISLATURE A governmental body primarily responsible for the making of laws.

LIBEL Written defamation of a person's character, reputation, business, or property rights.

LIBERALISM A set of beliefs that includes the advocacy of positive government action to improve the welfare of individuals, support for civil rights, and tolerance for political and social change.

LIBERTARIANISM A political ideology based on skepticism or opposition to almost all government activities.

LIBERTY The greatest freedom of individuals that is consistent with the freedom of other individuals in the society.

LIFE CYCLE EFFECT The theory that people change as they grow older because of age-specific experiences and thus are likely to hold age-specific attitudes.

LIMITED GOVERNMENT The principle that the powers of government should be limited, usually by constitutional checks.

LIMITED JURISDICTION Exists when a court's authority to hear cases is restricted to certain types of claims, such as tax claims or bankruptcy petitions.

LINE ORGANIZATION In the federal government, an administrative unit that is directly accountable to the president.

LINE-ITEM VETO The power of an executive to veto individual lines or items within a piece of legislation without vetoing the entire bill.

LITERACY TEST A test administered as a precondition for voting, often used to prevent African Americans from exercising their right to vote.

LITIGATE To engage in a legal proceeding or seek relief in a court of law; to carry on a lawsuit.

LOBBYIST An organization or individual who attempts to influence legislation and the administrative decisions of government.

LOGROLLING An arrangement in which two or more members of Congress agree in advance to support each other's bills.

LOOPHOLE A legal method by which individuals and businesses are allowed to reduce the tax liabilities they owe the government.

LOOSE MONETARY POLICY Monetary policy that makes credit inexpensive and abundant, possibly leading to inflation.

MADISONIAN MODEL A structure of government proposed by James Madison in which the powers of the government are separated into three branches: executive, legislative, and judicial.

MAJORITARIANISM A political theory holding that in a democracy, the government ought to do what the majority of the people want.

MAJORITY LEADER OF THE HOUSE A legislative position held by an important party member in the House of Representatives. The majority leader is selected by the majority party in caucus or conference to foster cohesion among party members and act as spokesperson for the majority party in the House.

MAJORITY OPINION A court opinion reflecting the views of the majority of the judges.

MAJORITY RULE A Basic principle of democracy asserting that the greatest number of citizens in any political unit should select officials and determine policy.

MANAGED NEWS Information generated and distributed by the government in such a way as to give government interests priority over candor.

MATERIAL INCENTIVE A reason or motive having to do with economic benefits or opportunities.

MEDIA Channels of mass communication. .

MEDICAID A joint state-federal program that provides medical care to the poor (including indigent elderly persons in nursing homes). The program is funded out of general government revenues.

MEDICARE A federal health insurance program that covers U.S. residents age 65 and older. The costs are met by a tax on wages and salaries.

MERIT SYSTEM The selection, retention, and promotion of government employees on the basis of competitive examinations.

MILITARY-INDUSTRIAL COMPLEX The mutually beneficial relationship between the armed forces and defense contractors.

MINORITY LEADER OF THE HOUSE The party leader elected by the minority party in the House of Representatives.

MONETARY POLICY The utilization of changes in the amount of money in circulation to alter credit markets, employment, and the rate of inflation.

MONOPOLISTIC MODEL A model of bureaucracy that compares bureaucracies to monopolistic business firms. Lack of competition in either circumstance leads to inefficient and costly operations.

MONROE DOCTRINE A policy statement made by President James Monroe in 1823 that set out three principles: (1) European nations should not establish new colonies in the western hemisphere; (2) European nations should not intervene in the affairs of independent nations in the western hemisphere; and (3) the United States would not interfere in the affairs of European nations.

MORALIST FOREIGN POLICY A foreign policy based on values and moral beliefs.

MUNICIPAL HOME RULE The power vested in a local unit of government to draft or change its own charter and manage its own affairs.

NATIONAL COMMITTEE A standing committee of a national political party established to direct and coordinate party activities between national party conventions.

NATIONAL CONVENTION The meeting held every four years by each major party to select presidential and vice presidential candidates, write a platform, choose a national committee, and conduct party business.

NATIONAL HEALTH INSURANCE A plan to provide universal health insurance under which the government provides basic health care coverage to all citizens. In most such plans, the program is funded by taxes on wages or salaries.

NATIONAL SECURITY COUNCIL (NSC) An agency in the Executive Office of the President that advises the president on national security.

NATIONAL SECURITY POLICY Foreign and domestic policy designed to protect the nation's independence and political and economic integrity; policy that is concerned with the safety and defense of the nation.

NATURAL RIGHTS Rights held to be inherent in natural law, not dependent on governments. John Locke stated that natural law, being superior to human law, specifies certain rights of "life, liberty, and property." These rights, altered to become "life, liberty, and the pursuit of happiness," are asserted in the Declaration of Independence.

NEGATIVE CONSTITUENTS Citizens who openly oppose the government's policies.

NET PUBLIC DEBT The accumulation of all past federal government deficits; the total amount owed by the federal government to individuals, businesses, and foreigners.

NEW ENGLAND TOWN A governmental unit in the New England states that combines the roles of city and county in one unit.

NONOPINION The lack of an opinion on an issue or policy among the majority.

NORMAL TRADE RELATIONS (NTR) STATUS Status granted through an international treaty by which each member nation must treat other members at least as well as it treats the country that receives its most favorable treatment. Formerly known as most-favored-nation status.

OFFICE OF MANAGEMENT AND BUDGET (OMB) A division of the Executive Office of the President. The OMB assists the president in preparing the annual budget, clearing and coordinating departmental agency budgets, and supervising the administration of the federal budget.

OFFICE-BLOCK, OR MASSACHUSETTS, BALLOT A form of general-election ballot in which candidates for elective office are grouped together under the title of each office. It emphasizes voting for the office and the individual candidate, rather than for the party.

OLIGARCHY Rule by the few in their own interests.

OMBUDSPERSON A person who hears and investigates complaints by private individuals against public officials or agencies.

OPEN PRIMARY A primary in which any registered voter can vote (but only for candidates of one party or the other).

OPINION LEADER One who is able to influence the opinions of others through position, expertise, or personality.

OPINION POLL A method of systematically questioning a selected sample of respondents who are deemed representative of the total population.

ORAL ARGUMENTS The verbal arguments presented in person by attorneys to an appellate court. Each attorney presents reasons to the court why it should rule in his or her client's favor.

ORDER A state of peace and security. Maintaining order by protecting members of society from violence and criminal activity is the oldest purpose of government.

OVERSIGHT The process by which Congress follows up on laws it has enacted to ensure that they are being enforced and administered in the way it intended.

PARDON A release from the punishment for or legal consequences of a crime; a pardon can be granted by the president before or after a conviction.

PARTY IDENTIFICATION Linking oneself to a particular political party.

PARTY IDENTIFIER A person who associates him- or herself with a given political party.

PARTY ORGANIZATION The formal structure and leadership of a political party, including election committees; local, state, and national executives; and paid professional staff.

PARTY PLATFORM A document drawn up at each national convention outlining the policies, positions, and principles of the party.

PARTY-COLUMN, OR INDIANA, BALLOT A form of general-election ballot in which all of a party's candidates for elective office are arranged in one column under the party's label and symbol. It emphasizes voting for the party, rather than for the office or the individual.

PARTY-IN-GOVERNMENT All of the elected and appointed officials who identify with a political party.

PARTY-IN-THE-ELECTORATE Those members of the general public who identify with a political party or who express a preference for one party over another.

PATRONAGE The practice of rewarding faithful party workers and followers with government employment and contracts.

PEER GROUP A group consisting of members sharing common social characteristics. These groups play an important part in the socialization process, helping to shape attitudes and beliefs.

PENDLETON ACT (CIVIL SERVICE REFORM ACT) An act that established the principle of employment on the basis of merit and created the Civil Service Commission to administer the personnel service.

PERMANENT CAMPAIGN A coordinated and planned strategy carried out by the White House to increase the president's popularity and support.

PICKET-FENCE FEDERALISM A model of federalism in which specific programs and policies (depicted as vertical pickets in a picket fence) involve all levels of government—national, state, and local (depicted as the horizontal boards in a picket fence).

PLURALISM A theory that views politics as a conflict among interest groups. Political decision making is characterized by bargaining and compromise.

PLURALITY A number of votes cast for a candidate that is greater than the number of votes for any other candidate, though not necessarily a majority.

POCKET VETO A special veto exercised by the chief executive after a legislative body has adjourned. Bills not signed by the chief executive die after a specified period of time. If Congress wishes to reconsider such a bill, it must be reintroduced in the following session of Congress. .

POLICE POWER The authority to legislate for the protection of the health, morals, safety, and welfare of the people. In the United States, most police power is reserved to the states.

POLICY TSAR A high-ranking member of the Executive Office of the President appointed to coordinate action in one specific policy area.

POLITICAL ACTION COMMITTEE (PAC) A committee set up by and representing a corporation, labor union, or special-interest group. PACs raise money and make campaign donations.

POLITICAL CONSULTANT A paid professional hired to devise a campaign strategy and manage a campaign.

POLITICAL CULTURE The collection of beliefs and attitudes toward government and the political process held by a community or nation.

POLITICAL PARTY A group of political activists who organize to win elections, operate the government, and determine public policy.

POLITICAL QUESTION An issue that a court believes should be decided by the executive or the legislative branch.

POLITICAL SOCIALIZATION The process through which individuals learn a set of political attitudes and form opinions about social issues. Families and the educational system are two of the most important forces in the political socialization process.

POLITICAL TRUST The degree to which individuals express trust in the government and political institutions, usually measured through a specific series of survey questions.

POLITICS The struggle over power or influence within organizations or informal groups that can grant or withhold benefits or privileges.

POLL TAX A special tax that must be paid as a qualification for voting. The Twenty-fourth Amendment to the Constitution outlawed the poll tax in national elections, and in 1966, the Supreme Court declared it unconstitutional in all elections.

POLLSTER A person or firm that conducts public opinion polls for a campaign.

PORK Special projects or appropriations that are intended to benefit a member's district or state; slang for earmarks.

PRECEDENT A court rule bearing on subsequent legal decisions in similar cases. Judges rely on precedents in deciding cases.

PRESIDENT PRO TEMPORE The temporary presiding officer of the Senate in the absence of the vice president.

PRESIDENTIAL PRIMARY A statewide primary election of delegates to a political party's national convention, held to determine a party's presidential nominee.

PRESS SECRETARY The presidential staff member responsible for handling White House media relations and communications.

PRIOR RESTRAINT Restraining an action before the activity has actually occurred. When expression is involved, this means censorship.

PRIVATIZATION The replacement of government services with services provided by private firms.

PRIVILEGES AND IMMUNITIES Special rights and exceptions provided by law. States may not discriminate against one another's citizens.

PROGRESSIVE TAX A tax that rises in percentage terms as incomes rise.

PROPERTY Anything that is or may be subject to ownership. As conceived by the political philosopher John Locke, the right to property is a natural right superior to human law (laws made by government).

PROPERTY TAX A tax on the value of real estate. This tax is a particularly important source of revenue for local governments.

PUBLIC FIGURE A public official, movie star, or other person known to the public because of his or her positions or activities.

PUBLIC INTEREST The best interests of the overall community; the national good, rather than the narrow interests of a particular group.

PUBLIC OPINION The aggregate of individual attitudes or beliefs shared by some portion of the adult population.

PURPOSIVE INCENTIVE A reason for supporting or participating in the activities of a group that is based on agreement with the goals of the group. For example, someone with a strong interest in human rights might have a purposive incentive to join Amnesty International.

RATIFICATION Formal approval.

RATIONAL IGNORANCE EFFECT An effect produced when people purposefully and rationally decide not to become informed on an issue because they believe that their vote on the issue is not likely to be a deciding one; a lack of incentive to seek the necessary information to cast an intelligent vote.

REALIGNMENT A process in which a substantial group of voters switches party allegiance, producing a long-term change in the political landscape.

REALIST FOREIGN POLICY A foreign policy based on an understanding of the nation's economic and security interests.

REAPPORTIONMENT The allocation of seats in the House of Representatives to each state after every census.

RECALL A procedure allowing people to vote to dismiss an elected official from state office before his or her term has expired.

RECESSION Two or more successive quarters in which the economy shrinks rather than grows.

REDISTRICTING The redrawing of the congressional district boundaries within each state.

REFERENDUM An electoral device whereby legislative or constitutional measures are referred by the legislature to the voters for approval or disapproval.

REGISTRATION The entry of a person's name onto the list of registered voters for elections. To register, a person must meet certain legal requirements of age, citizenship, and residency.

REGRESSIVE TAX A tax that falls in percentage terms as incomes rise.

REMAND To send a case back to the court that originally heard it.

REPARATION Compensation—monetary or nonmonetary (e.g., formal apology)—to make amends for a past transgression or harm.

REPRESENTATION The function of members of Congress as elected officials representing the views of their constituents.

REPRESENTATIVE ASSEMBLY A legislature composed of individuals who represent the population.

REPRIEVE A formal postponement of the execution of a sentence imposed by a court of law.

REPUBLIC A form of government in which sovereignty rests with the people, as opposed to a monarch.

REPUBLICAN PARTY One of the two major American political parties. It emerged in the 1850s as an antislavery party and consisted of former Northern Whigs and antislavery Democrats.

REVERSE To annul or make void a court ruling on account of some error or irregularity.

REVERSE DISCRIMINATION The charge that an affirmative action program discriminates against those who do not have minority status.

REVERSE-INCOME EFFECT A tendency for wealthier states or regions to favor the Democrats and for less wealthy states or regions to favor the Republicans. The effect appears paradoxical because it reverses traditional patterns of support.

RULE The proposal by the Rules Committee of the House that states the conditions for debate for one piece of legislation.

RULE OF FOUR A United States Supreme Court procedure by which four justices must vote to grant a petition for review if a case is to come before the full court.

RULES COMMITTEE A standing committee of the House of Representatives that provides special rules under which specific bills can be debated, amended, and considered by the House.

SAFE SEAT A district that returns a legislator with 55 percent of the vote or more.

SAMPLING ERROR The difference between a sample's results and the true result if the entire population had been interviewed.

SECOND BUDGET RESOLUTION A resolution passed by Congress in September that sets "binding" limits on taxes and spending for the following fiscal year.

SELECT COMMITTEE A temporary legislative committee established for a limited time period and for a special purpose.

SENATE MAJORITY LEADER The chief spokesperson of the majority party in the Senate; directs the legislative program and party strategy.

SENATE MINORITY LEADER The party officer in the Senate who commands the minority party's opposition to the policies of the majority party and directs the legislative program and strategy of his or her party.

SENATORIAL COURTESY In federal district court judgeship nominations, a tradition allowing a senator to veto a judicial appointment in his or her state.

SENIORITY SYSTEM A custom followed in both chambers of Congress specifying that the member of the majority party with the longest term of continuous service will be given preference when a committee chairperson (or a holder of some other significant post) is selected.

SEPARATE-BUT-EQUAL DOCTRINE The 1896 doctrine holding that separate-but-equal facilities do not violate the equal protection clause.

SEPARATION OF POWERS The principle of dividing governmental powers among the different branches of government.

SERVICE SECTOR The sector of the economy that provides services—such as health care, banking, and education—in contrast to the sector that produces goods.

SEXUAL HARASSMENT Unwanted physical or verbal conduct or abuse of a sexual nature that interferes with a recipient's job performance, creates a hostile work environment, or carries with it an implicit or explicit threat of adverse employment consequences.

SIGNING STATEMENT A written declaration that a president may make when signing a bill into law. Such statements usually point out sections of the law that the president deems unconstitutional.

SINGLE-PAYER PLAN A plan under which one entity has a monopoly on issuing a particular type of insurance. Typically, the entity is the government, and the insurance is basic health coverage.

SLANDER The public uttering of a false statement that harms the good reputation of another. The statement must be made to, or within the hearing of, persons other than the defamed party.

SOCIAL CONTRACT A voluntary agreement among individuals to secure their rights and welfare by creating a government and abiding by its rules.

SOCIAL MOVEMENT A movement that represents the demands of a large segment of the public for political, economic, or social change.

SOCIALISM A political ideology based on strong support for economic and social equality. Socialists traditionally envisioned a society in which major businesses were taken over by the government or by employee cooperatives.

SOCIOECONOMIC STATUS The value assigned to a person due to occupation or income. An upper-class person, for example, has high socioeconomic status.

SOFT MONEY Campaign contributions unregulated by federal or state law, usually given to parties and party committees to help fund general party activities.

SOLIDARY INCENTIVE A reason or motive having to do with the desire to associate with others and to share with others a particular interest or hobby.

SOVIET BLOC The Soviet Union and the Eastern European countries that installed communist regimes after World War II and were dominated by the Soviet Union.

SPEAKER OF THE HOUSE The presiding officer in the House of Representatives. The Speaker is always a member of the majority party and is the most powerful and influential member of the House.

SPIN An interpretation of campaign events or election results that is favorable to the candidate's campaign strategy.

SPIN DOCTOR A political campaign adviser who tries to convince journalists of the truth of a particular interpretation of events.

SPLINTER PARTY A new party formed by a dissident faction within a major political party. Often, splinter parties have emerged when a particular personality was at odds with the majority party.

SPOILS SYSTEM The awarding of government jobs to political supporters and friends.

SPRING REVIEW The annual process in which the Office of Management and Budget requires federal agencies to review their programs, activities, and goals and submit their requests for funding for the next fiscal year.

STANDING COMMITTEE A permanent committee in the House or Senate that considers bills within a certain subject area.

STARE DECISIS To stand on decided cases; the judicial policy of following precedents established by past decisions.

STATE A group of people occupying a specific area and organized under one government; may be either a nation or a subunit of a nation.

STATE CENTRAL COMMITTEE The principal organized structure of every political party within each state. This committee is responsible for carrying out policy decisions of the party's state convention.

STATE OF THE UNION MESSAGE An annual message in which the president proposes a legislative program. The message is addressed not only to Congress but also to the American people and to the world.

STATUTORY POWER A power created for the president through laws enacted by Congress.

STRAIGHT-TICKET VOTING Voting exclusively for the candidates of one party.

STRATEGIC ARMS LIMITATION TREATY (SALT I) A treaty between the United States and the Soviet Union to stabilize the nuclear arms competition between the two countries. SALT I talks began in 1969; agreements were signed on May 26, 1972.

STRICT CONSTRUCTION A judicial philosophy that looks to the "letter of the law" when interpreting the Constitution or a particular statute.

SUBPOENA A legal writ requiring a person's appearance in court to give testimony.

SUFFRAGE The right to vote; the franchise.

SUNSET LEGISLATION Laws requiring that existing programs be reviewed regularly for their effectiveness and terminated unless specifically extended as a result of those reviews.

SUPERDELEGATE A party leader or elected official who is given the right to vote at the party's national convention. Super delegates are not elected at the state level.

SUPPLEMENTAL SECURITY INCOME (SSI) A federal program established to provide assistance to elderly persons and persons with disabilities.

SUPREMACY CLAUSE The constitutional provision that makes the Constitution and federal laws superior to all conflicting state and local laws.

SUPREMACY DOCTRINE A doctrine that asserts the priority of national law over state laws. This principle is rooted in Article VI of the Constitution, which provides that the Constitution, the laws passed by the national government under its constitutional powers, and all treaties constitute the supreme law of the land.

SWING VOTERS Voters who frequently switch their support from one party to another.

SYMBOLIC SPEECH The nonverbal expression of beliefs, it is given substantial protection by the courts.

TARIFFS Taxes on imports.

TECHNICAL ASSISTANCE The practice of sending experts in such areas as agriculture, engineering, or business as aid to other nations.

TEMPORARY ASSISTANCE TO NEEDY FAMILIES (TANF) A state-administered program in which grants from the national government are used to provide welfare benefits. The TANF program replaced the Aid to Families with Dependent Children (AFDC) program.

THIRD PARTY A political party other than the two major political parties (Republican and Democratic).

TICKET SPLITTING Voting for candidates of two or more parties for different offices. For example, a voter splits her ticket if she votes for a Republican presidential candidate and a Democratic congressional candidate.

TIGHT MONETARY POLICY Monetary policy that makes credit expensive in an effort to slow the economy.

TIPPING A phenomenon that occurs when a group that is growing over time becomes large enough to change the political balance in a district, state, or country.

TOTALITARIAN REGIME A form of government that controls all aspects of the political and social life of a nation.

TOWN MANAGER SYSTEM A form of town government in which voters elect three selectpersons, who then appoint a professional town manager, who in turn appoints other officials.

TOWN MEETING The governing authority of many New England towns. Qualified voters may participate in the election of officers and the passage of legislation.

TOWNSHIP A rural unit of government based on federal land surveys of the American frontier in the 1780s. Townships have declined significantly in importance.

TRACKING POLL A poll taken for the candidate on a nearly daily basis as election day approaches.

TRIAL COURT The court in which most cases begin.

TRUMAN DOCTRINE The policy adopted by President Harry Truman in 1947 to halt communist expansion in southeastern Europe.

TRUSTEE A legislator who acts according to her or his conscience and the broad interests of the entire society.

TWELFTH AMENDMENT An amendment to the Constitution, adopted in 1804, that specifies the separate election of the president and the vice president by the electoral college.

TWENTY-FIFTH AMENDMENT A 1967 amendment to the Constitution that established procedures for filling presidential and vice presidential vacancies and makes provisions for presidential disability.

TWO-PARTY SYSTEM A political system in which only two parties have a reasonable chance of winning.

UNANIMOUS CONSENT AGREEMENT An agreement on the rules of debate for proposed legislation in the Senate that is approved by all the members.

UNANIMOUS OPINION A court opinion or determination on which all judges agree.

UNEMPLOYMENT The inability of those who are in the labor force to find a job; defined as the total number of those in the labor force who are actively looking for a job but unable to find one.

UNICAMERAL LEGISLATURE A legislature with only one legislative chamber, as opposed to a bicameral (two-chamber) legislature, such as the U.S. Congress. Today, Nebraska is the only state in the Union with a unicameral legislature.

UNINCORPORATED AREA An area not located within the boundary of a municipality.

UNIT RULE A rule by which all of a state's electoral votes are cast for the presidential candidate receiving a plurality of the popular vote in that state.

UNITARY SYSTEM A centralized governmental system in which local or subdivisional governments exercise only those powers given to them by the central government.

UNIVERSAL SUFFRAGE The right for all adults to vote for their representative.

UNORTHODOX LAWMAKING The use of out-of-the-ordinary parliamentary tactics to pass legislation.

VETO MESSAGE The president's formal explanation of a veto when legislation is returned to Congress.

VOTER TURNOUT The percentage of citizens taking part in the election process; the number of eligible voters who actually "turn out" on election day to cast their ballots.

WAR POWERS RESOLUTION A law passed in 1973 spelling out the conditions under which the president can commit troops without congressional approval.

WASHINGTON COMMUNITY Individuals who are regularly involved with politics in Washington, D.C.

WATERGATE BREAK-IN The 1972 illegal entry into the Democratic National Committee offices by participants in President Richard Nixon's reelection campaign.

WEBERIAN MODEL A model of bureaucracy developed by the German sociologist Max Weber, who viewed bureaucracies as rational, hierarchical organizations in which decisions are based on logical reasoning.

WHIG PARTY A major party in the United States during the first half of the 19th century, formally established in 1836. The Whig Party was anti-Jackson and represented a variety of regional interests.

WHIP A member of Congress who aids the majority or minority leader of the House or the Senate.

WHISTLEBLOWER Someone who brings to public attention gross governmental inefficiency or an illegal action.

WHITE HOUSE OFFICE The personal office of the president, which tends to presidential political needs and manages the media. .

WHITE PRIMARY A state primary election that restricted voting to whites only; outlawed by the Supreme Court in 1944.

WRIT OF CERTIORARI An order issued by a higher court to a lower court to send up the record of a case for review.